To Mike —

With prayers that we will someday, somehow, find a better way... than war.
And with warm personal regards,

your Friend!

Tom

November 2000

Searching

for the

Good

Searching

for the

Good

*A Young Man's
Journey to
War and Back*

Thomas A. Brewer

Quaise Publications, Wilton, Connecticut, and Nantucket, Massachusetts
Copyright © 2000 by Thomas A. Brewer

∞ The paper used in this publication meets the minimum requirements of the American National Standard for Information Sciences—Permanence of Paper for Printed Library Materials, ANSI Z39.48-1984.

Library of Congress Control Number: 00-091390

ISBN 0-9701339-0-1 (hardcover)

Book design by Diane Marshall, Coleridge Design, Kansas City, KS 66103

Jacket design by Alon Koppel, fusionlab.com
Jacket photograph provided by the author
Proofreading provided by PeopleSpeak

Printed in the United States of America
Thomson-Shore, Inc.

To my wife, Penny, whose love and friendship have endured the storm. Also to my deceased father, A. A. Brewer, who taught me to search for the good in all things. And to my children, youngest to oldest: Annie, Topher, Stacey, Kristin, Suzanne, and Caroline, who each in their own way has suffered the aftermath of war.

I also dedicate this book to the men of Alpha Company, Second Battalion 27th Infantry "Wolfhounds" and to all of the other Vietnam combat veterans who live with the memory of having fought for America in its most controversial war.

Contents

Contents

Preface

In 1967, at age twenty-six, I fought in Vietnam and was wounded two times. On my return, I was treated like a hometown hero. There were articles in the local press and speaking engagements. No one spit at me. No one turned the other way. I was proud to have given to my country, as had so many Americans before me. Having served in Vietnam even helped me land my first serious job.

In 1968, after the enemy's widespread but militarily unsuccessful Tet Offensive, the mood of the country shifted dramatically. Support for the war, which had been rapidly eroding, plunged. Then in 1969, the My Lai massacre—where U.S. soldiers slaughtered Vietnamese civilians, including women and children—became public. A growing number of pundits characterized the war as illegal and immoral, soldiers as low-class fodder for an evil self-serving war machine in Washington. GIs now returned but as "baby killers," not heroes, shunned and sometimes, allegedly, spit upon.

Over the ensuing years, the Vietnam vet was stereotyped as an unemployable, drug-addicted psychopath, never at peace with himself or anybody else. After the war, many books and movies picked up on and expanded on these themes. I began questioning my own service. Had I been part of something evil? Had I been brainwashed? Should I have resisted and fled to Canada to avoid going to Vietnam, as some others had done?

A select-few isolated events, sometimes heinous, that created sensational headlines and grabbed attention—like My Lai or an innocent child hit by napalm—were replayed by the media time and again. For many who were not there, these distortions are the truth about Vietnam. For me and many others who grew up in the patriotic 1950s and fought in the jungles and paddies of "Nam," there is so much more. We have our own Vietnams, our own stories, our own truths. Why did we go? What was it really like? What pain do we feel? How have we coped? What do we want our children to know?

This book is about me and my Vietnam, written at the urging of one of my children who wanted to know more about that period in my life and in our country's history. It is not intended to be an academic or political analysis of the war. Nor does it provide any profound answers to the many questions that still exist about Vietnam. It is about a patriotic young man who grew up during the post–World War II "fabulous fifties" and went to college and off to war in the turbulent sixties.

It's about returning, adjusting, and never forgetting. It's about the stuff of war and of life afterwards, of commitment and doubts, of sorrow, and of bad memories and good. It is about a man who suffered the horrors of ground combat, still carries the physical and mental scars of battle, and works hard every day at living a relatively normal existence.

I therefore argue that though a book about me, it tells the story of thousands like me. Anonymous men and women with stories like mine that are masked by the plethora of Vietnam War writings that dwell on the far side of soldierly conduct or on those who were psychologically crippled by the war. A personal meditation and a montage of one man's life, the book also portrays that multitude of citizen soldiers who served with honor in Vietnam, did their jobs, came home, and went on with their lives, in spite of much pain and torment.

Acknowledgments

I owe my heartfelt gratitude to many individuals who helped me with this book. George Fuller, a dear friend, read early chapters and encouraged me to proceed with the complete story. John Reaves, another dear friend and writer himself, provided creative guidance and editorial suggestions that gave life to my words. Davis Crippen, a friend and colleague of many years, provided encouragement as well as editorial expertise that made the writing eminently more readable. Other close friends—Sue Darow, Fred Johnson, Jane Johnson, Jack DeSoye, Noreen DeSoye, Benji McGowan, Mike Maurer, Alice Pearson, and Carolyn Watt—reviewed the first complete version of the manuscript and provided essential feedback that was needed to refine the writing for a broader audience. Retired Lieutenant Colonel Steve Ehart reviewed the manuscript, validated basic assumptions, helped me fill in memory lapses, and provided key insights and critical suggestions that could come only from a 27th Infantry Wolfhound who fought alongside me in Vietnam. Retired Colonel Calvin Neptune also reviewed the manuscript and provided valuable input from a seriously wounded Vietnam veteran's point of view. Former Sergeant Alfred "Luke" Serna, another Wolfhound there with me, provided insights into the Mahar-Clouse story included in the Epilogue, an incident that was first introduced to me by Steve Ehart. Sergeant Serna and Platoon Sergeant Gary Pearce, also there with me, were kind enough to provide some of the photographs that have been included.

To all whose contributions have enriched this book, I am forever grateful.

Thomas Brewer
Wilton, Connecticut

Part One

Dustoff

Zulu

By the ninth of July 1967, I thought of myself as a battle-tested combat soldier. Crouched in the doorway of a Huey helicopter skimming over the green sea of jungle in War Zone C, I led the forward elements of Alpha Company into Landing Zone Zulu. I had been fighting with men in the elite Second Battalion 27th Infantry Regiment, the legendary *Wolfhounds*, since arriving in Vietnam early in the year. These were tough, well-trained soldiers, part of the Army's 25th "Tropic Lightning" Division out of Hawaii. Based now in Cu Chi, South Vietnam, they had as much experience and success fighting the Vietcong (VC) as any of the American outfits. As well-trained, highly motivated jungle fighters and one of the first army units to arrive in Vietnam, they had few equals.

Alpha Company, in particular, had participated in some of the bloodiest battles of the war. We'd seen a lot of action together, fought in numerous battles. Each time, I was shaken by the savagery of battle. Like many other infantry company commanders and platoon leaders, I had come to terms with never getting out of Vietnam alive or in one piece. To do our jobs, we had to gamble with our lives. And the odds were frightening.

We knew we would be hit. It was only a matter of when. How badly. How many times. Would it be a slug from a Russian AK-47 or a rocket-propelled grenade whistling among the trees before it exploded? Or would it be a white-hot shell fragment from an exploding mortar? Or a land mine? Or one of a dozen ingenious booby traps set by the enemy on the jungle floor, somewhere under the green waves slipping away below us?

On our way into Zulu, I wondered, as always: will today be my day? If hit, will I die quickly, or slowly and in pain? If wounded, will my manhood be intact? Will I lose a leg or an arm? Will I be blinded or paralyzed? Our world was small and full of violence. We didn't ponder the right or wrong of the war. We fought and killed to survive. Approaching the landing zone (LZ) I was drenched in sweat, my heart drumming loudly in my chest. We were on our way, once again, to confront the enemy. I knew what I had to do, I told myself, and was ready to do it.

■ ■ ■

I went into Zulu with the first lift of six helicopters. I was in one of the lead choppers. Each of the other five carried five to six men of Alpha's third platoon and two door gunners armed with M-60 machine guns. Heavily armed helicopter gunships led the way. It would take three more lifts to get the rest of Alpha into Zulu. But first we had to secure the immediate area, or the company might be cut to pieces before they hit the ground.

My two radio operators were at my side. Specialist Paul Singleton was a tall, lanky, no-nonsense farm boy from Ohio. Specialist Jerome Washington, a young kid from Georgia, was mild-mannered, small, and slight. Both were in their late teens. Though I had just turned twenty-six, they referred to me as "the old man." Their job was to carry the radios we needed to communicate with each of our three platoon leaders and with higher headquarters.

Across from us sat Lieutenant Ernie Petre, our artillery forward observer. We all thought he looked like a character in a Hollywood war movie: lean, tough, leathery. He had earned his commission in officer candidate school, after serving nine years as a sergeant. I think it contributed to his professionalism and coolness in the field. His radio operator was anything but cool. Specialist Jim Alverez was angry most of the time. He'd dropped out of high school in Philadelphia and, as he put it, "I don't take any crap from no one." Alverez maintained contact with the artillery fire-support base that Petre contacted when we needed the heavy guns to get us out of a tough situation. Petre and

Alverez never let me forget that while the infantry was the "queen of battle," the artillery was king. Their job was always putting the balls (artillery rounds) where the queen wanted them.

The five of us were tight, like family. We were the company's command group, in charge of directing the action once on the ground. It was critical that we stay close together at all times. We ate together, slept together in foxholes, and risked our lives together. We shared our private thoughts. And we were prize targets. Because of the telltale antennas on all the radios we carried, it was easy for the Vietcong to spot us quickly and concentrate their fire. They knew if they could wipe us out, they might radically tilt the outcome of a firefight and gain the praise of their comrades. So each time we flew into an LZ, we felt like a big red bull's-eye was painted on our chests, saying "shoot here."

Our fears were always the same. Will the LZ be *hot,* with dug-in enemy soldiers firing on us as we jump from the choppers, dangerously exposed and burdened by the radios and other heavy equipment we carried? Will we be together on the following day? Who will leave the LZ on a litter, who in a body bag?

■   ■   ■

May and June had brought a significant increase in enemy activity throughout the Wolfhound Area of Operations (AO). The AO included Hau Nghia and Tay Ninh Provinces, VC-infested War Zone C, the Iron Triangle northwest of Saigon, and the dreaded Ho Bo Woods. Intelligence reports indicated that VC units were being reinforced and joined by regular army units from North Vietnam in preparation for a major offensive. This was to become the famous Tet Offensive of early 1968, which altered the course of the war.

Intelligence reports also indicated that a heavily armed VC battalion was operating in our AO with the sole mission of destroying the Wolfhounds. And near the village of Loc Ninh, just days before, Zulu, one of our patrols, encountered a booby-trapped sign. It read, "Go No Further 'A' 2/27 Wolfhound[s] All Will Die." The sign gave the offensive a very personal character. We were all spooked and on edge. It seemed that every day more and more letters were sent home. Many by Wolfhounds, like me, thinking that each letter could be the last.

In fact, we were now in constant contact with the enemy. Every movement across the AO was cautious and tentative, slowed to a crawl by sniper fire, mines, and booby traps. Firefights were frequent and sometimes intense. Casualties on both sides were rising. The Vietcong were everywhere—in the trees, in tunnels and in bunkers, behind rice paddy dikes, hidden in the villages and hamlets as we passed through. We called them Charlie, VC, gooks. At night, their loudspeakers penetrated the eerie silence of our defensive positions with propaganda designed to destroy our will to fight. Hanoi Hannah pleaded with us in her sexy and melodic voice. "Oppose orders to set off on raids! Oppose fascist officers! Demand to be given a decent job, not the people-killing job! Oppose the Johnson-McNamara war policy! Make love, not war!"

■ ■ ■

On our way to Zulu, the Hueys flew high above the deep green tapestry of the jungles and rice paddies of War Zone C. All we could hear was the *dut-dut, dut-dut, dut-dut, dut-dut* of the chopper's rotor blades. Off in the distance, gray clouds of smoke and dirt marked the LZ, as artillery pounded the earth just over the horizon.

We neared the landing zone and could hear the exploding shells. Banking to the left, we began our rapid descent. The artillery lifted. Air Force jets zoomed in, smothering the jungle below with cluster bombs. They filtered down through the green canopy before exploding in a torrent of fragments, shredding anything in their way. Helicopter gunships followed, right behind the jets and ahead of our landing. They chopped up the LZ with rocket and cannon fire, sending great clods of dirt into the air. As we made our final approach, our door gunners hammered the perimeter of Zulu with M-60 machine-gun fire.

It seemed that all hell was being visited on this place, that nothing could live through the storm of metal and explosives. And yet we knew from experience that the worst might still be waiting for us. The VC might come up from their holes and tunnels to cut us down as we leaped from the chopper and scrambled across the small clearing, suddenly vulnerable. Or they might have vanished as quietly as they appeared. Leaving to fight another day.

Now almost over the LZ, the chopper swung down. I shouted, "Lock and load." Crouched in the doorway, we clicked off the safety mechanisms on our weapons. The earth rushed up to meet us. We got ready to jump. We could smell the cordite, taste the smoke. The machine dropped abruptly to five feet above the ground. We had three seconds to get out before dangerously exposing the crew to enemy fire. One by one we leaped into the green inferno, drenched with sweat and pumped full of adrenaline. Every man had to quickly orient himself and dash to a nearby crater for cover. Still no incoming fire. Were we safe for now?

Singleton handed me the radio handset. "Alpha Three-Six, this is Alpha Six, over." I made contact with Lieutenant Steve Ehart, with the third platoon. He sounded like his usual cool, earnest, Midwestern self. He was okay. Every one of his men in the first lift was accounted for. Nobody was down.

Suddenly we started to pick up sniper fire. It seemed to be coming from the tree line to the north of the LZ. I ordered a quick move out, staying as low as possible. Ehart's platoon peppered the jungle ahead of us with M-16 rifle fire and M-79 rifle-propelled grenades. We hoped to keep the VC pinned down. After hastily securing the perimeter, our superior firepower enabled us to neutralize the incoming fire.

The next job was to bring the rest of Alpha Company into Zulu. We spent forty-five tense minutes getting everybody else on the ground and safe. But it was starting to look like the VC had disappeared. Okay, I thought. So far, so good.

I reported to battalion headquarters that Zulu was secure and that Alpha was moving out in the direction of the small village of Tan My. The village, a known VC stronghold, was the suspected headquarters of the 169th VC Battalion. Our mission was to find them and to destroy them. It was a classic *search and destroy* operation.

■ ■ ■

With the men spread out, we advanced in two parallel columns toward our objective north of the landing zone. It was very tough going. The trails were mined and booby-trapped. In places they were lined with punji pits—camouflaged holes with razor-sharp bamboo stakes, each poisoned with buffalo dung. The dung ensured that any wound would be infected and perhaps deadly to the poor soldier impaled on the stakes. As always, we had two point men up front in each column. The first carefully searched the ground, step by step, for booby traps and mines. The second scanned beyond and up into the trees, looking for snipers. One man couldn't perform both functions and have any chance of staying alive.

We hacked our way through heavy vegetation and bamboo thickets. Blood trails were everywhere, left by VC wounded or killed by the heavy firing going into the LZ. It was sweltering and humid. The jungle steamed. Swarms of mosquitoes attacked us from every direction. We stopped only to destroy enemy bunkers and tunnels with grenades and C-4 plastic explosive or to evacuate new replacements who had collapsed from the heat, not yet acclimatized.

The hours crawled by, infinitely slow. We came to a small gorge choked with vines. At the bottom flowed a mud-filled stream. We hacked our way down the slippery gorge. Then, holding our weapons high above our heads, we slid down the bank of the stream and sloshed into the murky, chest-high waters. At first, the cool wetness was a huge relief from the heat. But the feeling didn't last long. Schools of leeches surrounded us, poking at any opening in our jungle fatigues, slithering through to reach the skin underneath. It was a peculiarly intimate kind of terror. I can honestly say that I never saw any of Alpha's men panic in battle. But leeches on our peckers was something else entirely. Everyone went crazy. We stampeded across the stream to the relative safety of the opposite bank, quickly stripping to remove the stubborn bloodsuckers, some of them up to six inches long.

We moved out again for Tan My—more hours of painful progress. Then, at last, we broke into a large clearing of rice paddies checked with small dikes and bounded with banana trees, palm, and sugarcane. We halted the company. The village was about two hundred meters in front of us. It seemed peaceful enough. We saw no human beings. A few indifferent water buffalo snorted around in the paddies. Closer to the village, pigs and ducks foraged. Where were the people? It was unnaturally quiet. We took it as a bad sign.

I thought about leaving the men in a column and crossing to the village on the paddy dikes. But we would have made too good a target for a machine gun. And the dikes were often mined. So we spread the men in Alpha's first platoon out into a line formation and increased the distance between one man and the next. Then I directed the rest of the company to wait in the woods, with listening posts for security placed on each flank and to our rear.

■ ■ ■

The tension increased; no one said a word. I took a couple of deep breaths. With a hand signal I directed the first platoon to move forward. We moved ahead slowly. Extreme caution. A few drops of rain condensed out of the air and struck the ground. At that moment —*crack, crack, crack*—incoming fire, from the direction of the village. Suddenly bullets were zinging by, spitting up dirt and cutting at the bark of nearby trees.

We scattered and ran for cover, legs pumping. Abruptly I found myself tossed upwards, flying through the air, hurled effortlessly by an explosive blast I never really heard. I landed on my back in a ditch. The world was blurry. My glasses had been blown off. I was stunned and disoriented. I can remember thinking, what the hell happened?

I sat up. Looking down, I saw blood gushing out of my right boot. My foot and lower leg were numb. I heard fearful shouts from nearby, "I'm hit, I'm hit!" and the anxious groans of the others in the command group. It was total confusion. Noise, cries, gunfire, and men rushing everywhere. I felt helpless. I couldn't stand up or locate a radio to find out what was happening. What were we up against? I tried to pull myself, hand over hand, toward what looked like my glasses sticking up in the mud.

After what seemed like an endless period, I reached the glasses and put them on. Our company medic appeared on my small horizon—a movie-star-handsome guy with dark hair and a thick handlebar mustache, Specialist Bert Hale. I demanded information. He told me Petre, Alverez, and Washington were all hit by the same blast that tore me up, but not as badly. Ehart and my other platoon leaders had Charlie under control for the moment.

Hale put a tourniquet on my leg to slow the bleeding. He quickly looked at the damage, gasped, and told me not to look. He bandaged the wound as well as he could and shot me full of morphine. The pain was just beginning. Slapping me on the shoulder, he said: "It looks pretty bad, sir. You'll be going home. I hope you don't lose your foot."

Night was falling fast. Finally a *dustoff* helicopter, used for evacuating soldiers wounded or killed in action, arrived at the LZ. It came in fast and dropped to the ground. I was quickly placed on a litter. The litter was strapped to a pod on the outside of the chopper. I was high on morphine. As the whirring rotor blades lifted me up, it seemed like a giant dragonfly was snatching me from harm's way.

But Charlie wasn't through yet. Sporadic VC fire followed us as we ascended. Tracer bullets were flying by on all sides. Through the morphine haze, my anxiety rushed up. I was sure I was going to be hit again. I closed my eyes and waited for the impact. It didn't come.

Moments later, we were in clear sky and safely out of the range of small arms. I looked down at the battlefield, ribbons of smoke lingering over the clearing. I remembered the tired, brave Wolfhounds waving us off. A storm of emotions fought the drug. I was sad that I was leaving them to fight without me, angry at the chance that took me away. At the same time, relief was beginning to get stronger: I'm still in one piece; I didn't get killed.

The more the blades of the chopper beat out the miles and the farther away from the battle we flew, the more of a hazy blur it all became. It seemed almost a distant dream or a freakish hallucination. I couldn't seem to decide. Was I still in it? Was I still a part of it? Or was it all over? A nerve-settling calm crept in, embracing the whole of my body and mind. I remember thinking, as I fell in and out of consciousness, I am getting out, I'm getting out alive—I'm on my way back to the world . . . I'm safe. Then everything went black.

■ ■ ■

Time proved me wrong. I might have been safe from the war, but not the horrors of war. Over thirty years later, Vietnam is still with me. It's a part of me. It won't let go. Lurking deep in the recesses of my soul—a schizophrenic ghost from the past—it haunts and torments me at the slightest provocation.

At other times, it rises up to remind me how lucky I am to be alive. Occasionally, paradoxically, I think of the good that has come from my experiences in the Army and in Vietnam. And I wonder how much of my good fortune in life, since the war, was the child of those experiences.

Part Two

The Journey Begins

Willow Run

At eight years old, I was sitting on the crumbling front steps of the place where we lived. It was a tired, soot-stained brick apartment house in downtown Pittsburgh. I was very excited.

Each day, streetcars rumbled and clanked on their hard steel wheels as they passed in the street right below my window. And since mid-June, my routine had been the same. Whenever I heard a streetcar coming, I dashed through the dark hallway and down three flights of stairs, threw open the front door, and paused on the steps, waiting for the car to stop. I watched the people get off, face by face. Was Dad one of them?

My father, then unemployed, had left in June to look for work in Michigan, promising to return for us when he found a job. Each day, for weeks, I had walked back upstairs, my head hanging low, my eyes counting the steps. I reported to my mother, "He isn't back."

But maybe this day was different. Mom had packed four battered suitcases containing all that we owned. She and my younger brother, Dick, and my older sister, Sally, were waiting on the steps with me. Today, we all thought, he really is coming to get us. Sitting there, watching pillars of steel-mill smoke rise into Pittsburgh's slate-gray sky, I wondered, where are we going; what will my new life be like?

After what seemed hours, a black 1942 Ford sedan pulled up. Dad was at the wheel. In a matter of minutes, the suitcases were loaded, and we all piled in, chattering, apprehensive. The car rolled forward down the grimy streets of Pittsburgh and away. It was August 1949 and we were on our way to Willow Run, Michigan.

■ ■ ■

Like many other working-class families moving to Michigan in search of work, we first settled in the government housing project known as Willow Run Village. The rambling maze of tiny dilapidated row houses, with coal stoves and ice boxes, adjoined the huge Willow Run automobile assembly plant.

The plant was originally designed and built by Henry Ford. But in 1949, it was owned by Kaiser-Frazer, a giant automobile company that has almost disappeared from memory. Later, the factory was purchased by General Motors.

It was the dawn of the post–World War II era, the "fabulous fifties." The U.S. auto industry reigned supreme in the industrial world, emerging from the war stronger than ever, an unparalleled leviathan of manufacturing. It would be many years before Detroit, just a few miles from Willow Run, would be threatened by automobile makers in Japan and Germany.

In boom times, new cars emerged from the monstrous Willow Run facility at a rate of one per minute, twenty-four hours a day, seven days a week. Many of the men from our community who had fought in the war now worked at the plant, building cars. The wages were high, and it seemed that everyone we knew either had a job there or wanted one.

But in spite of the plant's prominence as an exemplar of America's peacetime industrial might, local residents still called it "the bomber plant." During World War II, the mighty B-24 Liberator bombers, the terrifying warplanes used to help free Europe from Hitler's grasp and beat the Japanese in the Pacific, were built at Willow Run. At the height of the conflict, they had rolled ponderously down the plant's mile-long assembly line, one after another, each swarmed over by a small army of workers, many of them women. The bombers couldn't be built as fast as the automobiles, but they were built fast enough to help us win the war. At its peak, the bomber plant employed tens of thousands of workers.

When growing up, we were told that even "Rosie the Riveter" had worked at Willow Run. During the war, Rosie had become both famous and familiar to every American, a symbol of determination and hope, of hard work and good spirits in tough times. She was featured in government films promoting war bonds and in the "We Can Do It!" posters, plastered all over offices and factories, posters that symbolized American women working in the defense industry. It was a symbol and an experience that would change American society in the postwar era. But in 1949, that wasn't so obvious. With the men back from the war, most of the women who had worked alongside Rosie, making the weapons to fight the war, were now at home raising their contributions to the baby-boom generation.

■　　■　　■

Looking back, I think the people of Willow Run represented the spirit of post–World War II America, particularly in those years, the early half of the 1950s.

We had just been through a war in which America had triumphed, not just because we fought, but because we worked our way to victory, united as never before. We believed that honest, hard work made any dream possible.

We had little in the way of material wealth. But spending and leisure weren't part of the equation. Life centered on family, church, school, and community. It was a spirit that shaped me, a set of core beliefs that have guided my actions for all my years.

The threat of war was still real and physical. Every so often at school an alarm siren would go off, signaling a mock atomic attack. "Duck and cover," our teacher would yell. Then all the other children and I would scramble under our desks to protect ourselves from flying glass. We knew it was possible that our country, and our homes and schools, might be destroyed at any time.

But we weren't too worried. God was on our side. School began with the Pledge of Allegiance to the Flag, all of us singing "God Bless America," and hearing an early morning prayer. The national controversy over prayer in schools was still in the future.

And yet, science and mathematics were high on the list of important subjects in school. We were told that studying science was crucial to our futures and to the future of America. The country wasn't resting on its laurels after the second of the wars to end all wars. We felt like we were in a race, still fighting, still competing with the Russians to be the most powerful and influential nation in the world. The bomber plant at Willow Run was a constant reminder of the military and industrial strength of our nation and the role our community had played in helping to win the war. The people in our town, the people my family knew, were deeply and sincerely patriotic. We believed that our country was the greatest and most generous nation on earth. Though we considered peace to be constantly at risk, we were optimistic about our futures. As we watched the Cold War develop, the arms race accelerate, and Communism spread around the world, we still believed that America was invincible.

■   ■   ■

As a young boy, I often played cowboys and Indians or war. When my brother and I played war with our friends, the bad guys were always the Japanese, never the Germans. I'm not sure why; perhaps it was the early war movies we watched dramatizing war in the Pacific. I always ended up on the side of the good guys—the Americans. And the good guys always won.

Our pretend battles took place on an island somewhere in the Pacific. The beach was our backyard, grown muddy with countless battles. Using cornstalks as logs, we built defense bunkers in a large drainage ditch that ran alongside the yard. Behind the ditch was a wooded area, which became the jungle. As we stalked each other through the green tropical jungle or crouched in the bunkers waiting for the enemy, we carried wooden toy rifles. Our hand grenades came from the garden: large, juicy, overripe tomatoes. One of us always carried a small American flag.

Acting as courageous American soldiers, we charged across the beachhead, shouting "Bang-bang-bang." We tossed our hand grenades into the bunkers, while dodging those hurled at us by the Japanese.

When hit by the juice, skin, or seed from a hand grenade, we were counted as either wounded or killed, based on the size of the tomato stain. Years later, in another tropical jungle, no more or less real to me than this one, I would be wounded by a hand grenade while fighting an Asian enemy.

Sometimes, in our pretend wars, prisoners were taken. If we Americans got captured, the enemy tortured us. Our captors first marched us through the woods in single file to a large willow tree. They ordered us to remove our shirts. We had to hang by our hands from a low branch, feet off the ground. Then one of the Japanese soldiers, using a willow switch, administered five very hard lashes across our bare backs. We could stop the torture at any point by crying "uncle" and dropping from the branch. Though the stinging lashes hurt and sometimes caused welts, we never cried uncle. To capitulate meant giving secret information to the enemy and endangering our friends—something we could not do.

Sometimes the Americans captured the Japanese. We didn't torture them. We gave them candy cigarettes. We were the good guys.

It seemed like the most exciting and important thing in the world, fighting for your country, being brave, and being tough enough to withstand torture. Most of all, being honorable. That's what we were taught, what we saw in the black-and-white war movies, what we absorbed from the thoughts and words and stories of the people of Willow Run. It's what we believed.

■ ■ ■

By the late 1950s, we had moved to Belleville, just a few miles from Willow Run. Dad's job situation changed for the better. Since arriving in Michigan, he had managed the lunch counters in two "five and dime" stores, partnered in a failed diner, and toiled long hours in an aluminum foundry. Now he was settled into a more secure civil service position, managing the food-service operations at a state mental hospital. Mom worked as the night-shift nursing supervisor at the general hospital in Ypsilanti. Sally, who later became a nurse herself, was wowing the boys as the lead cheerleader at the high school.

My brother, Dick, who would soon run on the track team with me and later avoid going to Vietnam, was finishing up in junior high. I had stopped playing little boy games like cowboys and Indians and war. I was a teenage boy in high school, true to nature.

High school sports, rock and roll, and trying to "get a little feel" were high on my priority list of extracurricular activities. On Friday nights during the fall and winter, it seemed as if the whole town turned out to see my teammates and me play football and basketball. It was thrilling to hear the roar of the hometown crowd, everyone supporting us and cheering us on to victory. Later in our lives, some of us found as soldiers fighting for victory in the biggest contest of all, war, that the home crowd didn't always support us. And they seldom cheered.

After the games we went to the sock hops in the high school gymnasium, where we danced the night away to the tunes of some of the early icons of rock and roll like Buddy Holly, the Platters, and Elvis Presley. At the dances and the parties held after the games, we drank soft drinks or fruit punch. Alcohol, let alone drugs, had not yet hit the Midwestern high school scene.

When I turned sixteen, I learned to drive my Dad's blue and white '56 Chevy, his first-ever new car. I thought I was pretty cool. It wasn't hard to get a date for a drive-in movie with a car like that. Oh, the memories I have of making out in the back seat, necking, and frantically trying to undo bras, but never going all the way. The sexual revolution was nowhere in sight, and "good girls" vowed to stay virgins until marriage.

As my class approached the end of our senior year, we were apprehensive about what lay ahead, but we knew we could handle it—we were all grown-up. Most girls seemed to look forward to becoming good wives and homemakers, boys to getting a job in Willow Run or entering the military service. A relatively small number of kids in my class planned on going to college. I was one of them. I wanted to become a doctor.

■   ■   ■

On graduating from Belleville High School in 1959, I felt the mood in and around Willow Run, and indeed around the nation, starting to change. The world was now clearly divided into two major camps: the Free World and the Communists. The struggle was more than competition. There was a tension that was deadly and all consuming, global in scope. More than anything else, it shaped our picture of the world from Willow Run.

We had watched America and its NATO allies fight Communist aggression in Korea, but not to victory. There was still a festering truce, a standoff at the Thirty-eighth Parallel, which separates North and South Korea. The good guys hadn't won. We heard about the Communist Vietminh forces defeating the French at Dien Bien Phu, in far-off Vietnam. But we didn't really understand its significance. Asia was still far away, but getting closer with every war.

The Iron Curtain, a heavily patrolled border of tank barriers, barbed wire, minefields, and armed fortifications separating Communist Eastern Europe from Western Europe, was now firmly in place. Nikita Khrushchev, Russia's crude and aggressive leader, seemed bent on enslaving the entire world under Communism. He was on the march in so-called wars of liberation in Southeast Asia, Africa, and South America.

With the Russian launch in late 1958 of Sputnik, the first earth-orbiting satellite, America was now chasing Russia in the race to outer space. We were both developing long-range missiles capable of reaching across the oceans to touch each other's towns and cities. For the first time in history, America was at serious risk from war with a foreign power. The U.S. Strategic Air Command had B-52 bombers loaded with nuclear bombs in the air twenty-four hours a day all around the globe—waiting for the order to drop them somewhere. We considered ourselves behind in the arms race. We would have to work hard to catch up.

The threat of a nuclear war was very real. It was present, palpable. In the papers every day, in the movies, and on the radio, we talked about it. We found it hard to believe that it would not happen someday. We just didn't know when or how or whether America would be able to retaliate effectively if Russia struck first. Just six months before my graduation from high school, Cuba, a mere 100 miles off the coast of Florida, fell to Fidel Castro and to Communism. The whole southeastern United States was in striking distance of his warplanes. The enemy was knocking at our door.

Families like ours participated in community civil defense exercises simulating the aftermath of atomic attacks. We learned how to identify the symptoms of radioactive fallout and how to administer first aid. We boiled water to purify it. We practiced outdoor field cooking in simulated contaminated areas. I learned how to bake bread in a fifty-five-gallon metal barrel over an open fire in the woods. We assumed, during the exercises, that our town no longer existed, that most everyone had been killed or injured. It was very serious business.

■　■　■

During the summer between high school and college, I too joined the legions of people from our community who had worked, or were then working, at "the bomber plant." I landed a job spot-welding fenders on the new Chevrolet Corvair, a compact automobile many times smaller than the giant B-24 bombers that had rolled off the same assembly line.

Spot-welding is pretty boring. You can get a lot of thinking done on the line. As the metal bodies inched by, in the flash and glare of the welding machine, I often thought about how the people must have felt working at the plant during the war, about how their work helped win the war and saved the world. I was pretty proud to be working there, too, part of the history of Willow Run.

I also thought about the backyard battles of my childhood. I knew that the time in my life when wars were just memory or imagination was long gone. There were real wars still happening in the world. I was convinced, as we all were, that America might soon fight in another real war against the Communists. I loved my country. I believed in our leaders and in the spirit of Willow Run. I knew that if called to fight, I would go.

The Fateful Decision

As a child growing up, in and around Willow Run, I was often asked by other children, "What did your dad do in the war?" I hated that question. It seemed like nearly everyone's dad had been in the Army, Navy, Marines, or Air Corps. But not my father. He'd never served in the armed forces at all.

At the time he received his induction notice, he was the civilian manager of the officers' club at the Naval Air Station in Pensacola, Florida. That's where the Navy trained pilots for duty on aircraft carriers. At my father's request, strings were pulled. His induction order was rescinded.

Dad often showed me pictures of himself with many of the Navy's top brass at the lavish banquets and officers' club parties he had organized on their behalf. He had a smile on his face and an arm around their uniformed shoulders. I remember wondering—in my little boy mind—how he could be enjoying himself when so many men were going and dying in the fighting overseas. One time, I asked Dad why he didn't go into the service. He said, "Son, I had a family. My first duty was to them."

I wanted my father to be a hero, like I thought the other boys' fathers were. Instead, I thought, he took the easy and safe way out of the war. It always bothered me. I sometimes wondered, Is my dad a coward? Later, as an adult, it didn't seem so simple.

■   ■   ■

In the fall of 1959, I left my job at the bomber plant in Willow Run. I was going off to college. But I wasn't going very far.

Living on campus at a big name university was out of the question. There simply was no money for that in the family budget. The college was Eastern Michigan University in Ypsilanti, Michigan. The campus was only a few miles from our house on Borgstrom Street. So I lived at home in the same old room and commuted by car to classes every day.

There was little in the family treasury for tuition and books, either. Earning the cash to stay in college was as inevitable and inescapable as going to classes and studying. And it often consumed more of my life.

During the school year, I flipped hamburgers at the student lounge in Mckinney Hall. As a member of the varsity track team, I worked on the university's grounds maintenance crew. Off campus, I cashiered and stocked shelves at Bailes' Pharmacy. I also did landscaping at a nursing home. During summers, I worked as a state park ranger tending to the campgrounds and woodlands of W. J. Hayes State Park, a two-hour drive to the west of Ypsilanti.

I had enrolled in the premedical program, which made its own grueling demands for class time and study. So there wasn't much breathing room left for parties, pep rallies, and hanging out on campus. In fact, there was no time at all. It was hard not to feel left out, and I usually did.

There was one other inescapable obligation. EMU, like many state colleges and universities, is a land-grant school. It sits on public land given years ago to the State of Michigan by the U.S. government for the purpose of building a state college. When I went to college, land-grant schools were required by law to offer a four-year Army Reserve Officers Training Corps (ROTC) program. All male students attending a land-grant college were required to enroll in Basic ROTC during their freshman and sophomore years.

Thus, twice a week, while crisscrossing EMU's bucolic ivy-laden campus, we wore the Army-green uniform of an ROTC cadet. It was the first time in my life, but not the last.

■ ■ ■

In the beginning, most freshmen regarded ROTC as a dreadful chore and even an embarrassment. We felt that we looked lousy in our drab, baggy uniforms. Worse yet, it signaled to everyone on campus our lowly status as underclassmen. But gradually I changed my mind. I started to like the training. The curriculum included leadership topics such as developing responsibility and loyalty and setting an example. I thought these could help me all my life. Other subjects, like close-order drill, radio communications, map reading, and marksmanship, seemed concrete and tangible, even fun. It was a welcome change from the dry and general academic course of study required during the first two years at a state university.

Normally, I would have been finished with ROTC and been out of the Army-green uniform after my second year at school. Like most students entering the basic program, I planned to drop ROTC after my sophomore year. At the time, relatively few juniors and seniors enrolled in the advanced program, which was voluntary. Graduates of Advanced ROTC received a second lieutenant's commission in the U.S. Army Reserve and were obligated to spend two years on active duty after graduating from college. That wasn't part of my life plan.

But late in my freshmen year, I learned that the Army paid the postgraduate education expenses for individuals who successfully completed the advanced program. For me, postgraduate meant medical school. And medical school, I knew, was going to be very expensive. The family budget would be no help, and flipping burgers wasn't going to make it either.

All of a sudden, ROTC looked different to me. It was a path to the future, a means to an end. If I didn't have the money when I graduated, which seemed overwhelmingly probable, the Army could pay my way through medical school. When the summer of my sophomore year at EMU ended, I faced the decision: Join Advanced ROTC or drop the military life altogether.

It wasn't a decision made in a vacuum. Even running between classes, jobs, and ROTC, I was acutely conscious of world events. Willow Run had made planes for a war where the U.S. and Russia were allies. But that alliance had quickly deteriorated into a bitter struggle on a global scale. Now, in 1961, the Cold War was intensifying. Russia had resumed aboveground nuclear testing, after not doing so for several years. Relations between the United States and the entire Communist Bloc of nations were severely strained. John F. Kennedy, president for nearly a year, had loudly and publicly vowed to stop the worldwide spread of Communism.

Soon after taking office, Kennedy was faced with Communist aggression in Laos, in a part of the world that seemed very far away to Americans then. But he swiftly fulfilled his vow by sending military aid and advisers. Their mission was to help the established government in Laos resist the rebellion. And in April of that year, a small army of anti-Castro rebels, aided by the U.S. government, launched what became the doomed invasion of the Bay of Pigs in Cuba.

During that summer of my decision, there came an even more serious blow to peace, a major escalation in the struggle. The Communist East Germans, with Russian support, constructed the Berlin Wall.

It was a dreadful symbol and a terrifying reality—a twelve-foot-high concrete barrier with barbed wire and other deadly traps on top. The wall was guarded twenty-four hours a day by East German soldiers and guard dogs, searchlights, and rifles and machine guns. The people of East Berlin were prisoners behind the wall. Many East Berliners tried to visit relatives or seek freedom in West Berlin by climbing over or tunneling under the wall. If detected, they were shot.

Watching from Willow Run, many of us were alarmed at what was going on around the world. We became convinced that a real war, a hot war, might break out at any time. It seemed that Khrushchev and the Communists were landing one punch after another and that we might lose the fight to save the Free World. More and more able-bodied young American men were being drafted for two years of military service somewhere in the world.

After thinking about it for a long time and talking it over with my family, I decided to enroll in Advanced ROTC. We reasoned that I was killing the proverbial two birds with one stone. If I gained acceptance to medical school, the Army would pay my way. If not, I would serve my two years of active duty—which now seemed certain with or without ROTC—as a commissioned officer, rather than a draftee. It seemed like the logical decision, somehow inevitable and inescapable.

On returning to school in September to begin my junior year, I went to the ROTC office and signed up. All juniors in the advanced program were required to schedule a thorough physical examination at Fort Jackson in Detroit. When we reported for the physical, we took our place in a long line of new recruits. We stripped to our skivvies and proceeded from station to station in the typical hurry-up-and-wait fashion of the Army. We were questioned, weighed, measured, poked, pricked, electrically monitored, X-rayed, and eyeballed.

It took almost three hours to complete the examination. I didn't know why, but we were left totally naked for over an hour. It was chilly and my penis shrunk up like a turtle's head, peering out of its shell. It was humiliating. I kept wanting to hide it with my hands. What a wimp I must have looked like. The whole excruciating process seemed eternal, but it finally ended.

The results? Except for my eyesight, I passed with flying colors. But my eyes were a major problem. Having worn thick glasses since childhood, I tested 20/450 in one eye and 20/500 in the other. I was near-blind.

At the last station, a nerdish private first class looked up at me, flashed a big grin, and gave me a thumbs-up. Then, he stamped the top page of my physical examination report, in large red letters: "Not Eligible for Combat Arms: Infantry, Armor, Artillery, Corps of Engineers, and Signal Corps." Of course, I thought. The Army didn't want a soldier in the heat of battle who couldn't see without glasses. What if the glasses were knocked off and broken and he was suddenly helpless, a burden to his comrades?

So I couldn't go into combat. So what? I didn't care. After all, my grand plan was to go into the Medical Services Corps. I was going to serve my time in the Army as a medical student and then as a doctor. My eyes wouldn't be a problem. I carried a copy of that report back to the ROTC office at school. It was placed in my "permanent file."

■ ■ ■

Now that I was officially in the Advanced ROTC program, I saw a real difference in the content and quality of the instruction. We studied world affairs, applied leadership, counterinsurgency, and small-unit tactics. The instructors were top-notch sergeants and junior officers. Several had seen combat in Korea. All were true professionals, as well as excellent motivators.

One of them, Master Sergeant Frank Maki, became a valued mentor and a close friend. Frank's crew-cut good looks, military bearing, and combat decorations made him a come-to-life recruiting poster. But it was his direct and active commitment to duty, honor, and country that I remember most. Later, as a young officer, I tried very hard to emulate the example he set. In the summer of 1971, then-Captain Frank Maki was killed by enemy fire in Vietnam.

I worked hard at ROTC and received high grades. Our class was preparing for summer camp, scheduled for July and August, at Fort Riley, Kansas. At summer camp, we would go through our basic training, similar to training that raw recruits and draftees experience.

I was beginning to feel like a soldier, but I still saw the Army as just a means to an end, a more important end—a career in medicine. I studied just as hard all year to keep up my grade point average in my premedical subjects. My plan was to go to the University of Michigan's College of Medicine in Ann Arbor. To gain admission, it was crucial that I do well on the standardized Medical College Admissions Test, which I'd have to take early in my senior year. That was my real goal, the prize I was holding up in my mind's eye.

■　■　■

In mid-July 1962, I left my summer park ranger job and boarded a bus with other ROTC cadets from EMU for Fort Riley, Kansas. When we arrived, most of us were asleep in our seats. It was early in the morning. We awoke to the shouts of a burly drill sergeant: "Wake up, girls; get out and form a line, belly-button-to-butt, you miserable good-for-nothing pinheads!" We stumbled out and lined up, yelled at and taunted each step of the way. "Double-time haaach, get moving, college boys!"

We ran to the supply center, stopped at the door, and entered one at a time. We moved in a line, right-to-left, past piles of boots, socks, underwear, fatigue pants, shirts, helmets, packs, and webbing. At each pile we stopped, yelled out our size, and caught what was thrown at us. When we had all our gear, we formed up outside in another belly-button-to-butt line, our arms overflowing with clothing and equipment. Then we double-timed it 500 yards to the Third Platoon, G Company barracks.

I dropped a boot.

"Give me twenty-five, you clumsy four-eyed ballerina," yelled the sergeant. I dropped to my knees, laid down my load, and barked off twenty-five push-ups. Then I picked up my stuff and ran to catch up. "You better catch them, four-eyes, before they get to that barracks, or it's fifty more." Just as I caught them, I dropped my other boot. That terrifying voice was even more scathing, "You a slow learner, four-eyes. Get your skinny ass back to where you started and give me 100 more."

It took awhile for me to do the agonizing push-ups. So by the time I got to the barracks, the sergeant's instruction on how to keep our gear in footlockers was already under way. A few minutes later: "Four eyes, show us how a soldier folds underwear."

"Sergeant, I missed that."

"You got four eyes and you still can't see. Give me fifty."

"Yes, Sergeant!" and down I went, barking off fifty more push-ups, my arms straining and aching to give way with each push.

And so went the rest of the day. I was yelled at, humiliated, and punished physically until lights out and Taps. Lying in my army cot staring up at the wooden ceiling, I was physically and emotionally exhausted—and trembling. I wondered if I could hold myself together. Would I make it through the training? I wanted to quit. Go home. I knew they were trying to break me. But why was I the one? The one, out of all the men in my platoon, who was mocked and verbally attacked where it hurt most, in that area of my self-image where I was most easily humiliated. Since I was a kid, I had always felt inferior because of my glasses.

All night long I lay awake, flat on my bunk. Exhausted as I was, all I could think about was what the next day was going to be like. I was convinced I couldn't go on with it. Toward morning, I thought about my father. Whenever I complained to him about someone or a situation I was faced with, he would say, *"Non illegitimis carborundum."* When I asked him what that meant, he said, "Don't let the bastards get you down."

Just as the sun came up and Reveille sounded, I resolved to stick it out. In spite of everything, I would beat them at their own game. I couldn't bring myself to quit and give them the satisfaction of my failure. Somehow I found the determination to get up and face the day. I don't quite know how I did it, but with no sleep, running on pure nervous energy, I somehow met the challenge of the next day. And I met it again on all the following days.

Six weeks later, at the summer camp graduation ceremony, I was named the top cadet in my platoon and in my company of over 200 men. I had achieved the highest scores in all areas of training: physical conditioning, weapons, marksmanship, communications, map reading, chemical warfare, tactics, and leadership. Standing on the platform in front of the whole camp, I thought to myself, four-eyes had come quite a long way since that first long day and night.

■   ■   ■

In spite of that moment of pride, or perhaps because of it, I was even more determined to become a doctor. I wasn't eager to repeat that kind of line-soldier experience. So in September 1962, when I returned to school for my senior year, I was ready to put all my energy into preparing for medical school.

But on my first day back, there was a message for me to report to the ROTC office. The commanding officer, Colonel George Murray, was waiting for me.

He announced that he was promoting me to cadet colonel and commander of cadets. I was now the student leader for over one thousand cadets at EMU. Murray said the combination of my high class standing, summer camp achievements, and faculty leadership ratings made me the outstanding candidate. Murray also told me that the

Army was awarding me the first-ever scholarship for an EMU student showing outstanding promise as a future Army officer.

For a moment, I didn't know what to say. Then I told him that I was honored, and that I needed the money, but that my intentions were to pursue a career as a doctor. He reminded me that a career in the Army and a career in medicine were not mutually exclusive; I could pursue both directions at the same time. Of course, I thought. I didn't have to choose between them.

Outside the narrow focus of my life and plans, the world continued to be split in two by ideology. Just a month after I returned to school, the Russians moved long-range missiles into Cuba, giving Castro the capability of launching a nuclear attack on the United States. In response, President Kennedy ordered a naval blockade of Cuba and demanded that the Russians dismantle Cuba's nuclear weapons. Khrushchev threatened an attack. The citizens of Willow Run and the entire world watched and waited, fearing World War III.

After several tense days at the brink of a possible Armageddon, Khrushchev backed down, and the Russians complied with Kennedy's demands. The Cuban missile crisis was over. But I think that America had come closer to nuclear war than ever before. And perhaps ever since.

The missile crisis and my new responsibilities in ROTC distracted me during the first two months of my senior year, but I was still able to throw myself into the stressful ordeal of applying to medical school. I did well on the standardized Medical College Admissions Test and applied to the University of Michigan and two other top schools. I was very confident about my chances of getting accepted. I believed that solid academics, leadership, athletic achievement, and having worked my way through college were enough to get me into one of the better schools.

I was wrong. Not a single acceptance. I received rejection letters from all three schools to which I had applied. I was disappointed and astonished. How could I have been so confident and so mistaken?

Several months later, I met a member of the University of Michigan Admissions Committee through a mutual friend, Harry Hidenfelter, my high school football coach. I learned from the committee member that all of the qualifications of which I was so proud were, of course, helpful. However, most everyone applying to a top-ranked school could boast much the same—and more. I learned, to my dismay, that getting into a top-ranked medical school took more than I was able to provide.

Without the immediate prospect of medical school, I was faced with the harsh reality of going directly into the service—on the very day of graduation from college. My plans for medical school would be placed on hold. I was in a state of disbelief. Was this really happening? What was I going to do?

I now had to make a decision I hadn't expected at all. I needed to select the branch of the Army for my tour of duty. There was, however, an obvious and logical choice. Given my interest in medicine, my family and friends assumed that I was going to select the Medical Services Corps, where I could serve in an administrative capacity even though I wasn't a doctor.

I didn't. I chose the infantry.

■   ■   ■

Like many other infantry officers I knew who had made the same choice, I don't know if I can completely explain that decision. The infantry, the so-called queen of battle, was arguably the riskiest branch and the most dangerous choice we could make. There were many reasons that I gave myself. Not getting into medical school was a big one. There were many others. I was influenced by an old book that I read two months before making my decision: the Tower Books 1943 edition of *Living Philosophies: A Series of Intimate Credos*. In it, Albert Einstein writes of his and of all mankind's lives being dependent on the labors of those that have gone before us and that he, we, often borrow too heavily from the work of others. Though he wasn't referring specifically to military service—he was a committed pacifist—his words stuck with me, moving me as few others had.

JFK was also a factor in my thinking. During his inaugural speech in 1961 and on several other occasions, he had said to all

Americans, "Ask not what your country can do for you, ask what you can do for your country." His words inspired me. I thought of the freedom and the way of life my family and I enjoyed. I didn't want to borrow from the many that had died fighting to preserve our way of life. Odd as it may seem, I reasoned that if I could not serve my country as a doctor, saving lives in the event of war, I had to risk my life—as others had before me.

In the end, perhaps the most important influence on my decision was my father's own choice, long ago. At some very deep level, I knew I couldn't take the easy road as, to me, my father had taken during World War II.

■   ■   ■

It wasn't an inescapable decision. In fact, the Army didn't make it easy for me. To qualify for the infantry, I needed to take another physical examination and pass it with flying colors. I had already taken a second physical at the beginning of my senior year. Like the first one, because of my abominable eyesight, it was stamped "Not Eligible for Combat Arms . . ." in large red letters.

This time I was determined to pass muster. Before leaving for Detroit for my third examination, I took my glasses off and put in my newly acquired contact lens. Of course, contact lenses wouldn't be any better in combat than glasses, but perhaps I could fake my way through the examination. On the long ride to Fort Jackson, I sat on the bus and looked out the window, wondering if I could pull it off. The examination was as endless and excruciating as before. The eye exam station was the last stop in the exam process. I walked into the tiny office. The eye specialist quickly said, "Read the top line of the chart on the far wall."

I responded, "A P F C."

"Now read the bottom line."

I said, "H K N S."

"Congratulations, soldier. The Snellen chart shows you have 20/20 vision."

The specialist didn't ask any questions or look into my eyes to check them further. He just marked 20/20 for both eyes on my physical examination report. Then he gave the report to me.

I walked the report down the hall to the medical records file clerk. He pulled my file and placed the new report on top of the two previous reports. The "Not Eligible . . ." notation was still clearly visible on each of them. I took my copy of the results back to the ROTC office at school. It was placed in my permanent file.

I still wonder if anyone ever reviewed it and found the discrepancies.

■　■　■

One month before graduation, Colonel Murray informed me that two others and I would graduate as Distinguished Military Graduates (DMGs). As DMGs, we would be eligible for a Regular Army (RA) commission, similar to a West Point graduate. If we accepted an RA commission, we would be obligated to serve three years on active duty, rather than only two as reserve officers. After the three years, all we would need to do is initiate some routine paperwork resigning our regular commissions and accepting reserve commissions on inactive status.

Murray went on to say, I think as an incentive, that individuals accepting an RA commission could choose the country they preferred for their initial assignment. In fact, that had a strong appeal to me. I had always wanted to see Europe, and I'd studied four years of German as part of my premedical work. An extra year seemed, at the time, a small price to pay for the opportunity to see Europe. I accepted the RA commission and requested Germany for my assignment.

I graduated from EMU on June 8, 1963. I was commissioned, on that day, a second lieutenant in the Regular Army. During the swearing-in process, I raised my right hand and swore that I would ". . . defend the Constitution of the United States of America from all enemies, foreign and domestic. . . ."

Mom, with a proud smile on her face, pinned the gold bars of a second lieutenant to the epaulettes on my new summer-tan dress uniform. Sergeant Maki was the first to salute me: "Congratulations,

Lieutenant Brewer—sir." As Army tradition required, I presented him with a brand new one-dollar bill.

Colonel Murray hosted a postcommissioning reception for all the new lieutenants and their families. Later, in the afternoon, Mom and Dad threw a backyard barbecue party in my honor for neighbors and friends. The next day, I left for Fort Benning, Georgia, where I was to receive additional training prior to my departure for Germany.

I felt at the time, in spite of all my carefully considered choices, that I was being swept away by events. Events that were way beyond my control.

Fort Benning

"**F**ollow Me," said the letters on the large white-on-royal-blue sign arching over the main gate. Follow Me was the creed infantry officers live with and for during their time in the Army.

It was June 10, 1963, two years since the summer of my decision to enter Advanced ROTC and just two days after my graduation from college in Michigan. I had just arrived at the entrance to Fort Benning, Georgia, the headquarters for the U.S. Army's Infantry School. The Infantry School is where the Army trains its officers to lead soldiers in fulfilling the infantry's mission.

The world has changed much since 1963, as has the means of waging war. I would guess the infantry's mission may have also changed, perhaps grown in complexity. But back then, the mission of the infantry was deceptively simple: "To close with and destroy the enemy." Other branches of the Army existed primarily to support the infantry and its mission. Logistical units kept the infantrymen supplied. Tanks, armored vehicles, and helicopters transported them to the battle. Artillery provided the firepower necessary to support the engagement on the ground. Engineers built roads, bridges, bases, and airstrips. Medical units cared for the wounded.

But it was the infantryman who had the bloody job of engaging the enemy, eyeball-to-eyeball, and destroying him with rifle fire, grenades, machine guns, rockets, bayonets, pistols, and sometimes with his bare hands or anything else he could find.

The infantry officer's job is to accomplish the mission, while tending to the welfare of his troops—in that order. The mission is the first priority. It's not a healthy or natural way to think. All human beings want to live. But in ground combat, the chances of losing your life are very high. So the infantry officer must find a way to lead his soldiers into and through the savage chaos of battle, conscious that he or any one of them may die. He must keep the mission, not survival, foremost in his own mind and the minds of his troops. Because the mission always comes first.

So the two words painted on the crescent-shaped sign over the entrance, in white on royal blue, have a very special meaning to an infantry officer. Follow Me is the infantry officer's motto. It means leadership by example. In combat, an infantry officer must show courage and gain the respect of his troops by going first into battle. He must be aggressive, competent, and determined. But above all, he must be selfless as he and his men close with and destroy the enemy.

By the time I left Fort Benning, Follow Me was as much a part of my personal values as my Midwestern upbringing.

■ ■ ■

As I rolled up to the gate to the Infantry School in my white Volkswagen Beetle, I was stopped by two smartly uniformed military policemen, MPs. One of them bent over and squinted at me through the rolled-down window of the car.

"Can we help you?" he said. I handed him the documents from the Department of the Army that directed me to report to Benning. He looked at the orders, then suddenly shot upright, standing rigidly at attention, and saluted me. "Sorry, sir, I couldn't tell you were an officer with your civvies on! Welcome to Fort Benning."

The MP directed me to G-1, the personnel office for the school. He raised the gate and saluted me again as I drove away.

I discovered I was somewhat uncomfortable. I had just received my first salutes as an officer from someone I didn't know. It seemed that just by arriving I had been promoted to another level of humanity. "Am I really worthy of a salute?" I thought, as I passed through the gate into my future.

I rolled past row after row of two-story, yellow-beige barracks buildings on carpets of green lawn. I saw churches with tall steeples, marching fields, firing ranges, and obstacle courses. In the distance stood multistory administration buildings with the U.S. flag, the Fort Benning flag, and regimental colors flying high. Lined up with lawns and small sidewalks sat block after block of identical housing units for people assigned to the fort on a permanent basis. Traffic on the roads was busy and monochromatic; Jeeps, trucks, buses, and sedans painted an identical shade of olive-drab crisscrossed my path at every stop sign.

Everything was orderly and clean; there wasn't a speck of trash or litter. And it seemed to go on forever. Benning was a giant city in itself, spanning the horizon, perhaps larger than any of the towns I grew up in. Everywhere I looked groups of soldiers were marching or running to the cadence count of drill instructors and platoon leaders: "Hup-two-three-four, hup-two-three-four, hup-two-three-four. . . ." Many of the groups wore the uniforms of allied nations. I imagined a sense of purpose, even history, in the air.

As I made my way nearer to G-1, I thought about the next couple of months. It was only mid-June. The nine-week-long Infantry Officer Basic Course, IOBC-4, that I was scheduled to attend didn't begin until August. After IOBC, I was scheduled for a month of airborne (called parachute or jump) training and nine weeks of ranger training. As an individual option, new Regular Army officers were required to attend at least one of these special schools. I was eager to learn what I would be doing until August.

When I finally found G-1, I parked the car and walked slowly up the steps. I hesitated, took a deep breath, and entered. At that moment I was very conscious that a boundary was being crossed. I was stepping over an invisible line. This was for real. Now, I was in the Army. Not training for it, not headed for it. In the Army.

At the front desk, I was welcomed by a dutiful staff sergeant. He in turn introduced me to the personnel officer, the jocular Major Rollins. In the first few minutes of an orientation by Rollins, I learned something new. My three-year overseas service obligation did not, in fact, include my time at Fort Benning. The clock started the day I left the United States for Germany.

My orders called for me to depart in late December. Until then, I was on "temporary duty in route to my permanent station." Though I was still proud to be serving my country, I wasn't really that interested in spending any more than three years with Uncle Sam. Six weeks would pass before I started IOBC-4. I quickly considered my options. Three other IOBC classes were scheduled ahead of IOBC-4. I put it to Rollins. "Can I attend an earlier IOBC?"

He chuckled genially. It appeared to be his characteristic approach to difficult questions, or perhaps he just enjoyed saying no. "That's not possible," he said. "You're on orders for IOBC-4 because it is the only session designed specifically for Regular Army officers, West Point graduates, and Distinguished Military Graduates, like you, from civilian colleges."

I tried another approach. "Can I go to airborne training before IOBC?" He smiled again. "Negative. You might get injured and not be able to start IOBC-4 on time."

"Okay," I said. "What about ranger training?" Rollins was still genial. "Negative, for the same reason. But as an RA officer, you're only required to attend either airborne or ranger training after IOBC-4, not both. Are you sure you want both?"

I did, I thought, but not if it was going to extend my stay at Fort Benning, which wasn't counted in my three-year obligation. At the time, my commitment to the Army still seemed like something that was under my control. So I decided to drop ranger training. This saved me only a few weeks, given my overall schedule and the start dates for the training courses I was scheduled to attend.

It appeared that nothing else could be done to shorten the wasted weeks or enable an earlier departure. "What, sir, am I supposed to do between now and IOBC-4?"

The major chuckled some more. He seemed to enjoy his job. "Just hang around," he said. "Try to keep yourself busy."

I couldn't believe my ears. And I certainly didn't see any humor in my predicament, not then. The immediate reaction was a flush of anger, though I kept it to myself. I had been ordered by the Army to active duty immediately on graduation from college. I had packed up; said good-bye to home, job, friends, and family; and driven to Fort

Benning. And now I was going to sit on my butt, while getting paid to pretend I was busy. "What a waste," I thought. Up to this point, I thought that the Army was a *gung-ho*, fast-charging outfit. I had just experienced my largest dose ever of the Army's "hurry-up-and-wait" syndrome. It wouldn't be my last.

■ ■ ■

During my first week at Benning, I spent my days just killing time—walking around the base, watching others being trained, reading anything I could get my hands on, and playing many games of billiards at the officers' club. Lots of other guys were in the same predicament.

Perhaps in retrospect, it might have seemed like a vacation. But after working four jobs to get through college, pushing myself as hard as I could to get good grades in both academic subjects and in ROTC, I had trouble adjusting to having nothing to do. Each day seemed a week. I was bored stiff. I kept thinking of all the taxpayer money going to support my temporary life of leisure.

I had to find something. The following week, I met a Captain Johnson, who was also on temporary duty. He was filling the time by escorting foreign army officers who were attending advanced infantry training at Fort Benning on trips to the NASA Space Center in Cape Canaveral, Florida. At the cape, they toured America's rocket launch facilities. Afterwards, they were entertained at generous parties thrown by civilian contractors attached to NASA. The contractors worked on the Saturn rockets, one of which would later take Neil Armstrong to the moon.

I asked Johnson if I could help him out. Two days later, with Johnson's help, I was organizing a trip to Canaveral for thirty officers from various allied nations.

We escorted several groups in July. It was interesting, and it alleviated the sense of waste. We frequently talked with the foreign officers, all of whom spoke some amount of English. They were from places like West Germany, France, Great Britain, Italy, several South American countries, Turkey, Greece, and also Iran, a nation that would later become our enemy. It was pretty cosmopolitan for a twenty-two-year-old from Michigan.

The topic that most concerned the visitors was the state of civil rights and race relations in the United States. Martin Luther King Jr. and other civil rights activists had recently caught the attention of the world. In the spring of that year, King and his followers had peacefully marched for desegregation in Birmingham, only to be beaten back by fire hoses and club-wielding policemen. And there was talk of an August march on Washington, D.C. It was at this march where King would deliver his eloquent and much celebrated "I Have a Dream" speech, about freedom and equality and courage in the face of oppression.

Yet in June, President Kennedy had delivered a famous speech of his own, the "Ich bin ein Berliner" speech in West Berlin, celebrating freedom and his identification with the oppressed citizens of East Germany. The Allied officers questioned us time and again about why we Americans preached freedom and democracy to others around the world, while treating our own black citizens so poorly. Neither Johnson nor I had any answers. And for the first time in my young life, I could see how outsiders viewed our actions as Americans. Our behavior was often very much at odds with the ideals we tried to transport to other nations. For a young man from Willow Run, it was one of the first introductions, outside of the classroom, to the reality that the world contained a multitude of valid viewpoints.

■　■　■

On a hot and humid third of August, just days before IOBC-4 started, I married my first wife, nineteen-year-old Kathy Kellogg of Detroit. She had been my on-again, off-again girlfriend during my last two years of college. I had called her during a lonely spell, soon after my arrival at Benning, and asked her to fly down and marry me. She said yes, without hesitating.

Since I was already at Benning, with time on my hands, I made all the arrangements. It was a small wedding, so all we had to worry about was scheduling the facilities and making sure that everyone was able to get there and have a place to stay. It went smoothly. We were married at the base chapel and held a small reception at the officers' club for our immediate families and some of my new Army buddies. I recall Kathy's family being quite excited about her marrying an Army officer ready to whisk her off to Germany for three years.

We honeymooned at an inexpensive motel outside of Calloway Gardens, Georgia. Both of us were virgins. Consummating the marriage was a protracted nightmare. She was tense and I too eager, and certainly not sensitive enough to her needs.

It was only two days, but I was glad when it was over. I think she was, too. We left the motel a day early and moved into a small studio apartment in downtown Columbus, Georgia, just minutes from the base. As was the case with much of the temporary housing outside an Army base, the place was filthy. We spent two days cleaning and painting till we dropped from exhaustion. Then it was time for IOBC-4 to begin.

For the next three months, including nine weeks of IOBC and three weeks of airborne training, I was gone from dawn to dusk and often away on night and weekend maneuvers. I was immersed body and soul in the rigorous training. Even when I was home, I had to spend much of my time studying, polishing my brass and shoes, and prepping my uniforms.

Kathy was over a thousand miles from home, with no family or friends nearby, nobody to talk to, and nothing much to do. She was very unhappy. I can't blame her, though at the time, I didn't understand why she wasn't the vibrant new bride I thought she should be. We struggled, tried to console each other, and looked forward to Germany. We thought things would get better.

■   ■   ■

The course of training in IOBC—a highly concentrated extension of my ROTC training—was aimed at turning me and my classmates into infantry troop unit commanders. It was to prepare us to be "leaders of men in combat," as it said in the Army manuals.

Initially, we concentrated on advanced training in basic soldiering such as physical conditioning, marksmanship, bayonet training, map reading, compass work, explosives, escape and evasion, chemical warfare, and small-unit tactics. After we mastered the basics, we focused on the leadership skills necessary to accomplish our mission as infantry officers.

The knowledge and the dedication of all of the instructors at Fort Benning were impressive. Like those in the Advanced ROTC program, they were a top-notch group of young officers and seasoned noncommissioned officers. All were highly trained and experienced in the topics they taught. However, I found that it was the sergeants on the faculty who taught me and my classmates how to become good leaders—how to take infantrymen into combat and bring as many back as we could. Many of these noncommissioned officers had seen action in Korea. They were capable small-unit leaders themselves. They knew, firsthand, what it takes to lead men in battle.

One of the first things we learned about leadership was the importance of gaining the respect of our troops. Soldiers go into battle because of the Army's system of discipline. But the maintenance of that fighting spirit needed to win the day stems from the respect and loyalty that a unit has towards its leader. Gaining the respect of our troops wouldn't be easy. We would have to know our jobs well and set a good example. If we tried to bluff it or couldn't demonstrate competence, morale would suffer and casualties might rise. And we were told to never ask our troops to do something we wouldn't do ourselves. If they experience hardship, share it with them. Stay calm when the going gets tough. And demonstrate in everything we do a strong sense of personal responsibility and loyalty to our troops—and also to those above us in the chain of command.

Becoming good instructors was yet another area of intense focus during our IOBC experience. We studied the psychology of learning, how to design effective training, and how to teach our troops by using proven instructional methods. Much of our time as young officers would be spent as instructors working, with our sergeants, to teach the soldiers in our units all they needed to know as combat infantrymen.

Our instructors stressed over and over again how important it is to keep our men informed; it's critical to building high morale and effective teamwork. We learned to show each man how his job relates to other jobs. The goal was to build a sense of mutual support and teamwork.

For me, one of the most important things that we learned at Fort Benning was to know our men and to take care of them. It was a lesson that would come back to me again and again in Vietnam and later in life. Army units, numbering hundreds or thousands, are still made up of individual human beings, each with a different personality and different capabilities. Knowing each one as an individual would help us build the best teams possible. It would also help build trust in us as leaders. If we earned their respect and their trust, our troops would follow us into battle.

As our training progressed, I could see that the principles of leadership we were learning might also apply later in civilian life, with one very big difference. In the Army, men's lives would depend on how well we performed.

■   ■   ■

The nine weeks of IOBC-4 training ended. All that was left before I shipped out to Germany were three weeks of airborne training. By comparison to the leadership classes, airborne was resoundingly physical.

The instructors seemed intent on keeping our hearts and lungs working at maximum overload. We double-timed it, ran everywhere, and did hundreds of push-ups and sit-ups each day. And they wasted no time in preparing us to throw ourselves from an airplane into empty space.

During the first week, we learned the five-point parachute-landing fall by jumping from a low platform without a parachute. By the end of week two, they had us jumping from a thirty-two-foot-high tower, up and down like a yo-yo, while attached to a bungee cord suspended from a steel cable. At the start of the third week, in preparation for our first of five jumps from an airplane, we learned the parachutist song, sung to the tune of the "Battle Hymn of the Republic." As I remember, here are the first verse and chorus:

There was blood up on the risers,
There were brains up on his chute,
Intestines were a-hangin' from his paratrooper boots.

Gory, gory, what a hellava way to die,
Gory, gory, what a hellava way to die,
Gory, gory, what a hellava way to die,
And he ain't gonna jump no more.

I landed hard on my first jump. I felt a sharp pain in my left foot as it struck a rock hidden in the tall grass where I fell.

By the time I got home that night, I could hardly walk. I put ice on my foot for several hours and watched it turn black-and-blue.

What should I do? If I went to sick call to have the foot examined and treated, I might be prevented from jumping the following day, and every day thereafter until it healed. If that happened, I would be recycled back to the beginning of jump school. I would have to go through the full three weeks of training again before leaving Fort Benning.

Unacceptable. I wanted desperately to complete my five successful jumps, graduate from airborne school, and be awarded the coveted silver wings of an Army parachutist, on schedule.

The next morning, I wrapped the abused foot as tightly as I could with several rolls of one-inch adhesive tape, creating a cast-like enclosure. I borrowed a larger left boot from a friend so my foot could squeeze inside.

I made the next four jumps with my "cast" on. The instructors didn't seem to notice. The pain was almost unbearable, but not as much as the thought of going through the entire training again and wasting all that time before I could depart for Germany.

Later I learned that I had fractured several small bones.

■ ■ ■

The day after graduation from jump school, Kathy and I packed everything we owned into our Volkswagen Beetle. Then we set out, with our ironing board sticking up through the sunroof, for Kathy's home in Detroit. I was granted a short leave before my departure for Germany. Her home would be our base until I left.

We pulled up to the curb in front of her mother's Tudor-style house on Detroit's west side. Kathy jumped out. As she ran in to say hello, I started to unload the car. I took the ironing board first and started limping across the small lawn toward the house.

The front door flew open. "Hurry, hurry up, Tom," Kathy shouted, "something has happened to President Kennedy."

I hobbled in as fast as I could with my sore foot and set the board down in the foyer. Just as I peaked into the living room, where everyone was huddled around the black-and-white television, I heard news broadcaster Walter Cronkite say, "President Kennedy has been shot during a motorcade in Dallas."

I gasped. A cold chill pierced my shoulders and back; my skin pricked up with goose bumps. With my back against the wall, I slid down onto the floor. My breathing sounded loud in my own ears. It was November 22, 1963.

For the next three days we were glued in front of the television. We watched the nightmare unfold. We saw the police take Lee Harvey Oswald into custody. We learned of Oswald's trips to Russia and Cuba before the shooting. And even more incredibly, we saw Jack Ruby step from a crowd in Dallas and shoot Oswald as he was being moved from one jail to another. Like millions of other people around the world, we had trouble believing what we were witnessing.

When I left three weeks later for Germany and my first troop assignment, I was sure, in my mind, that the Communists had assassinated Kennedy through Oswald. I was not alone in that conviction. There was a quiet hysteria in America as everyone held their breath and waited for the consequences.

I thought about all that I had learned at Benning and about the state of the Free World I was pledged to protect—the hot Cold War, the assassination, the missile crisis, and the standoff at the Iron Curtain in Europe. I wondered, will there be a real war, will I be given a mission to "close with and destroy the enemy"? Most of all I wondered, am I ready—am I ready to have men follow me into battle?

Gelnhausen

The repeating wail of the alert siren ripped into my sleep at three o'clock in the morning. It had been a long two-and-a-half years since I left Fort Benning for Germany. My dreams that night could have been of my much anticipated trip home.

I bolted from bed and pulled on my Army fatigues and boots. Then I dashed down the stairs, grabbed my heavy field jacket, and ran out the door into the deep black of the night. After jumping onto my bicycle, I leaned on the pedals and bounced down the cobblestone path that led from my apartment to the main street. I had to reach Coleman Kaserne, and quickly.

The *kaserne,* an old German Army post, was now used by the American Army. The alert siren meant I had less than thirty minutes to get to Bravo Company, headquartered at the *kaserne.* The procedure had been drilled into us. The siren could sound at any hour, day or night.

I jumped off the bicycle and leaned it against the wall outside of Bravo's headquarters. After making sure that all of my troops were present and accounted for, I got into my Jeep at the head of Bravo's column of sixteen armored vehicles. MPs were directing traffic on the road out of the *kaserne.* Then I led Bravo into its appointed slot in the steady stream of olive-drab vehicles: Jeeps, tanks, armored personnel carriers, self-propelled howitzers, and supply trucks.

Within minutes, the whole organism, miles long, was snaking slowly through the fairy-tale villages of southern Hesse, in darkness under a star-filled sky. A sizable fraction of the American Army was on the move, headed for the border between West Germany and East Germany to confront the massive Soviet armies stationed there.

Two hours later, we had reached our designated area. We moved into defensive positions. I sat in my Jeep and stared through my binoculars across the Iron Curtain, close enough to see them, rows and rows of Communist tanks and soldiers, staring back at me from the other side.

It was May 1966, and this was the last of many combat alerts I had participated in since coming to Germany. In just one week, I was to depart for a new duty station back in the United States.

On my bicycle, peddling down village streets to the *kaserne* under those fairy-tale stars, I had hoped, as always, that this was just another practice and not the real thing.

■　　■　　■

I had first arrived in the town of Gelnhausen two-and-a-half years earlier, at Christmastime in 1963. It was home to the Third Armored Division's 48th Infantry Dragoons, to which I was assigned. Kathy, then five months pregnant with our first child, Caroline, joined me two months later. Gelnhausen is a medieval village, small and quaint, walled with stone. It sits on the Kinzig River, approximately twenty miles northeast of Frankfurt, Germany. In 1963, the tiny community found itself highly strategic, just a short distance from what was then the Iron Curtain.

The Berlin Wall had been in place for over two years and East-West relations were heavily strained. President John F. Kennedy was assassinated in late November 1963, just one month before my arrival. The German people of Gelnhausen spoke of him often, as a hero. As I did at the time, many of them also thought that Communists had been behind the plot to kill Kennedy.

The consensus among the military's top brass was that if war broke out, it would happen in Germany. Along the border of West Germany, Soviet forces outnumbered NATO forces at least ten to one. The European countries were relatively small and densely populated; it wouldn't take long for the huge Soviet mechanized force to overrun West Germany and France. The speed of the Nazi advance in World War II, which crushed France in six weeks, would be nothing compared to this modern juggernaut.

Our mission in Gelnhausen was to help defend against a Soviet armored attack through the Fulda Gap. The gap was a broad valley through the mountains on the border of West Germany, which had become critical to NATO planning in Europe. It offered the shortest invasion route between the Communist armies of Eastern Europe and Paris. It was felt that if the Soviet Army wanted to strike at the heart of democratic Europe, it would be through this narrow passage. It followed that our little medieval town, with its toy stone walls, was on the front lines of the Cold War.

But we were massively outnumbered in terms of conventional forces: soldiers, guns, and tanks. By ourselves, we had no chance of defending the Fulda Gap. In an attempt to balance the opposing forces, NATO planners had decreed the use of nuclear weapons. In my battalion of the 48th Infantry, we were equipped with Jeep-mounted Davy Crockett cannons, which fired tactical nuclear warheads. These were relatively small nuclear devices that would explode over the battlefield, destroying tanks and soldiers, and indeed anything in their limited radius of destruction.

Tactical nuclear weapons were intended to help us fight a delaying action against our numerically superior foe. Senior NATO commanders maintained that without nuclear weapons, Soviet tank divisions could crush us. And yet nobody could guarantee that the Soviets, once nuclear weapons were used, would not escalate the conflict to strategic nuclear weapons, including long-range bombers and missiles striking directly at the United States. It was scary to think that we were ready to start a nuclear war if the Soviets crossed the border.

■　■　■

The daily routine at the *kaserne* meant long hours with our soldiers, assuring their physical fitness and professional readiness for what might lie ahead. An officer's annual efficiency rating, and thus his future career, depended heavily on combat readiness.

I was struck by the diversity of the soldiers under my command. They came in all sizes, shapes, and colors, from all walks of life, from city ghettos and heartland farms. Some had not finished high school, while others had college degrees. Some were ex-criminals. My job, first as platoon leader and later as company commander, was to train them, motivate them, and take care of their needs. If necessary, I had to discipline them.

A continuing challenge for all of us was mechanical readiness, keeping our tanks and armored personnel carriers in top mechanical shape. Day in and day out, we performed maintenance and tested equipment. Inspections from higher headquarters were frequent. It was no good having the best weapons in the world if they didn't work on the one day you needed them.

When not at the *kaserne*, we participated in war games, massive field exercises that could last weeks or months. In the heat of summer or the freezing cold of winter, Bravo Company would mobilize to far-off villages with storybook names like Grafenwohr, Hohenfels, and Wildflecken. As part of an exercise, we might be pitted against other NATO forces, like the West German or French troops. They often played the role of the Communist aggressors.

Together, we fought large mock tank battles, reminiscent of the bloody mechanized conflicts of World War II—battles in which the formidable German armored divisions had ranged across the landscapes of Europe, fighting American Sherman tanks from the assembly lines of Detroit or Russian T-1s built by factories in the Urals. Now Germany was our ally, and Russia the enemy.

At the time, we were impressed with the realism of the simulated battles, or what seemed to us like realism. Generals and staff officers developed elaborate plans at the strategic and tactical level. The plans were carried out with the utmost precision. There were umpires, and pretend casualties were counted on both sides. We used blank ammunition. Ground was gained or lost and missions accomplished based on the unit's overall tactical proficiency. Success was measured by the hills and towns we captured. Seizing and holding territory, good old terra firma, was always of utmost priority.

Later, in Vietnam, some of us would find a war where the reality was very different. Winning and losing was not a matter of territory and objectives. A different concept, *body count*, was the official measure of success. And in that real war, we would come to realize that it is not planning and precision but arrant chaos that characterizes most battles and raw courage that determines the outcome.

■ ■ ■

I was lucky to be sent to Germany. It was considered a prime assignment. The junior officer ranks in the division included many highly motivated West Point graduates, as well as Army ROTC graduates, like me.

In retrospect, it seems that all of us, myself and the young officers I met there, came from a bygone era, an era that may have ended with the Vietnam War. We believed, heart and soul, in America. We believed in its leaders and in America's place as the leader of the Free World. We thought of our stand in Germany as a symbol for the world, a testament to America's determination to protect the rights of free people.

I was moved by the esprit de corps, devotion to duty, and patriotism of my peers. Most of them would later fight in Vietnam. Some would die. Many of the West Pointers that I knew who had chosen the Army as a career, and survived Vietnam, would later leave the service, disillusioned.

Our social lives in Gelnhausen were fairly simple and circumscribed. Activity centered on the officers' club, where parties and dances were frequent in a sort of country club atmosphere, or on informal get-togethers at a friend's apartment. With all of us thousands of miles from home and living in a foreign country, we relied heavily on each other for moral support and friendship.

At the same time, we viewed the opportunity to see Europe as a tremendous benefit. Many of us wouldn't have had the opportunity were it not for the Army. We organized auto and train trips as a group to places like France, Italy, Great Britain, Spain, the Netherlands, and Denmark. Many of us learned to ski at the Army's ski resort on the Zugspitze, Germany's highest mountain, located in the Bavarian Alps near Garmisch-Partenkirchen. And each year a gang of us invaded Munich during Oktoberfest to raise a little hell. We drank our fill of beer while listening to *oompah-pah* bands dressed in lederhosen shorts. Then we sang German beer-drinking songs till early in the morning. As we stumbled our way home, we always managed to cop a few souvenir beer steins from one of Munich's largest and most raucous beer houses, the Hofbrauhaus.

When not on duty, we played hard and had fun. As someone who worked his way through college and missed out on a lot of the social life along the way, I relished the camaraderie that existed among the young officers in Gelnhausen. I look back on the days spent with them as some of the best times of my life.

■   ■   ■

Up until mid-1965 we didn't hear much in Germany about Vietnam, other than an occasional reference on the Army's radio station or in the *Stars and Stripes*, the Army newspaper. Only a small number of American advisers were in Vietnam. No one in Gelnhausen seemed too concerned about the conflict. We all assumed it was just a limited effort. And it was nothing by comparison to what we would face if the Soviets burst across the border. But by midyear, President Johnson had sent the first American ground troops to Vietnam. Sporadic reports of American casualties were beginning to reach us.

In July, my company commander was unexpectedly transferred back to the States, early, to train recruits for Vietnam. As a first lieutenant, I then assumed command of Bravo Company, normally a captain's job. The same thing was happening in all the units at Coleman Kaserne, indeed, all over Germany. First lieutenants, like me, found themselves commanding infantry companies. All of the captains were being shipped back to the states to help with the buildup for Vietnam.

In November, we learned of the battle in the Ia Drang Valley in the Central Highlands of Vietnam. Two battalions of the Seventh

Cavalry, Custer's old unit, were decimated. Hundreds of Americans lost their lives in one of the bloodiest battles of the entire war. It was reported that American wounded caught on the battlefield by the North Vietnamese were either beaten to death, bayoneted, tied up and shot in the head, or cut apart with machetes.

By the end of the year nearly 200,000 American troops were in Vietnam. The U.S. government was denying reports that it was reducing the commitment of American troops to Europe. Those of us in Germany had a hard time believing the reports. While it was true that the actual number of Army divisions had not changed, this was not the case with troop strength. It appeared that all of the brigades, battalions, and companies making up a division were operating with about half the normal troops. Many of the units were commanded by officers holding a lower rank than specified in Army regulations. Soldiers at all levels were returning to the States or other duty stations far faster than they were being replaced.

In spite of what was happening, I still believed that I would complete my tour in Germany. I planned on leaving the service in late 1966, after serving my three years in Germany. When I accepted my Regular Army commission, I was assured that I would be released from active duty after three years, unless there was a major war. All I had to do, ninety days before my three years ended, was tender my resignation as a Regular Army officer.

I had served one year more than required as an ROTC reserve officer and Vietnam was not considered a major war. So I was confident that I would be discharged as planned. Furthermore, President Johnson and Secretary of Defense Robert McNamara were assuring the American people that the "conflict" in Vietnam would be over soon. At the time, I didn't have any reason to doubt them.

However, in January 1966, an ominous pattern emerged. Many of the Regular Army company-grade officers, lieutenants and captains, who had left Gelnhausen during the summer of 1965 were now on their way to Vietnam.

Reserve officers with two-year obligations were serving out their complete tours in Germany. Afterwards, they were discharged from active duty. But RA officers were seeing their tours in Germany cut short.

After rotating back to Army training centers in the States, they spent six months training new recruits. Then they went to Vietnam.

So I was caught by my own decision in college years ago. I could have been a reserve officer, but I had chosen the Regular Army commission and training, and I was bound by that commitment.

Without giving up hope, I was beginning to question my confidence that I would be allowed to leave the Army as originally planned. I put my chances at no better than fifty-fifty.

■　　■　　■

During our 1966 winter war games, Field Exercise Silver Talon, my battalion was under the command of Lieutenant Colonel John Norvell. He had assumed command only a few months earlier. Colonel Norvell had recently returned from a tour of duty as a military adviser in Vietnam. He had also served earlier in his career in Korea, having seen action with the 27th Infantry Wolfhounds. He was quick to gain the respect and ear of all the young officers, who were eager to learn something firsthand about what was going on in Vietnam.

Each night, after the day's operations, we sat around a kerosene space heater in the command tent listening to his Vietnam stories. He spoke often of the challenges of trying to help South Vietnamese troops, ill-equipped and poorly trained, to fight their war against the tenacious Vietcong. We saw him as a straight shooter who didn't attempt to glorify war, or even justify it. He was a career West Pointer dedicated to his profession and eager to give us any advice he could, much of it on how to stay alive if we ended up in Vietnam. While he never said it, I think he questioned the soundness of our early policies in Vietnam.

On one occasion during Silver Talon, Colonel Norvell became very upset with a decision I had made regarding one of the soldiers in Bravo Company. At the time, I thought he was cruel and indifferent. I later realized how right he was to dress me down for my actions and how important the lesson was that I learned from it all.

Private First Class Sandler and his platoon sergeant, Sergeant Ogilvy, had approached me two days after we got into the field.

"Lieutenant Brewer, Sandler has a problem. We need to talk to you about it," said Ogilvy.

"What is it, Sandler?"

"Sir, my wife is ill," said Sandler. "I need to return to Gelnhausen to be with her. She's pregnant, and I'm afraid something might happen to the baby."

"I'm very sorry about your wife, Sandler, but can't a friend's wife stay with her?" I asked.

"She hasn't really met anyone yet and I'm really worried about her. Please, sir, can I go?"

"How can you get there? It's five hours away," I said.

"We would have to send him back with one of the Jeeps," Ogilvy said.

After exploring the alternatives with Ogilvy, we concluded that the only way for him to return was by Jeep. I authorized the trip and asked Ogilvy to see to it that a Jeep and driver be made available so Sandler could leave immediately. Then we could have the Jeep and driver back early the next day.

Later that day, a Jeep belonging to the battalion's reconnaissance platoon was declared destroyed by one of the umpires. Colonel Norvell, code name Tango Six, called me on the radio.

"Bravo Six, this is Tango Six. Over."

"Tango Six, Bravo Six. Over," I responded.

"Bravo Six, I need to requisition a Jeep from you. We've got Red Force in front of us; I need to send recon up to take a look. Over," Norvell said.

"Tango Six, negative. Don't have one. Over," I replied.

"Bravo Six, you brought them all with you, didn't you? Over."

"Tango Six, Bravo Six, roger, but I had to send one back. Over," I said.

After briefly describing the circumstances regarding my decision to send the Jeep back with Sandler, I could tell that Norvell was annoyed. He told me to report to him in the battalion command post (CP) at nineteen hundred hours (seven in the evening).

At the end of the day, I reported to the CP as directed. When I entered, Norvell asked everyone else to leave the tent.

"Lieutenant Brewer, reporting as ordered, sir," I said as I saluted. "At ease, Brewer," Norvell said, his brow furrowed, staring critically into my eyes. "You did a stupid thing today by letting yourself feel sorry for Sandler. There are times in combat when a Jeep can be more important than one man's problems. If this were the real thing you could have gotten a lot of people killed by sacrificing a Jeep needed to scout out the enemy."

"I didn't know it would be needed, sir," I replied.

"When you're in a real battle, Lieutenant Brewer, you never know what you might need from minute to minute," Norvell said. "Don't ever make a decision one minute that might jeopardize the lives of your men the next minute; do you understand me?"

"Yes, sir," I said. Norvell excused me. I left the tent, my pride hurt, thinking he was a jerk. After all, it wasn't a real war and I thought that, given the circumstances, I was looking out for the welfare of my men.

A few days later, during one of our nightly officer chats, Norvell referred to the Sandler incident. He said that since we were simulating war conditions, I should have handled the situation differently: Tell Sandler that we would contact one of the officer's wives in Gelnhausen. Ask her to visit Sandler's wife and offer assistance. If a true emergency developed, we would send him back. Until then, we needed him and the Jeep to accomplish our mission.

After thinking, repeatedly, about the Sandler incident, I came to the conclusion that Colonel Norvell got angry at me as a way to get my fullest attention on a very important point. Then he used the incident as a teaching point for me and the other young officers under his command. The Sandler incident, and the way Norvell handled it, helped me do a better job at balancing the two critical, sometimes conflicting, priorities facing a commander: accomplishing the mission *and* maintaining the welfare of the troops. It helped me time and again in Vietnam, where the lives of my men were at stake, and later in the business world, where the jobs of my employees were at stake.

When Silver Talon ended, it did so on a high note for me. Colonel Norvell presented Bravo Company with an achievement award for "exemplary tactical proficiency" during the six-week-long exercise. We had achieved all of our objectives while taking a small number of "casualties." All of us in Bravo worked hard in preparation for Silver Talon; it was nice to get some recognition for our efforts. But the Sandler incident wasn't forgotten, not by me.

■ ■ ■

A week after we returned to Gelnhausen from the exercise, I received orders from the Department of the Army that directed me to report, in June, to the Third Basic Combat Training Brigade at Fort Leonard Wood, Missouri.

I was leaving Germany six months before my tour of duty was over, like so many other officers—the ones who had been assigned to Vietnam. I still intended to submit the paperwork for my resignation. But I had to accept the very real probability that my original plans had gone awry, that I would soon find myself on the way to Vietnam. It seemed inescapable.

Kathy was happy to be leaving. For her it had been a long two and a half years. As the only officer's wife in our group without a college degree, and the only new mother, she often hinted at not fitting in with the other wives, particularly at wives-only functions when the other officers and I were in the field. I tried to understand her feelings and reassure her, though I'm sure, not being in her shoes and experiencing her frustrations firsthand, I was nowhere close to being up to the task.

When I finally left Gelnhausen in early May of 1966, Colonel Norvell hosted a going-away party for me and several others who were departing the battalion. I was one of the last to leave the party, after drinking all too many flaming brandies and singing "I Left My Heart in San Francisco" over and over again, in poor imitation of Tony Bennett.

On my way out the door to Colonel Norvell's residence, he shook my hand, slapped me on the shoulder, and said, "Good luck, Brewer. If you get to Vietnam and end up in the 25th Division, try to get into the Wolfhounds."

"I will," I said. "And thanks, sir, for all your help."

Selectively Retained

I tore open the official-looking letter from Dow Corning, a subsidiary of Dow Chemical. After a polite opening, the letter announced that "those with whom you interviewed were very much impressed by your background and qualifications; therefore, we would like to offer you a position in either Technical Sales or Professional Personnel at a rate of $675.00 per month. We understand that it will take you approximately ninety days to process your resignation from active duty in the Army. If you accept our offer, we will hold the position for you until your release from the service."

It was June 6, 1966, and we were staying at my parents' home in Ypsilanti, Michigan, after returning to the States from Gelnhausen. Technically, I was still in the Army, but mentally it seemed like I had one foot outside the door.

I had taken a two-week leave en route from Germany to Fort Leonard Wood and spent all of that time looking for a job. The economic realities of life were looming larger and larger. Our first child, Caroline Marie, was born in Germany during the spring of 1964, and now Kathy was pregnant again. With a growing family and no rich relatives in sight, medical school would have to wait. I needed a job, and soon. The letter from Dow Corning made all the difference in our prospects.

Two days later we left Michigan, eager to reach Fort Leonard Wood. I planned to process my resignation as soon as possible—and say good-bye to the Regular Army.

■   ■   ■

On June 10, we arrived at Fort Leonard Wood's Third Basic Combat Training Brigade. After taking a few days to get settled, I assumed command of a basic combat training company. As company commander, I was responsible for "the training, administration, billeting, counseling, and discipline of 220 to 300 basic trainees." In other words, I had to teach a gaggle of teenage American boys, eighteen and nineteen years old, how to kill enemy soldiers with rifles, bayonets, machine guns, pistols, hand grenades, rocket launchers, and their bare hands.

It was a skill that seemed more and more practical. At the time, America's troop commitment to Vietnam was growing rapidly. These boys might have to fight and defend themselves in a few months. So I took my job seriously, even though I hoped to be leaving active duty soon.

The trainees came from all over America and from all walks of life. Some were draftees, but many were volunteers. Most were white. Much has been written about the preponderance of black soldiers serving in combat units during the Vietnam era. My experience was different. The majority of men serving in the infantry units I commanded, over a period of four years, in Germany, the United States, and Vietnam, were white Caucasians. A small percentage were black; some were Hispanics and some Asian-Americans. To me, the mix of enlisted men in the Army seemed to mirror the U.S. population as a whole.

After eight weeks of basic training, all my trainees would move on to advanced training. Many would then go to Vietnam. Most would be sent as individual replacements for soldiers killed or wounded in Vietnam or for soldiers completing their mandatory twelve-month tour of duty.

That was a feature of the Vietnam experience that distinguished it from previous American wars. In all of our other conflicts, the young men in a unit trained together, shipped out together, and fought together. That was a key factor in the fellowship, esprit de corps, and morale of Americans in combat. But the majority of those who served in Vietnam, after the initial buildup, went there as individuals.

This often resulted in a sense of loneliness and isolation, an alienation that characterized many a soldier's tour of duty in Vietnam. This was particularly true when a man first joined a unit as a replacement. "Short-timers," soldiers with only a few weeks or months left before returning home, were often leery of a "fucking new guy" (FNG). They didn't want to be teamed with someone lacking combat experience, who might do something stupid and get them killed. It takes a long time to establish confidence and trust between the men in a combat unit. In Vietnam that time wasn't always available.

■　　■　　■

But none of this was going to affect me, I thought. On June 20, I sent a letter to Dow Corning accepting the job offer. On June 22, I submitted the necessary paperwork tendering my resignation from the Regular Army, under the provisions of Army Regulation 635-120, effective October 1, 1966. Regulation AR 635-120 provided for the release after three years on active duty of Regular Army officers commissioned through ROTC. My three years were up on June 8. Major Roberts, my battalion commander, and Colonel Gooding, my brigade commander, sent my request forward.

But their cover letters recommended that my request be disapproved: "in view of the present critical need for experienced and well-qualified officers at the unit commander level and with no foreseeable alleviation of the situation, the retention of Captain Brewer on active duty is considered in the best interest and current needs of the military." I had been promoted from first lieutenant to captain on June 30, prior to the date of their cover letters.

When my paperwork reached Major General T. H. Lipscomb, who was commander of the United States Army Training Center and Fort Leonard Wood, he recommended approval and sent my request up the line to Fifth Army Headquarters. At the time, I thought that Roberts and Gooding were kissing up by not recommending approval and that Lipscomb was fair minded and perhaps better able to apply Army regulations to a case like mine. I was still optimistic. I began making plans for leaving active duty.

Through the rest of the hot Missouri summer, I worked hard with the drill sergeants to make ours the best company in the battalion. Then, on August 29, I got the news. In Washington, the Department of the Army had disapproved my resignation. According to the Department, "the critical needs of the Army mandate that you be selectively retained on active duty for another eighteen months with a new ETS of March 31, 1968." ETS meant "End of Time in Service."

The Army had just recently instituted what later became a highly controversial "selective retention" program. Some Regular Army officers in my category were being released after three years. But others were selectively retained due to the "needs of the service." Most of those retained on active duty had similar backgrounds. We had all served as company-grade unit commanders, in combat-ready units, in countries like Germany and Korea. We were considered ripe for Vietnam.

So in spite of my careful plans, I was still entangled by my own choices and by the tides of history, circa 1966. Even though the notice from the Army had not mentioned Vietnam, I fully expected to get orders soon.

When Dow Corning learned of my change in status, the company assured me that it would still have a job for me on my eventual discharge from the service. In fact, the company seemed pleased that I would have my service behind me when I returned. It had recently been experiencing the inefficiencies that went with hiring and training American college graduates, only to see many of them get drafted soon after they joined the company.

■　■　■

On September 4, my disappointment was mixed with happiness over the birth of our second daughter, Suzanne Elizabeth. Caroline now had a sister to grow up with. I felt a very lucky man to be blessed with these two healthy little girls.

But just nine days later, on September 13, I received a set of priority orders from the Department of the Army. They directed me to report, in early 1967, for Jungle Warfare Training in Panama's Canal

Zone. After completing training, I was to report directly, without delay, to the 25th Infantry Division in Cu Chi, South Vietnam.

I sat on the couch in the living room, stunned. Across the room, loving pictures of my mother and father sat on the television looking down at me as I sat staring at the orders. Kathy had taken Caroline with her to the post exchange to do some shopping. Suzanne was sleeping in her bassinet just down the hall. Through the living room bay window, I could see the afternoon shadows growing longer. The house was silent. I could almost hear my heart beating against my chest.

At that moment there was something unreal and dream-like about what was happening. Many images ran through my mind, all the things that seemed to lead inevitably to this moment. I remembered playing war with my brother in the muddy backyard in Willow Run and how I used to feel about my father not serving in World War II. I remembered all the scenes from the Cold War while I was growing up, the constant sense of dread from the threat of Communism, and all the politicians and presidents who voiced America's commitment to the ideals of freedom and democracy. I remembered the stark images of the Berlin Wall and the East Germans shot by Communist soldiers while trying to escape, over or under the wall. I remembered John F. Kennedy's pledge, and Lyndon Johnson's after him, to take a stand against the spread of Communism in Asia and around the world.

And I recalled my own choices, conscious or not. Joining ROTC and faking my eyesight during my physical exam so that I could join the infantry. Struggling so hard to excel in all the military training that I was offered the RA commission. Going to Germany and making myself into one of the "experienced and well qualified officers at the unit and commander level" that the Army now needed so critically.

I thought, for a long while, about the oath I took to defend America against all enemies, foreign and domestic. I realized that I had spent much of my life preparing to fight the Communists, if it ever came to that. It had, and I was mentally prepared for it—or at least I thought I was.

Kathy and Caroline returned. I handed the orders to Kathy. Without looking at them she tossed them on the couch. "I know what they say," she said. "I can tell by the look on your face." She was more angry than sad; then she said, "I knew this would happen. You'll never be let out of the damn Army. I hate it; I want to go home." Caroline started to cry.

■ ■ ■

The next several months were difficult. I wanted to spend as much time as I could with my family before going to Panama. But the time was just not there; I had used most of my leave looking for a job on returning from Germany. And there would be one last surreal bureaucratic blunder that would soak up much of the remaining weeks.

One morning, I arrived at company headquarters. There was a line in front of the door. More than a hundred of my trainees were waiting to see me. I was shocked at how many were standing there; normally there were only three or four in a single morning. I wondered, what was up?

First Sergeant Whipple showed me a new Army regulation that he had just posted. It proclaimed that homosexual soldiers were not authorized in the Army, and it directed that all soldiers claiming to be homosexual be immediately discharged. The result was predictable. Soldiers have excellent survival instincts. A hundred of the most intelligent stood outside my door. They had calculated that it would be better to leave the service with a general discharge for being homosexual than to die as a heterosexual in Vietnam.

With commanders all over the training center experiencing the same dilemma, it didn't take long for the Army to see what a dumb regulation it had written. It was immediately rescinded and replaced with a revised rule. However, the new version was not much better—it required a great deal of time to enforce.

As I recall, it specified three categories of suspected homosexual soldier: self-proclaimed, accused by a fellow soldier, or caught in the act. Only those caught in the act were to be immediately discharged. The other categories would be investigated. With the posting of the revised regulation, things calmed down, slowly. But it took me a lot of time, away from family, to deal with the mess.

When I did have some time to spend with the children, it was very emotional for me. I played with them and often held them close. All the time I was thinking that in a few months, I would leave and might never see them again.

While the children slept, I read everything written about Vietnam that I could get my hands on. If I had to go, by God, I was going to prepare myself as best I could. There had to be some way to increase my chances of returning home.

I was beginning to realize that little of my training applied to Vietnam. What I had learned in Germany was how to fight a conventional war, using tank tactics from World Wars I and II. Even at Fort Leonard Wood, we focused only on basic training. The Vietnam conflict was an unconventional war, being fought against an unconventional enemy, in jungle terrain that made conventional armor and weapons systems ineffective. The rules had to be very different.

I read all of the Army's after-action reports on infantry battles in Vietnam. I read every book I could find, including *Street without Joy* and *Hell in a Very Small Place* by Bernard Fall; *The Making of a Quagmire* by David Halberstam; and *Peoples Party, Peoples War* by General Vo Nguyen Giap, North Vietnam's much revered military leader.

It was clear that the Vietcong and North Vietnamese Communists were a dedicated, tenacious, and clever enemy with a lot of patience. They were committed to win the struggle, no matter how many years it took or how many generations of Vietnamese. It was also clear that the South Vietnamese military was inept and corrupt. Obviously, they would need a lot of our help to win the war.

I also read an article in *Harpers* magazine by retired General S. L. A. Marshall, where he described a key Vietcong tactic: always waiting until they outnumbered their enemy before moving in for the attack. In the article, he wrote of a battle in which an infantry company had been lifted by helicopter into a small jungle clearing. A platoon was left behind to secure the landing zone, while the majority of the company moved out in search of VC. The Vietcong watched the American soldiers from hidden positions until most of the troops had departed. Then they unleashed a vicious and decisive assault on the remaining Americans, now heavily outnumbered.

The article would be prophetic of my own experience in Vietnam. Soon after arriving, I found myself fighting to survive in a remarkably similar battle.

Christmas that year was a very sad time for me. It was just two weeks before I had to leave for Panama and then for Vietnam. Christmas carols proclaiming peace on earth and goodwill toward men seemed ironic and out of place. In front of the children, I acted as if I was in control of my feelings. But all the time I was fighting hard to hold back my crying. Still there were many times, when I looked in on Caroline and Suzanne, lying so innocently in their sleep, that tears slipped down my cheeks.

In January, it was time to go. In some ways, I was relieved. I wanted to get on with it. I wanted the sadness of leaving to end.

The day before I departed Fort Leonard Wood, Major Roberts and Colonel Gooding asked me to report to them in Gooding's office. They informed me that the Army had approved their recommendation that I be awarded the Army Commendation Medal for my company's achievements while serving with them. The citation read, "his company attained test results that far exceeded the stated United States Continental Army Command's goals in all graded phases . . . and his sincere devotion to duty resulted in a significant contribution to the overall training excellence of this command."

I was shocked; I felt strongly that if any award was handed out, it should have gone to the drill sergeants who did most of the training. Without their professionalism and loyalty, I would have accomplished very little. The same was true in Germany, and it was true of sergeants with whom I later served in Vietnam.

As I was leaving, I told Major Roberts and Colonel Gooding that I couldn't feel good about the award unless something was done for the top two drill sergeants that worked with me. Major Roberts assured me that it was customary to recognize the drill sergeants when they were reassigned, just as it had been with me. With this knowledge, I felt a little better.

■　　■　　■

My father had taken a job in Lansing, Michigan, and offered to rent us the place in Ypsilanti during the twelve months I would be in Vietnam. It was a very generous offer, for I'm sure he could have put the equity he had in the house to good use in Lansing. On January 5, I drove Kathy and the children to Michigan and settled them into my parents' home. I was grateful and happy that I didn't have to leave the family on an Army base, like Fort Leonard Wood, and that they could be close to relatives during my absence. I had heard that it was particularly difficult for the families that stayed on Army bases. The high concentration of military families made reports of deaths more frequent than in civilian communities. The impact on all of them was devastating, always wondering when their turn for bad news would come.

Dad and I didn't talk much about my situation. I think he saw it as unfortunate that I had to go to Vietnam, but it was my duty as an Army officer. We had talked briefly when I received the orders retaining me on active duty. He spoke of General MacArthur's "Duty, Honor, and Country" speech given several years earlier at a West Point graduation ceremony. It seemed ironic to me that he referred to the speech when he had not served in the military himself. And as he looked at me, with two children and going off to war, I wondered if he thought about his decision not to serve in World War II. Had the tables been turned, I know that I would have done so. I also wondered if way down deep he might have been living, subconsciously through me, a part of what he missed during "the good war."

Mom and Dad also took the occasion of my leaving to talk to me about their concerns for my safety. I had always been well-coordinated and athletic but also accident-prone. I injured myself frequently as a kid, taking risks I shouldn't have and often tripping over this or that in my exuberance. Even to this day, I have never stayed in a hospital for an illness, but there have been many trips to the emergency room for severe injuries. Both Dad and Mom assumed that the Army had trained me well. They knew I had been successful in previous Army assignments, but this was a real war, not the threat of war that I had faced in Germany. It seemed that their biggest fear—having observed me growing up—was that I would put myself in harm's way, unnecessarily, or get killed out of carelessness.

I don't remember the specifics of saying good-bye to my mother and father. I'm sure Mom would have hugged me and that Dad and I probably shook hands. Back then it was very uncommon for a grown father and son to hug and say they love each other, as is done so often today.

Before my final departure, I made arrangements to have my Army pay allotment sent home. I also took out a life insurance policy with New York Life for $10,000, a fair amount of money back then. The insurance salesman, a friend of my father, showed up the day before I left to sell me the policy. It seemed a morbid thing to be doing at that moment, but it was something that had to be done.

The last thing I did was write a letter to Caroline and Suzanne with instructions to open it only if I didn't return, and then only at an age when they could understand it. In the letter, I wrote of my joy at their births, my love for them, and my sorrow at not seeing them grow up. I asked them to be good girls, to do well in school, and to take care of their mother.

After an emotional send-off, with no good-byes permitted, I told everyone how quickly the time would pass. Then I left via bus for the Army's Military Air Transport Command at Charleston Air Force Base, South Carolina. From there I would be flown to Panama. During the bus ride, the picture of Kathy, Caroline, and Suzanne seeing me off as the bus pulled out of the station stayed with me. They were too young, the mother and the children, to be left without husband and father.

On the plane to Panama, I slowly began to insulate myself from thinking about my family, particularly the children. They were safe and well cared for. I had to begin focusing hard on what was ahead of me, on what I was going to learn in Panama, how I was going to fight and lead in Vietnam, and how I was going to make it home.

Panama

By the time I had left Fort Leonard Wood for my brief leave in Ypsilanti I had put being selectively retained behind me. Now it was time to prepare myself mentally and physically for what had become the inevitable—fighting the Communists in the jungles of Vietnam. But the closest I'd ever been to a jungle was watching a Tarzan movie, and I knew Vietnam was no day at the movies. So I was grateful when the Army decided to send me to the Jungle Warfare School located in the Panama Canal Zone. The school had a reputation for providing some of the most intensely realistic, and dangerous, survival training in the entire Army education system.

The narrow isthmus of Panama lies in the tropics at approximately the same latitude as Vietnam, on the other side of the world. The climate, weather patterns, and vegetation are similar. My prior Army experience included the rolling hills, manicured woodlands, and open meadows of Germany and the Ozark Mountains and endless farmlands of Missouri. The heat, humidity, and dense jungle terrain of Panama were something entirely different. They would help me get acclimated to the tropics before arriving in Vietnam.

By the time we completed our training, my classmates and I felt at home in the jungle. And we could see that the school's reputation was well deserved. It was reported that one student in another class died of a snakebite and another from drowning. Several suffered severe injuries from falls. In the short time I was there, I lost several pounds from hacking my way through heavy vines and thick vegetation.

It was a long way from the jungles in the pretend battles I fought as a child in Willow Run.

■   ■   ■

After the long flight from Charleston Air Force Base, our plane landed at Howard Air Force Base near the Bay of Panama on the Pacific side of the isthmus. As we approached, we could see dozens of ships in the sea-green bay below, all waiting to pass through the Panama Canal. On landing, we boarded a bus that took us about fifty miles to Fort Gulick, near the harbor town of Cristobal on the Atlantic side of the canal.

The tropical landscape was strange, new, and beautiful for me, as from another world. From a distance it seemed like a tapestry of a hundred shades and shapes of green. I was eager to get closer, to feel it, smell it, taste it.

At several spots along the way, we could see the canal and some of the locks with massive ships passing through them. I remember thinking how difficult it must have been to build the canal in a place like Panama, with its rugged mountains and dense vegetation. Always in awe of major construction projects, I marveled at such a remarkable feat of the early 1900s.

I also remember being shocked, as we passed through villages, by the incredible poverty and squalor that seemed to be everywhere. Swarms of purposeless people were living in small ramshackle huts made of corrugated metal and shabby scraps of wood or cardboard. Most of the dwellings seemed no larger than a small room. No signs of electricity could be seen. And there were no yards for the gaunt children to play in, only heaps of rotting garbage and layers of trash for them to poke at.

On our arrival at Fort Gulick, we were issued our gear, including water purification pills, salt tablets, a hammock, mosquito netting, a machete, maps, and a compass. The hammock was to sleep in, up off the ground, away from the ants and snakes. The mosquito netting was to keep off not only mosquitoes but also black widow spiders and scorpions.

After we packed all our gear in duffels, we moved by truck to a small base of operations deep in the jungle. Once there, we huddled in a small clearing surrounded by palmetto and banana trees, where we were briefed on the three weeks of intense training that was ahead of us. The instructors told us there would be classes and live exercises on small-unit tactics like patrols and ambushes. But the major emphasis was on "survival training" and how to "live off the land." By the time we finished we would learn that the jungle, seemingly hostile and forbidding, could be a friend in need. Everything you require to survive, water, food, and shelter, is available in abundant supply—if you know where and how to look for it.

■   ■   ■

The first and foremost principle that we learned was the importance of "the buddy system." Nothing was to be done alone. In rugged and sometimes hostile jungle terrain, it is easy to get hurt or disoriented. If you break a leg or an arm, get bit by a snake or a crocodile, cut yourself badly, or just get lost, you need someone with you to help you out. Otherwise, dying is quite easy. This simple but very serious truth was stressed over and over by our instructors. In order to make it second nature, we practiced the buddy system in everything we did, even in exercises that didn't appear to be dangerous, like building a lean-to in the base camp or going to the bathroom in the bushes.

By the time we all graduated, we each had our own stories of why the buddy system was so important.

Mine happened late in the course, while attempting to swim across the Chagres River during an escape-and-evasion exercise. My buddy, Captain James Meade, and I made a small raft to carry our rifles and to help as a flotation device during the crossing. We entered the river at a point where it was about 200 yards wide. The current was dangerously strong. I was swimming with my left hand and arm, while pulling the raft with my right hand. Meade was on the other side of the raft. As we neared the far riverbank, my hand slipped off the wet raft. The current sucked me downriver, through raging waters and away from the raft. I swam against the current toward the raft. I tired. My muscles ached. I went under, then bobbed back up. I thought, "This is it." There was a rush of panic. I bobbed again, this time coughing up water. Someone onshore yelled to me, "Tom, over here, grab the rope." It was Meade. He tossed the rope, I grabbed on. Had I been alone, I might have drowned in the Chagres River.

After the instructors were sure that every one of us in the class had internalized the buddy system, we learned about poisonous snakes, spiders, scorpions, crocodiles, and the carnivorous piranhas. Our instructors wanted us to be wary of the jungle's dangers, so often hidden and hard to detect, before we started navigating the forests, rivers, and swamps of the Canal Zone.

Most of the snakes, including boa constrictors, pythons, and various other nonpoisonous snakes, all of which we were persuaded to pick up and handle, represented no serious threat at all. But the venomous pit vipers were another matter. If we encountered a pit viper, with its trademark triangular head, we were told to treat it with a lot of respect and get the hell out of the way quickly.

One species of pit viper posed a particular danger. It is called the fer-de-lance, a French name meaning head of the lance. It grows up to eight feet long, and scales of gray and brown make it hard to see in the dim light of the jungle. We had been taught that most coiled vipers will slither away when the danger that caused them to coil is no longer present. But not the fer-de-lance. It will seek out and hunt a human or any other warm-blooded species. Using very sensitive heat sensors, the fer-de-lance stalks warm-blooded creatures near its habitat and strikes at first opportunity, killing its prey with a deadly venom that attacks the nervous system in a matter of seconds.

After we knew a little about the jungle's creatures, we learned the importance of palm trees. They can be used for almost everything you need. Coconuts provide coconut meat and milk. They also can be made into bowls and ladles, even weapons. Strips of leaves or palm fronds can be used for shelter, a sleeping mat, baskets, and clothing. Fibers from the bark and leaves can be used to make ropes and brooms. Heart of palm is a delicacy and can also provide water for drinking. To this day, I can't look at a palm tree without thinking about its usefulness.

Then we moved on to edible fruits and plants like bananas,

plantains, papayas, mangoes, litchis, pineapples, sugarcane, yams, tubers, roots, beans, and berries. And, last, to edible creatures like monkeys, iguanas, crocodiles, birds, snakes, and fish.

We had several picnics on the spot, to savor the delicacies we picked or caught. We trapped a monkey by cutting a hole in a coconut and placing a shinny piece of cigarette foil inside. We then tied a rope around it, hid in the bushes, and waited. Pretty soon a curious monkey stuck his hand inside to get the foil. The hole was engineered to enable a monkey to get an open hand into the coconut but small enough to prevent a clenched fist from getting out. The clueless monkey just held on to the foil while we pulled him in for supper. We ate many things that we never thought we could or would. Most of us preferred iguana tail. It's like the white meat of chicken.

After the first few days of learning what not to step on and what we could eat and not eat, it was time to turn our attention to moving through the jungle. We spent a lot of time on land navigation, using maps and a compass to get to a predefined objective. Much of the time, visibility was limited to a few feet in front of us as we hacked our way through dense vegetation. Over us were layers on layers of green forest filtering the light; it was called triple canopy jungle. I became a big believer in using two men, designated as pacers, to count the meters to landmarks along the way. We would average their individual counts for greater accuracy. This technique later proved invaluable in Vietnam during night patrols and raids.

We learned how to cross rivers and gorges using rope bridges or sliding belly-on-top across single ropes spanning the obstacle. We practiced rappelling down steep cliffs, some near waterfalls that made the wet rocky surface especially treacherous. And we learned how to cross major water obstacles by building rafts with tree limbs and our rain ponchos, to carry our gear and help us stay afloat while swimming long distances.

It was tough training but indispensable. Having not gone to Ranger training, it gave me and the others some of the confidence that we knew Vietnam would demand from us.

■ ■ ■

After our basic survival training, our education progressed to combat tactics. We simulated squad- and platoon-sized patrols, ambushes, and raids on enemy encampments. We studied how to use jungle terrain to our advantage. We learned how to stalk our enemy with stealth through heavy vegetation—slowly, quietly, and hopefully unnoticed. We learned how to detect trip wires for booby traps and flares.

We were also taught how to kill in the jungle, using stealth. You silenced a sentry with a knife or strangled him with a wire garrote without being detected. After all my Army training, it was in Panama that killing started to become a very personal, up-close, and dirty business for me. In the mechanized battles we simulated in Germany, the enemy was at a distance, way out in front of us, when we destroyed him with our tanks and machine guns. I didn't like the prospect of sneaking up close behind a man and feeling his life slip away in my hands.

■   ■   ■

The course of instruction at the Jungle Warfare School ended with a three-day escape-and-evasion (E&E) exercise designed to put all that we learned to practical use. After marching deeper into the jungle on the Pacific side of the isthmus, we were imprisoned in a makeshift POW camp with several bamboo cages. Our mission was to escape in small, even-numbered groups while the guards looked the other way. We then had to make our way northwest, across the isthmus to Fort Gulick, about fifteen miles from the POW camp.

Soldiers permanently stationed in the Canal Zone played the enemy. Their job was to find and return us to the POW camp, using foot patrols in the jungle and motorized patrols on all the roads. Our challenge was to evade them and to get to the fort in three days or less—while living off the land, eating and drinking only that which we could find along the way. There were no other restrictions, other than assuring that we practiced the buddy system. The hostile terrain that stood between us and Fort Gulick would test all we had learned to that point. If the enemy recaptured us, we were allowed to escape again and again. But to be awarded the coveted title of *Jungle Expert* we had to reach our objective prior to the scheduled end of the course.

Meade and I escaped and scrambled northwest for several kilometers. Then we circled back and around the POW camp. Next we headed southeast toward the port town of Balboa. We plotted our escape assuming that most of the enemy patrols were roving between the camp and Fort Gulick. Our plan was to go the other way. Once in Balboa, we would try to catch the train that goes back and forth across the isthmus. We planned to travel to Fort Gulick in leisure class. After all, there were no restrictions.

We made it all the way to Balboa without being detected, though we had to evade two patrols shortly after our "escape" from the POW camp. The biggest obstacle we faced was swimming the Chagres River. That's when I almost drowned and Meade threw me a rope. All we had to eat were some plantains and a few small pieces of leftover crocodile meat that we had saved from an earlier kill.

We were tired and hungry when we reached Fort Gulick, but not nearly as much as the others in our class who took a great deal longer. Some of the teams didn't complete the exercise in the allotted time. The secret to our success was advance planning. We had learned of the E&E exercise from a previous graduate of the school and devised our strategy prior to first leaving the fort for the initial orientation in the jungle. We took money for the train tickets with us and Meade and I both stashed a pair of civilian trousers and a pullover shirt in our packs. Then we hid them, wrapped in plastic, not far from the POW camp the day before the exercise began. We figured we would need a suitable disguise if we were able to get to the train. And we did.

There were two of the "enemy" soldiers watching as people boarded the train. We walked straight by them, undetected.

■　　■　　■

Our reward for having returned to the fort so quickly was a night on the town in Cristobal. And it was a wild town, full of sex-starved sailors from countries all over the world. Their ships were at anchor just offshore, awaiting passage to the Pacific Ocean on the other side of the canal.

It seemed that every other establishment was a bar or a club, stuffed with raucous entertainment, rowdy drunks, and prostitutes from all over the Caribbean. And on every corner were several uniformed members of Panama's National Police, just waiting to haul someone off to jail. It was like a scene out of an old B-movie.

Prior to our departure for town, we were advised to be very careful about the police. Relations between the U.S. government and Panama were at an all time low, stemming from Panama's desire to regain authority over the Canal Zone. The police were looking for any reason they could find to arrest a U.S. soldier. Just staring at a policeman was excuse enough to be arrested.

We weren't planning to paint the town red. All we had in mind was a quick reconnoitering around town, a few beers, and some Central American music. We just wanted to see what Panama, outside the jungle, was all about.

Just to be extra safe, Meade and I had asked one of the members of Fort Gulick's permanent party, an instructor named Captain Diaz, to show us around. Diaz knew the town well and spoke fluent Spanish. We figured that he could help us talk with the locals and keep us out of trouble by steering us clear of places that were known to be dangerous. He quickly accepted the invitation and joined us.

Soon after we arrived in the middle of town, we sauntered into a smoke-filled cafe packed with people. We pushed our way to the bar, where in spite of the crowd we found three seats. We each ordered a beer. We guzzled them down and ordered seconds.

A tall, thin, sultry-looking girl with almond-colored skin walked into the bar. She wore a red halter top with overflowing breasts, yellow short-shorts, and thigh-high leopard-skin pirate boots. She glanced over her shoulder at me and slowly formed her fleshy, crimson lips into a sexy smile. Then she wriggled through the crowd towards us. I smiled back and returned to my beer.

Seconds later, she was at my side, rubbing my thigh and whispering to me in Spanish. I couldn't understand what she was saying, but it was easy for me to figure out where she was going. I flicked my wrist to brush her off and turned away.

The next thing I remember is being helped up off the floor by Diaz and Meade, both of them laughing up a storm. They hurried me through the crowded bar and out the back door in order to avoid the police. I had a splitting headache.

Diaz told me that the girl in the leopard-skin boots had hit me in the head with her purse. He assumed she must have had a brick or a rock in her purse, since it knocked me momentarily unconscious. Apparently, local custom ruled that returning a smile to a prostitute was like agreeing to a date, leaving just the price to negotiate. In her view, according to Diaz, when I said no and turned away, I was insulting her in public. So she got even.

I had gone into town feeling like a macho jungle expert and was returning to the bosom of the Army after being incapacitated by the deadly purse of a spurned lady of the night. Her tactics were admirable. Obviously, there were other areas where I needed survival training. I was the butt of many jokes over the next two days. At the graduation ceremony, I was awarded the official Jungle Expert Badge and a special Cristobal Bar Hopping Novice Certificate, crafted by Diaz, complete with a cartoon that depicted me getting hit in the head by a nasty-looking babe. Sometimes I fantasize that the story has become legend at the Jungle Warfare School and is used to enlighten other trainees on stealth combat techniques.

■   ■   ■

After graduation, four of us left for California from Howard Air Force Base in Panama, arriving at the Oakland Army Terminal outside of San Francisco. We would have a short layover there before departing for Vietnam. I planned to make the most of my last day in America.

Last Day in America

I awoke, rubbing sleep from my eyes after only a few hours of fitful rest. It was early in the morning after the long flight from Panama. Looking down the two rows of bunks in the transient officers' barracks at the Oakland Army Terminal, I saw that only a few of the twenty bunks were occupied.

My bunkmates were three other infantry officers, all young lieutenants: Mofett, Dougherty, and Rumson, who had also just completed jungle training and were headed for the war. We all awoke at about the same time; no one said anything for a long while. I imagined the others were all pondering the same question as I was. How do I spend a day in San Francisco when in a little over twenty-four hours we would board a plane bound for Vietnam?

None of us had any idea what a jungle war was really like, but we knew as infantrymen that the probability of being killed was pretty high. Lying in my bunk watching particles of dust glide and collide in an overhead ray of sunlight, I wondered: How will I do in battle? Will I come home? Will I see my family again? Will I ever set foot on American soil again? I kept thinking, last day in America, last day in America.

"I don't know what you guys have planned," Mofett said, "but I've got one day left and I'm goin' to find me a hot California gal and shack up."

"Bullshit," responded Dougherty. "You couldn't find a girl that hard up if you had all year."

"Oh yeah? I've got the telephone number of an old college friend, a sexy blond, who told me to give her a call if I ever got to San Francisco. Maybe she'll feel sorry for me and try to make my last day a memorable one."

"Fat chance of that, ugly. California girls may be blond, but they're not stupid," said Rumson as he took out a bag of brown yarn and some knitting needles.

"You'll see, and you'll all wish it were you," Mofett shouted as he headed for the shower.

I was in a state of disbelief watching Rumson going through the pile of yarn and needles on his cot. I'd never known a man that knitted, much less an infantry officer.

"What are you doing, Rumson?" poked Dougherty.

"What's it look like? I'm going to knit some booties for my sister's baby. I've made them for all the babies in my family. I've got one more pair to do before I leave for Nam. I'm not going anywhere until I'm done."

"You've got to be kidding; you're a jungle expert. How can you knit?" asked Dougherty.

"I always wanted to do something no other man could do. My mom told me to learn to knit, and so I did. Can you knit?"

"No way. Don't want to."

"Then button up so I can concentrate," Rumson said, lifting his massive six-foot-three frame off the cot and staring with deep creases in his brow down into Dougherty's fearful eyes.

"Just one question: Why brown?" I asked.

"Everyone gives booties to babies: blue, pink, yellow, white. The way I see it is if I give brown, they won't forget who they came from."

I'd never met anyone quite like Rumson. I was glad that he was going to a different unit in Vietnam than I was going to. Something didn't seem quite right with him.

■　■　■

On the way to the shower, Dougherty, who like me was also married, said the only thing he wanted to do was go to Fisherman's Wharf and eat some good seafood. After that, he would decide whether he had the energy to try to hook up with someone. I knew the answer but asked anyway: "Aren't you married?" "Yeah," he said, "but my wife won't know. If she did, she would understand."

I told Dougherty that having never been to San Francisco, all I wanted to do was see as much of the city as possible. "Okay, Brewer," he said, "you're the guide." As we entered the shower, Mofett rushed out. "Have a good day, gentlemen," he said. "Don't do anything I wouldn't do. See you tomorrow morning."

I stayed in the shower for about fifteen minutes, thinking it was likely my last hot shower for a long time. I drove Dougherty out quickly with a few verses from "I Left My Heart in San Francisco." It's a song that, to this day, I still associate with that moment in time and with the feelings of the thousands of American soldiers who left the states for Vietnam through the gateway of San Francisco.

While I was destroying the verses, I made mental notes of what I wanted to do. Riding a cable car was at the top of the list, followed by seeing the Golden Gate Bridge. I also wanted to check out Haight-Ashbury, where the hippie movement was born.

I knew that I wanted to gorge myself with food, real basic American food: eggs and bacon for breakfast, a hot dog and a hamburger with fries and Coke for lunch, and then seafood and a steak with Dougherty for dinner. I also had a craving for popcorn and a good movie. Afterwards, we would hit some topless bars, have some beers, and then head back to the barracks. I felt a slight tinge of panic, wondering if I had time to fit it all in. *Last day in America.*

■   ■   ■

By the time I was dressed, Dougherty had a cab waiting for us. We asked Rumson if he wanted to join us. He held up two knitting needles with some brown yarn hanging down and said, "I can't. Got to finish these and get them in the mail before tomorrow." Dougherty looked at me and rolled his eyes; I shrugged my shoulders, and out the door we went.

In the cab and on our way across the Bay Bridge, into a still fog-shrouded San Francisco, I suddenly remembered that I wanted to call home. I had talked to my family before leaving for Panama, but I wanted to hear their voices one more time.

The cab driver told us that the best view of the San Francisco skyline was from Sausalito, just across the Golden Gate Bridge, to the north. He took us through the city and across the bridge to a little breakfast spot. We had our eggs and bacon while enjoying the view across San Francisco Bay, beyond Angel Island and Alcatraz, to the city's skyline. The fog had lifted and I could see the Golden Gate Bridge standing majestically off to the right. I remember thinking it was the most beautiful view that I had ever seen. It would be my memory picture of America. After eating, I scrambled to a pay phone and dialed Kathy in Ypsilanti, Michigan.

"Hello," Kathy said as she lifted the receiver.

"Hi, it's me. I'm in San Francisco and I leave early tomorrow. I wanted to say good-bye." Silence.

"Wait a minute, I'll put Carol and Suzie up to the phone so they can hear your voice." Carol was two and a half and Suzie just five months old. I could hear shuffling in the background as Kathy said, "It's Daddy."

"Hi, Carol; hi, Suzie. It's Daddy. I love you and miss you. Be good girls for your mom."

I heard baby talk from Caroline that I couldn't make out. I fought back tears. It was hard. I had said my good-byes in early January, before leaving for Panama. Saying them to the children a second time was painful for me.

Kathy got back on the line. "Take care of yourself," she said, "and be careful."

"I will. Please write," I replied.

"You be sure to write."

"Okay. I've got to go before I get too emotional."

"Me too," she said. "Bye."

"Bye." The phone went dead before I could say anything else. Dougherty was banging on the door to the phone booth. "Hey, let's get going," he said. "We haven't got all day."

I wanted to call my parents next, but it was early afternoon in

Michigan and I knew that Dad wouldn't be home from work. I decided to call later in the day.

We grabbed another cab, but just as we approached the Golden Gate Bridge to cross back into San Francisco, we decided to brave the gusting winds and walk across the mile-long bridge. On the other side, we would decide what to do next.

The cab driver must have suspected, from our short hair and our conversation in the back seat, that we were in the military. Pulling over to let us out, he asked, "Where are you guys stationed?" Dougherty told him that we had just graduated from the Jungle Warfare School in Panama and that we were leaving for Vietnam the next day. "Tough war," he said. "Can't tell who you're fighting. If it were up to me, I'd send all those hippies over there, not nice boys like you."

We thanked him for the ride, paid him a buck, and jumped out of the cab. He seemed eager to talk with us. As we walked towards the bridge, he shouted, "Hey, you know those hippies don't do anything but sit around all day and smoke marijuana. They don't contribute anything to this country. If someone's got to die, it should be them."

We didn't look back, just kept going. He was an angry man and we wanted our last day to be a good day. As he drove off, he shouted, "Be sure to get your shoes shined before you leave." We looked at our shoes; they looked acceptable. Dougherty looked at me and said, "What's with that guy?" "He's mad about something," I responded.

■　　■　　■

We were chilled walking across the gently swaying bridge, with its tall red-gold towers poking up into the clouds. To the south, the spectacular vista of San Francisco welcomed us. Under the bridge an endless parade of boats and other seagoing vessels churned wakes in the water below. We walked slowly. And we didn't talk much as we crossed.

I didn't know what Dougherty was thinking. My thoughts were of the beauty in being alive at that moment in time: feeling the damp, cold wind stinging at my skin; tasting the salt in the air; seeing the blanket of fog layered above the city, just beneath a robin's-egg-blue sky; watching one foot move in front of the other, step by step toward a goal. I was happy that I was fitting in as much experience as I could before the day was over.

It was thrilling for me to be in such a unique place. I had seen most of the United States, much of Europe, a piece of North Africa, and Panama before I arrived in California, but nothing compared with the beauty that surrounded me as I walked south across the Golden Gate Bridge. It took us about thirty minutes to cross to a spot where we sat down to decide what to do next. It was midmorning of our last day. The hours were slipping away.

"Let's check out the hippies in Haight-Ashbury," said Dougherty. "By the time we finish, it'll be time for lunch."

"I want to take a cable car ride."

"Brewer, do you see any cable cars?"

"No, sure don't."

"Okay," said Dougherty. "Let's get a cab and go to Haight-Ashbury, see what it's all about. Then have some lunch. We can find out where to get a cable car while we're eating."

"All right, let's go."

■　■　■

It was just a short cab ride from the bridge through the Presidio and onto Masonic Avenue. Then it was a straight shot down to the famous corner at Haight and Ashbury Streets. We were at the center of the hippie movement, flower children, and free love. Hippie people were all around: standing in doorways and on street corners, sitting on curbs, lying on the sidewalk, and strolling down the streets slowly.

Even though it was 1967 and the counterculture movement wasn't new, I hadn't seen many hippies. This was partly due to growing up and going to college in the conservative Midwest. But since college, I had spent most of my time on military posts outside the country. So for me, going into Haight-Ashbury was like going to a zoo, but for people, not animals.

Our first reaction was how out of place we looked, with our short military-style haircuts, close-fitting khaki trousers, checkered shirts, light-colored cotton jackets, and spit-shined black shoes. We were definitely "square." Everyone else had on a mix of psychedelic tie-dyed tops, ragged jeans, and lacy Victorian tops. Those girls not in jeans wore long cotton, wool, or satin skirts in deep colors. Many were barefoot with layers of filth on the soles of their feet.

Almost everyone had some kind of symbolism hanging from their necks: love beads, a peace symbol, or a heavy crucifix. In fact, peace signs were everywhere: painted on jackets and on shirts, sewn onto jeans, tattooed on skin, and scribbled on signs that many carried.

The long hair, mustaches, and beards on the guys made them look as though they were from a previous century. There was a General Custer, an Abe Lincoln, and several who had the face and eyes of a Jesus Christ. The pale expressionless faces and unshaved legs on many of the girls made me think of the poor in Appalachia. We could smell the sharp mix of body odor and marijuana everywhere. Nobody hid the joints they were puffing on.

We walked up Haight Street, looking for a place to eat. Many of the hippies looked at us with contempt in their eyes, whispered something, and then turned to look away. Most of the small shops, many hawking drug paraphernalia, had antigovernment and antiwar slogans posted in the windows. I was eager to talk to some of the hippies, to challenge them, but Dougherty discouraged me. It's a good thing he did; I have an argumentative streak in me. I'm sure that I would have found myself in a nonofficer-like predicament of some sort.

Less than an hour ago, we had left one of the most beautiful spots I'd ever seen. Now we found ourselves in what seemed like a pathetic and hostile country. We felt like foreigners. On the other hand, I knew that the freedom of expression I was witnessing was one of the freedoms I had vowed to protect as an officer in the U.S. Army.

We didn't find any cafes or restaurants that we could feel comfortable eating in. So after just a short walk we decided to head to Union Square and get hot dogs and hamburgers. Afterwards, a cable car ride. We were happy to leave Haight-Ashbury.

When we got to Market Street, I said to Dougherty, "Maybe that cab driver in Sausalito was right; Uncle Sam should send all the hippies to Vietnam."

Dougherty laughed, adding, "Fat chance of that. Anyway, I wouldn't want one in my foxhole."

■   ■   ■

On our way to Union Square, we picked up some postcards. We had lunch at a hamburger joint across from the cable car turnstile at Powell and Market Streets. I had two hot dogs with mustard and relish; an inch-thick hamburger; golden, thick fries; and a giant hot fudge sundae with peanuts, whipped cream, and a cherry on top for dessert.

I normally eat fast, but on that day I ate slowly, making each bite last as long as I could. *Last day in America.* I remember it as one of the best meals I've ever eaten.

After lunch, we walked the three blocks to Union Square, sat down, wrote our postcards, and mailed them. Then, sitting in an uncommonly warm winter sun, we planned the remainder of the day and watched people go by. The waitress had told us that the best view of the city from a cable car was on the Powell-Hyde line, up Nob Hill and then down to Fisherman's Wharf. Since we were eating dinner at the wharf, we decided to look for a good movie, watch it, and then take the cable car to dinner.

Steve McQueen was playing in the three-hour-long film *The Sand Pebbles* just up the street from us. We waited half an hour until it started, purchased our tickets and two large bags of popcorn each, and spent the afternoon watching the film.

The story, set in China during 1926, is a favorite of mine to this day. Seaman Jake Holman (Steve McQueen) and the crew of an American gunboat get drawn into China's civil war. Caught between warring factions and torn loyalties, the officers and the near-mutinous crew wage a valiant, but futile, attempt to represent American foreign policy in a hopeless no-win situation. In the end, many lives are destroyed or lost for a pointless cause.

After the movie, Dougherty and I both wanted a drink. It was a great movie, but sad. Maybe it was Holman's dying comment: "What the hell happened?" that did it to me, but I had a hollow feeling in my stomach. Brave men fighting for cause and country, all for naught. We were silent, everyone was silent, as we left the theater. I was thinking about how quickly things can come unraveled.

■　■　■

It was late afternoon of our last day. We crossed the street to a little bar to grab a quick beer. Just as the bartender handed us our beers, I heard a cable car rumbling up the tracks. "Drink up," I said to Dougherty, slapping him on the back. We quickly guzzled down our beers, dashed out of the bar, and hopped on a cable car running north on Powell Street.

We stood on the outer running board, holding on tightly, as the car clickity-clanked its way up through Nob Hill. Turning left, we passed the high-rises and steep streets of Russian Hill and went straight into the setting sun. What an incredible sight as we crested the hill and turned onto Hyde Street. We started our long, slow descent towards the wharves jutting out into the silver-watered bay to the north. To our right, we could see Telegraph Hill. Straight ahead was Alcatraz, jutting up from the water. Like a giant rock fortress, it was guarding the sun as it completed its journey to the horizon, far to the west of the Sausalito hills.

We got off the cable car at the end of the line on Hyde Street, just across from Fisherman's Wharf. We walked for a while, passing row after row of fish market stalls with containers of ice displaying smelly seafood. There were mounds of abalone, salmon, tuna, blackfish, halibut, Alaskan king crab, Dungeness crab, oysters, clams, shrimp, octopus, eel, and many other ocean delicacies. We purchased a pint paper container of shrimp and some cocktail sauce to eat while we scouted for a restaurant.

As the sky darkened, we settled on a small dockside cafe that offered a good view out over the water and along the trawler-laden docks. Neither Dougherty nor I had ever seen or eaten Alaskan king crab, so we both ordered the crab and a steak, served with corn and slaw. While we waited to be served, I went to a phone booth and called my parents in Lansing.

"Hello," my mother said as she lifted the receiver.

"Hi, Mom, it's me. I'm in San Francisco and wanted to say hi before I leave for Vietnam."

"Father, it's Tom calling from California," I could hear Mom yell to Dad. "Let me talk to him when you're through," Dad said in the background. "How are you?" asked Mom. "How was Panama? I'm so glad you called."

"I'm doing fine and having a great last day seeing the sights with another guy before I leave. Panama was tough training, but really builds the confidence."

"Please be careful when you get to Vietnam," Mom said. "And be sure to write to your father and me. We'll be praying for you."

"I will."

"Hi, son," Dad said when Mom handed him the phone. He always called me son on serious occasions.

"Hi, Dad, this is it. I'm on my way tomorrow," I said

"We are all proud of you, son," my Dad said in a crackly voice. "Don't do anything stupid. And remember, you have a family that needs you to come home"

"I won't, Dad. I'll be writing when I can and I'll be back a year from now. It should go fast." I asked him to say good-bye to my brother and sister.

"Okay," Dad said as Mom grabbed the receiver.

"Bye, Mom; bye, Dad," I said. "I'll miss you."

"Please be careful," Mom said imploringly. Then she and Dad hung up the phone.

I walked back to the table and quickly finished eating. Time was running out for Dougherty and me. We talked about what we had done so far during the day and how soon it would all end. We concluded that it would be a long while before we would again lay eyes on any American girls, so we figured that this was the moment to hit the topless bars. *Last day in America.*

■   ■   ■

Different countries in different times have designated different parts of the human anatomy as sexual icons. In Victorian England, it was an exposed ankle. In the Hollywood movies of the thirties, the smooth naked chests of Clark Gable and Tyrone Power shocked and titillated audiences. In World War II cheesecake posters, it was the fantasy legs of Betty Grable. In sixties America, it was bare breasts. The power of this icon has lessened in recent decades due to overexposure. But back in 1967, it was still strong, and the code word was "topless."

At twenty-five, I had never been to a topless bar. I'd visited my share of "go-go" bars with dancing girls in gilded cages, sporting white patent-leather boots and bikini outfits. But completely and publicly bare breasts were rare in Ypsilanti and Willow Run.

San Francisco was different. All day long, traveling through town, we had spotted numerous signs for topless bars, even topless restaurants. We decided that we had held our enthusiasm in check long enough. We grabbed a cable car back toward Union Square and jumped off in front of an appropriately sleazy-looking bar. This wasn't an establishment that was subtle about its attractions. Over the door was a bright, red-and-white neon sign that said "Topless A Go-Go, Tits Galore," and a sign in the window reading "Amateur Night—Win $20."

It was dark inside the bar. The ripe smell of cigarette smoke, stale beer, and cheap perfume hung in the air. We took seats opposite a long wooden stage that loomed a couple of feet above us. On the stage a bulbous dancer with bleached blond hair and heavy makeup was wriggling out of a bikini top to the tune of a song I can't remember.

As we watched her, she stared at herself in a mirror directly across from the stage and behind us. She wasn't very attractive to our eyes. Her breasts were large and sagging with shiny stretch marks accenting their drooping shape. We were young and she seemed old. I can remember feeling sad for her, having to earn a living displaying a body beyond its prime. I was uncomfortable watching her.

We hoped our luck would change. And it did. The next several dancers were young, flirtatious, and gorgeous, with bodies composed of tight curves. We were dazed, awestruck, horny, and beginning to feel the effects of several beers. Then the master of ceremonies announced that the amateur contest was about to start.

With our overworked eyes fixed exclusively on the stage in front of us, neither of us had noticed what was going on in the bar behind. Some of the empty tables had filled up with girls in groups of two to four. This was amateur night. They were the amateurs.

They came in all types. Some were hippie girls like the ones in Haight-Ashbury. Others were proper-looking girls I wouldn't have been surprised to see walking down the streets in my hometown or working in an office somewhere. There was lots of talking and giggling. It turned to silence when the MC announced the contest. He called out, "Who's going to be our first contestant?"

We could hear whispering and nudging. All the girls were waiting to see who would be brave enough to go first. Then drumbeats sounded, announcing the first contestant. A young woman, perhaps in her early twenties, with red hair and dressed in bell-bottom jeans and a heavy blue woolen sweater, walked slowly to the stage, giggling all the while. Every couple of steps, she glanced back to her friends for encouragement.

Up on stage, as she glanced around the room, her cheeks turned bright red; they almost matched her hair. Just as the music started, she tugged at the bottom of her sweater. She hesitated for a moment, her eyes shut tight. Then she quickly lifted her sweater up to her chin, revealing milk-white breasts with tiny pink nipples. She swayed to and fro with the music for about ten seconds, jerked down her sweater, opened her eyes, and dashed from the stage back to the safety of her friends. There were hoots and hollers and roars of laughter as everybody gave her a big round of applause.

Then it was time for contestant number two. And then three, and then four through nine. With each new contestant, the dance lasted a little longer and became more seductive. The last girl stripped, slowly, all the way down to her red lace panties. The MC had to escort her from the stage before she went too far.

It was time to pick the winner. All nine girls lined up on stage, removed their tops, and revealed their breasts. Most were pretty tipsy by then and seemed to have lost any initial modesty.

I can remember, as the very young man I was that night, being struck by the variation in breast size and appearance. It was deliciously obvious that they came in all sizes and shapes. I told Dougherty that I had my money on the girl with apple-breasts, small with a slight upward tilt and cotton-candy pink nipples. But Dougherty bet me a dollar that the last contestant would win because she had the largest bosom.

The MC moved from contestant to contestant, placing his hand over each head, calling for a round of applause—more hooting and yelling and clapping. And the girl with the largest breasts, the one who had stripped to her red lace panties, won the twenty-five dollars. I gave Dougherty his dollar; he used it to tip the winner.

By the time it was all over, Dougherty and I agreed that this was the best time we'd had all day and that we'd better head back to the barracks in Oakland while we could still walk. We left the bar and headed down the street in search of a cab.

■   ■   ■

But San Francisco wasn't through with us. After a few blocks, Dougherty blurted out, "Can you believe it, Brewer? I see a sign just up on the left. I think it says 'Topless Shoeshine.' Can you see it?" I looked, and sure enough, there it was. "I can't believe it," I said, and we picked up the pace, aiming our uncertain steps at the sign.

We stumbled through the door and climbed up into two side-by-side chairs covered in maroon Naugahyde, with metal footrests. We were greeted by two cute brunettes wearing tight shorts and, true to the sign outside, no tops. "Like your shoes shined?" one asked. "You bet," I responded. "It's the last shine we're getting for a long time."

Both girls were sweet-mannered, very well-endowed, and from the viewpoint of two young soldiers on their way overseas, incredibly sexual. They polished our shoes; we indulged our libidos. The task produced interesting studies in kinetic motion. As they worked the polishing cloths, their breasts bounced up and down, moved in and out, and swayed in wave-like motions, left to right and right to left. After the girls had shined our shoes—several times at our request—

we paid and gave each a two-dollar tip, a big gratuity back then. On our way out they kissed us on the cheek and wished us well in Vietnam. We hailed a cab for Oakland.

■ ■ ■

Back in the barracks, Rumson was sleeping like a baby with three pairs of newly knitted booties lined up next to his bed.

Mofett was nowhere in sight. We figured he must have shacked up with someone, or if not, he was still on the prowl. At one point in the topless bar, I had a fleeting thought that it would be nice to have a woman that night. I reasoned that I might die soon and nobody would hold it against me. But I quickly decided not to. If I did die in Vietnam, I wanted to go with a clear conscience. I didn't want to die knowing I had betrayed my wife.

I stripped to my shorts and slid slowly into bed, thinking that it was a damn good last day in America. I had done the things I wanted to do. Nothing important was left undone.

I tried to sleep. I couldn't. I thought about the men who had died fighting for a lousy cause in *The Sand Pebbles* and started to feel very much alone, far away, and strangely unconnected from those I loved.

My mind was clogged, the events of the day and in Panama churning over and over; I couldn't clear it. I was a little dizzy, the room swirling ever so slowly. I saw the bridge and cable cars, Mom and Dad, my children, blood-spattered sailors, Rumson's booties, hippies and peace symbols, turbulent rivers, hamburgers, dancing girls, snakes and jungle vines, the girl in the leopard-skin boots, helicopters, crocodiles, and Mofett with a big grin.

I tried counting sheep: *one, two, three, four, five;* it didn't work. I tossed and turned. I tried focusing only on a number: *one, one, one, one, one, one;* then thinking: *sleep, sleep, sleep, sleep, sleep, sleep.* None of my old techniques worked. I thought again about the topless shoeshine. Then I finally drifted off, thinking of how nice it would be to snuggle up to a pair of inviting breasts. So soft, so warm, so safe.

Part Three

In-Country

A Wolfhound to Be

N ext stop, Vietnam," the pilot said over the inter-
com as we lifted off from the Philippines. The
phrase hung in the air like a stale punch line. Over
twenty-four hours earlier, we had left Travis Air
Force Base in California, bound for Vietnam via
Hawaii and the Philippines. The Army had chartered our Boeing
707 from Braniff Airlines. The airplane was painted a bright and
bizarre plum purple.

There was, of course, a logical explanation for the color.
Braniff's marketing brainstorm, which didn't save it from ex-
tinction, was its fleet of weird-colored planes: orange, yellow,
green, red, blue, purple. The Army probably got a bargain. But
we felt at the time it was peculiar to be flying into a war zone in
something the shade of a grape. As I would later learn, it was that
kind of war, surreal and full of contradictions.

We had brief stopovers in Hawaii and the Philippines. We remained cloistered at the military bases while the plane was
being refueled and serviced. At least we were allowed to breathe
the exotic air. I was happy to add a few more faraway places to
the list of tourist stops to which the Army had treated me.

Only a small group of officers was on the plane, and at
twenty-five, I was probably the oldest of them. Most of the two
hundred soldiers filling the plane were enlisted men, like those
I had trained at Fort Leonard Wood. The vast majority were in
their late teens and early twenties.

Looking back, I have to find some objective standard to realize how young they really were. I think to myself, some were

about the same age as my son today, who is eighteen. In our summer tan uniforms, we probably looked more like a gaggle of Eagle Scouts and their scoutmasters, headed for a jamboree, than real soldiers going to fight a war. I don't like to imagine my son on such a journey.

But in the plane that day, spirits seemed high, almost like a party. There was a lot of masculine noise and fooling around. The stewardesses, in purple uniforms with pink silk blouses to complement the plane's color, were indulgent. They took the GIs' flirtatious, and occasionally lewd, comments in stride. They were deft at keeping the boys in line, without embarrassing them in front of their buddies. It was obvious that they had hosted many such junkets to the war zone.

Things changed after our takeoff from the Philippines and the pilot's announcement that Vietnam was the next stop. The joking and flirting stopped. The troops all settled down and stayed relatively quiet for the remainder of the trip. The young men seemed to retreat inward, all alone with their thoughts. Some wrote letters or just curled up in their seats. There were numerous requests for pillows, blankets, glasses of water, and bits of candy. It was as though they craved the attention of a stewardess, as a small child needs a mother's reassuring comfort in times of uncertainty or fear.

We found ourselves high in a night sky over Vietnam, and already we had left the normal pattern of existence. All the interior lights were shut off. We started a rapid, steep descent to avoid antiaircraft fire from Charlie's guns below. The plane dropped and lost altitude quickly, sinking as in an air pocket. I could feel my seat belt tighten around my waist as it strained to hold me down.

Looking out of a window and off into the distance, we could see occasional parachute flares illuminating portions of the night sky, like bright balls of golden fire drifting slowly, eerily, down to earth. Artillery shells exploded farther out, flashing against the endless black, as lightning does.

The plane leveled off. We touched down. Tires screeched; engines reversed. There was an ominous silence inside the plane. Nobody was talking. Everyone seemed to be in a dread-filled daze. We rolled to an abrupt stop.

"Welcome to Vietnam, gentlemen," the pilot said, "and good luck."

■   ■   ■

We scrambled out of the plane, huddling in small groups on the tarmac. It was late at night and very dark outside, but hot and humid anyway, like stepping into a hot sauna. It was the dry season with the great wet monsoons still months away. Now we could actually hear the *boom, boom, boom* of exploding artillery rounds that we could only see from the plane.

It was obvious that the war we were joining had no front lines. The distant explosions ripped through the night air on all four sides of the airfield.

The half-moon sky was clear and filled with an endless twinkling of overlapping oceans of stars. I'd never seen so many. I couldn't find the common northern hemisphere constellations that I knew, like Orion and the Big and Little Dippers. They had to be there, hiding somewhere in the swells. I felt a long way from the sky I was familiar with and a long way from Willow Run. As a child, I had often lain in the grass at night looking up at the heavens, wondering what they looked like to someone on the other side of the world. Now I was that someone.

A serious-looking buck sergeant led us across the tarmac. We filed into a shabby white wooden building. Inside, he took attendance and organized us into larger groups. Then we waited to board buses that would take some of us to the 90th Replacement Battalion in Long Binh.

On the opposite side of the building stood a line of soldiers waiting to board the plane that we had just arrived on. They were on their way home. I remember being struck by their appearance. Most wore an air of suppressed joy, eager to be leaving, relieved to have survived. But several looked old beyond their years, with lean bodies darkened by the sun and eye sockets that were too deep and shadowed. A few of them, wearing the crossed-rifles insignia of the infantry, just stared ahead with blank looks on their faces—faces that had seen and witnessed things they wished they had not.

I said good-bye to Mofett, Rumson, and Dougherty. They were all headed to different outfits. I never saw them again and I often wonder if they made it back.

Then we boarded our buses again. Mine was a standard Army vehicle, like a green school bus but mutated by the war. The windows were fixed with a heavy wire mesh to prevent Vietnamese kids, old ladies, and farmers from throwing grenades into our laps.

It jolted me like the artillery exploding in the night sky. I didn't get it. We had just flown halfway round the world to protect this country against the enemy, to be their saviors. Where were all the pretty girls dancing in the streets, cheering our arrival, and throwing flowers—like in the World War II movies when the American troops rolled into town to liberate the people from the oppressor? What kind of place was this?

■   ■   ■

When the bus arrived in Long Binh, it was daylight. I reported to representatives from the 25th Division G-1, the staff organization in Cu Chi responsible for assignments throughout the division.

I had assumed that orders were waiting for me, specifying the unit to which I was assigned. They weren't. I should have known that in a combat zone, it's impossible to know in advance precisely where replacements for infantry units will be needed.

I was interviewed by a young rear area staff officer, Major Dante. When Dante learned of my status as a Regular Army officer, he said, "You're lucky to be getting a combat command assignment. It'll be good for your career."

It was a remark that triggered all the inner ambivalence I felt about what I was doing. My first thought was, What a jerk, my career isn't in the Army. But the prospect of leading men in combat was very appealing to me. Another part of me thought, that's what I was trained for, it's my job. I would have been terrified had I known what combat really meant. But at that moment, I would have been disappointed with anything else.

"What kind of a unit do you want?" he asked. "We need someone like you in the First Battalion, Fifth Mechanized Infantry. Your experience with mech. units in Germany will be helpful."

I didn't like the idea of a mechanized unit, in spite of my time in Germany. Before I left for Vietnam, I had read about the difficulties the M-113 armored personnel carriers (APCs) had maneuvering in Vietnam's terrain. The boxlike vehicles presented an easy target for VC rockets and antitank teams. I didn't like the idea of being blown to bits, or burned alive, in a mobile coffin mired down in a swamp somewhere. In a leg infantry unit, I could at least hug the ground when the going got tough and enemy fire was heavy.

"Anything but a mech. unit," I replied. "Can I get into the 27th Infantry Wolfhounds?"

Ever since I had learned about the Wolfhounds from Colonel Norvell in Gelnhausen, something in me had been pushing me in that direction. Maybe it was pride, maybe it was machismo. I had told Norvell I would try to get into the Wolfhounds, and maybe I just wanted to stick to my word. He had served with the 27th in Korea and told me of their proud lineage as one of the most heavily decorated units in the Army. I respected and admired Norvell and saw it as an honor to be in the same unit in which he had once served.

In San Francisco, and on the long plane flight to Vietnam, I had thought a lot about what unit I would be serving in. Up to now, my career in the Army had been dictated on the one hand by what seemed to me to be practical, rational considerations and on the other by the vagaries of Army bureaucracy and American politics. In fact, there is usually not a lot of choice in the Army. You go where you're told and do what you're told. But today I had a choice, and I had just made it.

Major Dante didn't think highly of my judgment, evidently. He looked at me with a quizzical look, like *What's with this guy?* and said, "Captain Brewer, there's always a need for replacements in the Wolfhounds."

"Why's that?" I responded, honestly naive.

"High casualty rate," he said. "They're always getting into a lot of shit, always out of base camp, humpin' the boonies. No one ever sees them but Charlie. The second battalion of the 27th just took a lot of shit up near Tay Ninh. Ran into an NVA unit."

It didn't dampen my enthusiasm, although it probably should have. "I'll take my chances with them. I really don't want to be in a mech. unit. I liked it in Germany, but I need to round out my experience. It will be good for my career."

"Okay," Dante said, "you're on your way." He raised one eyebrow. "Better you than me." He filled in blank spaces and stapled papers together, translating my choice into official orders. He handed my papers to me and said, "There's a convoy leaving for Cu Chi in a few minutes. Try to get a ride out there ASAP."

■　■　■

The 27th Infantry has a long, distinguished, and fascinating history. In 1918, its members became the first Americans to face Communists on the battlefield, while securing the Trans-Siberian Railroad in the bloody Russian Civil War.

It is an episode of American military history that is little remembered and just as surreal as Vietnam. At the tail end of World War I, as Imperial Russia was collapsing, a small group of American soldiers was sent far from home, to the doorstep of Asia, in a futile effort to stem the tide of the Bolshevik revolution. Urged on by Winston Churchill, who foresaw the rise of Russia as a hostile power in alliance with Germany, the Allies attempted to support a counterrevolution of liberals, Cossacks, and former monarchists, a formless coalition labeled the "Whites." Fighting with the White forces in Siberia against the Red armies controlled by the Bolsheviks, the 27th Infantry did their best for a losing cause.

The anti-Bolshevik forces were divided, badly led, and politically inept. The Americans were evacuated down the same railroad they had been protecting. They were abandoned, rather than defeated.

But it was in Russia that the regiment earned its name. Like Russian wolfhounds, they were ferocious towards their enemies and kind to their friends. When the regimental insignia was designed it included the head of a wolfhound in gold, superimposed on a black rectangular shield. The Latin motto, *"Nec Aspera Terrent,"* meaning "No Fear on Earth," was inscribed below the wolfhound head in gold letters.

During World War II, the Wolfhounds served in the Pacific. They fought at Guadalcanal in the Solomon Islands, New Britain, and on Luzon in the Philippines. During the Korean War, the Wolfhounds saw early action against the North Koreans and fought valiantly against the Chinese Communists when they entered the war. When the Korean War ended, the regiment returned to Schofield Barracks in Hawaii, where it concentrated much of its efforts on jungle warfare training.

In 1966 the Wolfhounds went to South Vietnam with the 25th Infantry Division, where they were assigned to the Vietcong-infested Cu Chi district. They left in 1971, after sustaining some of the highest battlefield losses among army units fighting in Vietnam.

The Wolfhounds have been cited for valor many times during each of the wars in which they have fought. Today they continue their tradition as one of the most highly decorated units in the United States Army.

Immediately following World War II, the Wolfhounds served as part of the occupational forces in Japan. While there, they established a long-lasting relationship with the Holy Family Orphanage in Osaka. When I was in Vietnam, I and many others in the 27th Infantry allocated a portion of our paychecks to help support the orphanage. And to this day, soldiers in Wolfhound units all over the world still donate whatever they can to the orphanage.

■　■　■

I found the convoy of eleven olive-drab "deuce-and-a-half" (two-and-a-half-ton) trucks. I threw my duffel bag up into the back of one of the trucks. It was lined with half-inch-thick steel plates. A fifty-caliber machine gun was mounted over the cab. As I climbed in, someone said, "You might need these," and handed me a steel helmet, an M-16 rifle, and a flak jacket. I was on my way to Cu Chi, and it obviously wasn't like taking a ride down Sunset Boulevard.

Apparently, ambushes were all too common along Highway 1,

running northwest out of Saigon to Cu Chi and Tay Ninh and then into Cambodia. I didn't like the idea of getting ambushed. In all the ambush training I had received, none of it had focused on truck convoys. I thought it was odd that we didn't get some sort of orientation or briefing before we departed.

But I wasn't in command of the convoy and I was as green as I could be. So I figured, if we were ambushed, I would just get down and shoot at something. The whole process seemed reckless and irresponsible, but who was I to question the combat vets?

The road was choked with U.S. military traffic moving rapidly in both directions. Large fuel tankers, self-propelled howitzers, Jeeps, trucks carrying troops, trucks carrying supplies, and large tank-recovery vehicles towing disabled tanks created an endless river of olive drab.

At the same time, there was a constant stream of civilians, on bicycles, on motor scooters, in oxcarts, on buses, and on foot. They seemed fragile and slow, dangerously mixed in with the military vehicles.

There was both a great sense of urgency and a general malaise. Everyone was in a hurry to get somewhere, except for the occasional bike-riding South Vietnamese soldiers. They pedaled down the highway with an air of nonchalance, as if they were out for a Sunday ride.

The air smelled foul to me. I couldn't recognize the odor. Later, I came to accept it as the smell of Vietnam: dust, dying plant life, garbage, incense, rotting fish, human waste, and sometimes human death, all compounded together.

Hovering over the flow of humanity were thick, suffocating clouds of red-orange dust and grit, kicked up from the bone-dry road by all the traffic. The powderlike dust stuck to everything and everybody, like flour sticks to a baker.

I immediately had severe trouble with my contact lenses. I'd worn them successfully during my tour of duty in Germany and at the Jungle Warfare School in Panama. The lenses were a partial answer to my constant struggle in the Army with the problem of my eyesight. But now my eyes were burning from the dust and the glare of the sun. In a matter of minutes, they nearly swelled shut. I was forced to remove the lenses and put on my Army-issue prescription sunglasses.

I had brought two pairs of sunglasses and three pairs of regular glasses to Vietnam. I always carried extra glasses in my ammo pouch, in the event I had to replace a damaged pair in the field. I was as concerned about not being able to see, and therefore lead effectively, as I was about getting shot.

It didn't take me long to realize why officers with my eyesight were not supposed to be leading men in combat.

Through my reddened eyes, I stared at the landscape, trying to get some feel for the country. The road we took to Cu Chi cut smack through the 25th Division's main Area of Operations. To the south and west of the road lay the Vam Co Dong River, the swampy Plain of Reeds, and the great, wet, Mekong Delta.

At the beginning of the trip, I wondered why I had been sent to jungle training. The terrain we initially passed through was open, flat, and blanketed with rice paddies. It was monotonous.

Every so often, I could see the hint of a small village or hamlet hidden by dense vegetation: palmetto, banana trees, sugarcane, and bamboo thickets. Water buffalo moved slowly about, in search of water. Papasans, old men wearing black pajamas, worked some of the fields. I thought to myself, Are these the enemy—at night? The black-clad Vietcong guerrillas I would soon be fighting wore essentially the same garments as the peasant farmers. It was difficult to tell them apart. And, in fact, at the individual level they were often one and the same: farmers by day, fighters at night.

But soon the landscape changed. I saw, to the northeast, the woods and jungles of what the Americans called War Zone C and the Iron Triangle. The green treetops began their steady rise towards the Central Highlands, far to the northeast.

■   ■   ■

In time, I would become much more intimately acquainted with this particular landscape, studying it on maps, riding above it in helicopters, and humpin' across it.

As a company commander, one of the most challenging parts of my job would be to plan and conduct combat operations in what was extremely varied terrain. One day we would be hacking our way through dense jungle vegetation, and next day we might find ourselves slogging our way through the sucking mud and chest-high waters of the swamplands.

But one of the most terrifying features of the AO's geography was underneath the surface. There was a vast network of VC tunnels, honeycombing the earth, concentrated in and around Cu Chi base camp. In Vietnam, the Wolfhounds became renowned as "tunnel rats." Slithering down into holes in the ground in search of VC was a part of our daily regimen.

The tunnels were everywhere, containing troops and headquarters, caches of weapons and medical supplies. It was a common occurrence for us to set up a night defensive perimeter and then find ourselves being shot at from behind and within the perimeter. The VC just popped up out of well-camouflaged tunnel openings, shot at us, and then popped back down. If we missed the muzzle flash from their rifles, we couldn't tell from where the shots were coming. It was a constant threat that was very effective at wrecking our nerves.

In Wolfhound units, the average GI was too large to fit into the tunnels. So the soldiers selected to be tunnel rats were those who were small and thin, similar in stature to the Vietcong. When we found a likely hole, a tunnel rat climbed down into it. Armed with only a .45 caliber pistol and a flashlight, he was to search for whatever he could find. The openings were often booby-trapped with explosives. In heavy vegetation, poisonous bamboo vipers and spiders often had to be cleared away. Worst of all, a tunnel rat never knew who might be waiting for him, aiming to kill him, once the opening was clear and he looked in. It was very dangerous work. It took a great deal of courage.

It was another form of combat that wasn't covered in my training.

■　　■　　■

When our convoy finally arrived at the town of Cu Chi, the place was anything but a thriving metropolis. And it was no tropical paradise. It looked poor, dilapidated, and dirty. I can remember asking myself, what are we doing here, why did we come half way around the world to fight a war in a place like this?

The single dirt road that served as a main street was the color of Georgia red clay. Lined up on either side were a few one-story huts made of stucco or corrugated metal, painted in faded shades of green, orange, and ocher. Each of the shops and businesses had a short, flat roof extending four or five feet out to the street, offering protection from the sun and rain, and brightly lettered signs over the entrance: Kim-Lien, Viet Xuan, Hung Phat Vinh, and Cho Phuoc Heip.

A good number of locals were milling around the town. Mamasans—old ladies wearing baggy black trousers, tight-fitting white linen tops, and wide conelike straw hats—stood in the doorways of many of the shops, staring indifferently at us as we passed by.

Small groups of kids with outstretched hands shouted, "GI numma one, VC numma ten," as we rode by. In Vietnam, numma one meant good, numma ten meant bad. I'm pretty sure that when the Vietcong passed through, the kids switched the greeting: Vietcong numma one, GI numma ten.

On several of the corners, GIs were talking to seductive young girls with straight coal-black hair, dressed in bright-colored *ao dais,* showing off their Barbie-doll-like figures. At one point we stopped to let an old man pass who was driving an oxcart with five-foot-high wheels and sides made of straw mats. We saw no young men anywhere. Cu Chi town was traditionally very sympathetic to the VC, so we all speculated that the young men were away hiding or fighting, and we would soon learn that our assumption was correct.

After the short ride through Cu Chi town we arrived at the entrance to the 25th Division's main base camp. I was immediately struck by its size. It looked as if an olive-drab tent city a couple of miles in diameter had been plunked down in the middle of nowhere. Row after row of army tents, built on wooden platforms and surrounded by walls of sandbags, housed the GIs. Quonset huts were everywhere. Motor pools, airfields, and makeshift medical facilities completed the picture.

The whole compound was guarded by heavily armed GIs in

large camouflaged bunkers, like small hillocks of sandbags, that surrounded the camp. Massive, self-propelled howitzers stood well behind and between the bunkers. The area for 300 meters in front of the bunkers had been cleared of all vegetation to permit good visibility and interlocking fields of fire. It had the desolation of a moonscape. Multiple rows of coiled concertina wire, barbed and razor-sharp, lay between the bunkers and the wooded area to the far side of the cleared area. The line of trees at the edge of the woods had been defoliated with Agent Orange so that enemy troops who might be massing for an attack could be spotted. It would have been suicide for anyone to launch a full-scale attack across such killing fields.

When I arrived at headquarters, a Jeep was waiting to take me to the area of the base camp occupied by the Wolfhounds. The driver showed me the Wolfhound Tactical Operations Center (TOC) and then took me to the officers' quarters.

The quarters consisted of a row of about twenty small round shelters, called hootches, made of straw with conical roofs. They were up off the ground supported by eighteen-inch stilts to keep the water and mud out during the rainy season. The side walls were made out of straw mats, which could be opened out and held up by poles to let fresh air in. I didn't realize it at the time, but I would come to regard these quarters as the Ritz by comparison to where I would be spending 90 percent of my time.

I tossed my duffel bag into a hootch, onto one of the two bunks inside. Then I reported to the TOC for my initial assignment.

■　■　■

On my way to the TOC, it seemed pretty quiet and empty in the Wolfhound section of the camp. When I arrived, I learned why.

The battalion executive officer, Major Dudley, was studying a large map of the Wolfhound AO. Several radios sat nearby, each on a different frequency. I could hear a number of transmissions coming through simultaneously.

Dudley welcomed me to the Wolfhounds. He pulled me over to the map and showed me current positions of various units. The entire battalion was participating in Operation Junction City in Tay Ninh Province, to the north of Cu Chi. Junction City was one of the first and largest American-led operations where hard-core North Vietnamese troops were encountered. Up until then, much of the fighting had been against local VC units.

Dudley informed me that I would be taking charge of Alpha Company when its commanding officer returned from the field in two to three weeks. In the meantime, I was to be acting S-3, the battalion operations officer. The permanent S-3 was in the field leading one of the companies where the CO had been wounded.

Dudley explained that as acting S-3, I would have lots of opportunities to get shot at by the enemy, and this was desirable. The idea was that I should become accustomed to being under fire before taking command of Alpha Company, where, as Dudley said, "all eyes will be on you when the shit hits." In fact, I was glad of the chance for a dress rehearsal, weird as it sounds. For all my training, I didn't really know how I would act when under fire. Nobody does until it happens.

In the meantime, I had a job to learn. As acting S-3, I represented the battalion commander on all operations matters. I was to maintain radio contact with all field units and maintain the battalion's situation map in the TOC. The map showed the location of all Wolfhound units, adjacent units, and supporting units. I also coordinated communications and liaison with higher, lower, and adjacent headquarters units.

As I settled into the job, coordinating tactical air support consumed much of my time. It was extremely important that the individual coordinating tactical air strikes know the location of all friendly units. It was the only way to ensure that our troops weren't hit with bombs or napalm from friendly planes. Another of my air-support functions was to coordinate and participate in missions where helicopters were needed to lift troops into and out of an operational area.

My first day as acting S-3, I found myself in an L-19 Bird Dog observation plane flying over the Wolfhound AO, near Tay Ninh. The L-19 was a small single-engine plane with rocket launchers mounted to the underside of each wing. The plane was piloted by an Air Force forward air controller (FAC) attached to the 25th Division.

When a ground unit was in trouble and a close-in tactical air strike was needed, the FAC guided the jets to the target. To make this possible, he had to work closely with the infantry company commander or platoon leader on the ground.

The ground troop commander contacted the FAC in the Bird Dog by radio. He described the target, provided the map coordinates for the strike, and indicated the color of smoke he would use to mark the location of the friendly troops. The FAC radioed the pilots, usually flying F-100s armed with bombs or napalm, and gave them the map coordinates of the target.

Most often, neither the friendly troops nor the target, nearly always enemy troops, could be seen clearly from the air by the high-speed jets flying just above the treetops. So as the jets approached the target area, the forward elements of the friendly ground troops marked their position by igniting a colored smoke grenade, typically yellow, orange, or purple.

At the same time, the FAC precisely marked the enemy target by firing rockets with white phosphorus (Willy Peter) warheads. The jets zoomed in and dropped their ordnance in and around the rising plumes of white smoke created by the white phosphorus.

I helped coordinate the process to assure that other friendly units in the AO were not in the target area at the time of the strike. It all happened very rapidly because tactical air strikes were often needed when an embattled unit was close to being overrun. And air strikes were potentially very dangerous for friendly troops. During ground combat in Vietnam the exact location of the opposing forces changed rapidly and frequently.

Coordinating an air strike was almost like a surgical procedure. There was a team of experts working together in a confined area, under a lot of pressure. Time was of the essence. Our job was to neutralize the problem without destroying the surrounding organs and killing the patient. One slip and you had a disaster on your hands.

After we finished several air-support missions for the Wolf-hounds, the FAC flew me all over the 25th's AO. Flying in the Bird Dog at a low altitude gave me an appreciation of the terrain.

Later, when I was on the ground leading Alpha Company, I was grateful to have had such a thorough aerial reconnaissance. When I looked at an area on my maps, I was able to see much more than just two dimensions; I could visualize the contours and vegetation of the land itself.

■　■　■

It was late when we arrived back at the base camp. Someone else had radio watch at the TOC, so I went straight to my hootch, tired and eager for some sleep.

There I met my hootch-mate, a second lieutenant whom I will call Donald Young. A platoon leader in the Medical Services Corps (MSC), he was responsible for about thirty medics assigned to Wolfhound ground units. Young had been in the field when I arrived at Cu Chi.

Lieutenant Donald Young turned out to be one of the nicest people I have ever met. We talked for a while. He spoke mostly about his fiancée back in the states and his plans to do medical research when he completed his tour of duty in Vietnam. He was an extremely positive person for being in the middle of a war. I thought at the time it was because, as a member of the MSC, his job was saving people, not killing them.

Young introduced me to the 25th Division officers' club, not far from our hootch, the very appropriately named Lack-A-Nooky Club.

Inside a large tent, sitting on a raised wooden floor, was actually a small mahogany bar with six barstools. There was even a real live bartender. At one end of the bar stood several bottles of liquor. Behind it was a cooler filled with beer. The roof was draped with camouflaged parachute cloth, the sides with battle streamers. Several small tables with chairs were scattered about. Cigarette smoke hung in the air. I could hear music coming from a now ancient reel-to-reel tape recorder sitting on a table in the far corner. In the background was the steady humming of the electric generator sitting outside the tent. Six officers were in the club, glassy-eyed from drink, telling war stories.

At first it seemed odd to me: officers in the rear area with such amenities, while men were dying in the field. I had a fleeting thought about my father throwing parties during World War II for the Navy's top brass at the officers' club in Pensacola.

Later, on the few occasions I returned to base camp from the field, I was glad there was a place to relax and have some fun, if only for a few hours. But I resented some of the officers who were frequently in residence, those with rear area assignments that kept them from the field. The troops I commanded called them *rear area motherfuckers.* Some of them talked a good game but had no idea what it was really like as an infantryman in the field, fighting the war.

Young and I finished that first evening over a couple of drinks, sitting at the bar. A couple of mechanized infantry officers, jaded and cynical, spent a lot of words trying to irritate us. They talked in mock sympathy of the tough life of the Wolfhounds in the jungle, always humping the heavy packs and equipment and taking such high casualties. They boasted about how they preferred riding in comfort and safety, surrounded with protective armor, rather than hoofing it in the bush, and how great it was to carry extra rations to the field in their APCs, and even coolers filled with beer.

They were trying to get under my skin, and they succeeded. Back at the hootch, I struggled to fall asleep. The air shook with the thundering *boom, boom, boom, boom* of salvo after salvo of outgoing artillery. The thoughts went round and round in my head. A lot of them were second thoughts about my decision to join the Wolfhounds. Had I done something honorable or something stupid? And if it were honorable, would anyone notice in this surreal and cynical war?

Why?

The night after my visit to the Lack-A-Nooky with Lieutenant Young, I had been asleep for several hours when I heard the *splat, splat, splat* of nearby mortar explosions. I jumped up, grabbed my steel helmet and rifle, and slapped Young on the shoulder. "Did you hear that?" I shouted, "Let's get the hell out of here."

"I heard it," Young said as he jumped up to follow me out of our fragile hootch into the dark of night. Nearby was a dug-in shelter, where we would be safe from the incoming fire.

I had scrambled up and out in my bare feet and boxer shorts, but Young took a few seconds to throw on a shirt and trousers and jump into his boots. I could hear the telltale sound of mortars popping out of their tubes, far beyond the perimeter of the base camp. I ran a few steps into the blackness, fearful of where the next shell might land. Then I turned to make sure Young was following me.

Just as I faced in his direction, a mortar round exploded behind him, throwing dirt, smoke, and razor-sharp shrapnel everywhere. His mouth dropped open and his eyes widened; then he stumbled forward and collapsed just a few feet from me. I thought, Oh, God, if only he had moved a little faster.

I rushed to him and lifted him up, with my right arm around his back—it was wet—and his left arm over my shoulders. He didn't say anything. He wasn't moving. I thought he had passed out. He was heavy. I tried to drag him. I went down.

People were racing to the shelters. I screamed out, "Medic, I need a medic. Please help me!" Someone pointed me in the direction of an aid station bunker about fifty meters away. More rounds landed *splat, splat;* steel fragments whizzed by. I was rooted to the ground by Young's weight.

I grabbed the arm of the next guy rushing by. "Help me get him to the aid station," I pleaded. "I can't carry him that far." The soldier took Young's other arm; we dragged his motionless body to the aid station and pulled him down through a small opening in the sandbags.

A medic rushed to us. As together we laid Young down, his eyes staring straight ahead, I put my hand on the back of his head to support it. I felt a warm spongy ooze. I quickly removed my bloody hand. It looked like Young had taken shrapnel in both his back and his head, where I could see what appeared to be a hole in his skull. The medic checked Young's heartbeat and pulse. He had trouble finding it. Nearly panic stricken, he said Young wasn't going to make it. He called for help. Young looked pale; his life was slipping away.

I gasped, looked away, and tried to hold back the sour taste of bile. Then I vomited in the far corner of the bunker. I couldn't stop thinking, had he not been between me and the mortar fragments that might take his life, it could have been me. It would have been me.

When I stopped vomiting, a medic checked me over—I was covered with blood and dirt. He found a small laceration on my right shoulder and a puncture wound on my left thigh with a small chunk of shrapnel in it, the size of a pea.

The wounds were so minor I hadn't even noticed them in all the confusion. A doctor removed the fragment from my leg with a large pair of tweezers, cleaned the wound, stitched it up, and put a two-inch bandage around my thigh. Then he closed the cut in my shoulder with a large butterfly bandage.

By the time the doctor finished with me, the mortars had stopped. I was on my way to the Wolfhound's TOC with two very visible bandages. I was still dressed in only my olive-drab boxers and my helmet. I was in a state of high anxiety; I didn't know what to expect next. I knew that a mortar attack often preceded a ground attack, so I was imagining Charlie and his hordes coming at us out of the darkness at any moment.

■   ■   ■

Crouched over, my rifle in my left hand, I dashed close to the ground from shelter to shelter on my way to the TOC. As I quickly jumped inside each shelter and looked around, the inhabitants seemed pretty calm, or at least they were until they saw a nearly panic-stricken barefoot captain wearing only his skivvies, his helmet, and some bandages appear from nowhere, then disappear again. I'm sure I looked like a pretty foolish rookie.

When I arrived at the TOC, the officer on duty stared at me and chuckled. "What happened to you?" he asked.

My adrenaline was pumped and I was angry about Young. "Nothing happened to me," I shouted. "What the hell's happening on the perimeter?"

The grin disappeared from the officer's face. He explained that Charlie was throwing a few mortars at the base camp, again, and that some sappers (suicide bombers) had tried, unsuccessfully, to come through the wire at Ann-Margret, a portion of the perimeter named after the sexy entertainer who had visited Cu Chi with Bob Hope in 1966. He said it happened every couple of months but that they never followed with a full-scale attack. He assumed Charlie knew that many of the combat units were out of base camp up near Tay Ninh and that he wanted to take advantage of the opportunity.

I took a deep breath and tried to calm down. I told him about Young. He said he had no idea that anyone had been seriously hit. He was truly sorry for the way he acted when I walked in. He then briefed me on the status of the Wolfhounds in the field and said that the best thing I could do was go and get some sleep. I was due to relieve him at the TOC at sunrise, just three hours away.

■   ■   ■

On my way back to the hootch, I could see people emerging from the shelters, dispersing, and going their separate ways, back to their own tents and Quonset huts. Life at the base camp was returning to normal.

Off in the distance, high in the sky outside camp, I saw Puff the Magic Dragon pouring fire on the jungle, targeting the suspected location of the VC mortar team. Puff was a converted AC-47 cargo plane mounted with Gatling-type rotating machine guns. It fired thousands of red tracer bullets per minute, like fire from a dragon's mouth, hence the nickname. But I thought at that moment the bullets looked more like a giant stream of red piss coming from an angry, ugly monster hovering high in the night sky.

Still farther in the distance I could see the soft glow of flares lighting the sky above other likely targets. Several artillery batteries fired round after round into the dark. I suspected that it was all futile, that the VC had long since dropped into a tunnel or been smart enough to move quickly out of the area from where they had fired on us.

I thought what a strange and tragic night it was. And how unprepared I was for any of it. The Army had trained me well for dozens of different theoretical situations. My instructors taught me what to do in armored campaigns and house-to-house battles in Germany. They trained me to fight in the jungle. But none of that training really had much to say about what I should do in this particular situation, in a mortar attack on a giant city-sized base camp in Vietnam.

Oh, I knew that, in theory, when you're under mortar or artillery fire in the open you should get out of the target area quickly, or crouch down into your foxhole and just pray nothing lands on you. But nobody had briefed me ahead of time that Cu Chi base got mortared periodically, that a full ground attack seldom followed, and by the way, Brewer, here is the way to a shelter.

I couldn't help thinking about what a figure I must have cut, racing around in my underwear, looking for some VC to shoot at. I was extremely happy that the Alpha Company's Wolfhounds, the men I was soon to command, were still in the field and hadn't witnessed my crazy antics.

■　　■　　■

Back at my hootch, I stared down at the ground where Young had fallen. Dark spots in the dirt marked his let blood. I stood in a trance, seeing him as I did when we first met, not even thirty-six hours ago. I saw him sitting on his bunk, with his brown hair and boyish grin, talking of his fiancée and his life as a medical researcher after Vietnam. I saw him at the bar at the Lack-A-Nooky, speaking with pride of his medics in the field and how he respected their courage and professionalism under fire. And then I saw him with the medics bent over him frantically trying to save his life.

I shut my eyes in disbelief and took a deep breath. I couldn't believe his life might end, snuffed out so quickly, so completely. The whole thing seemed a horrible nightmare. I wanted to waken and find him still talking to me.

I somehow lifted my trembling body into the hootch and collapsed on my cot, weakened from fear and gut-wrenching emotion. Then I struggled up, put on my jungle fatigues and socks, and placed my boots next to the cot—I never slept in base camp again in only my boxers.

I lay back down on the cot and looked up at the straw roof above me. I thought about the reality that had just been demonstrated to me, how at any time a mortar could fall from the sky and end my life, as it might end Young's. I was afraid of going to sleep on my back, looking upwards, and possibly having my face blown off as I slept.

I turned over onto my stomach. To this day I can't fall asleep in bed on my back, as I had my entire life before the mortar attack.

I wasn't able to sleep. I kept thinking of Young and how he might die. He was committed to doing good things for mankind and now he might be gone forever, before he had a chance to make the contributions to life that he was capable of making. I wondered about all the other young men that had already died or would die in Vietnam. What would their lives have been like, what dreams were buried with them? I didn't know Young's parents, but I thought of their pain if he died and when they learned of his death. I thought of his fiancée, her great sorrow.

I had trouble making sense of it, putting all that had happened together. Young, an ROTC officer like me, probably had the same options as I did regarding his branch of service. But he had chosen the Medical Services Corps, a branch of the Army whose job is to care for the wounded, whereas I had chosen the infantry, in spite of my dream of becoming a doctor. Though combat medics are often exposed to enemy fire, they don't purposefully seek out and engage the enemy. That's the infantry's purpose in life. Yet there he was, near death, or already dead, in base camp. And I, the proud infantryman, had only a few scratches.

It just didn't seem right that God should let a person like Young die. I thought, Why, why—why him, not me?

In just the few days that I had been in Vietnam I had already tasted how rotten and unjust war can be—how it could randomly touch anyone, with devastating effect.

In less than an hour my life had changed forever. I had never seen a person near death before, much less in such a mangled condition, lying right in front of me, in my hands. I could feel an anger and hate swelling up inside me, so strong and quick that it took control of me. I perceived Young's mortal wounds as an act of cowardice by the VC. I thought, it wasn't the typical infantryman's kill-or-be-killed scenario. They just lobbed a few deadly mortar rounds into a heavily populated base camp and then ran away. They didn't care who got killed or maimed.

My attitude towards the war was profoundly changed from that moment on. Suddenly the conflict was intensely personal. Politics and patriotism—the spread of Communism, the role of American democracy—be damned. None of that was relevant.

I knew now what I had to do when I first came face to face with the enemy. There was no longer a doubt or question in my mind. I would kill as many as I could, as fast as I could. And I was eager to get on with it.

Eagle Flight

The Huey pilot was flying slow, in wide overlapping circles, as an eagle soars in search of its prey. We were drifting above the tapestry of jungle and rice paddies in War Zone C. Our prey were the enemy troops, VC or NVA, hidden under the rippling green surface of the tropical forest. This was my first *eagle flight* mission.

It was dawn of the third day after the mortar attack on Cu Chi. The air was already hot from a blazing red-orange sun perched on the horizon. I had no idea what to expect. My adrenaline was pumping hard, and the steam heat produced rivers of sweat.

Captain Rob Robertson of Delta Company was with me in the Huey. Our first job was to act as bait, to goad the enemy into revealing their positions by shooting at us. Then we would swoop down on them as an eagle does. But now we were exposing ourselves, expecting at any moment the whine and thud of bullets piercing the thin metal skin of the helicopter.

Crouched next to the open door of the Huey, I was sitting on top of my flak jacket to protect my vitals from a round slamming violently up through the bottom of the chopper. In my right hand, I held a Willy Peter grenade.

Several kilometers to our south, and well out of visual range, were two heavily armed gunships circling Hill 42. Robertson's second platoon, commanded by Lieutenant Ritchie, was circling in six other choppers just south of the gunships. They were all waiting to hear from us, waiting for the radioed order to sweep over the horizon and down on the unsuspecting enemy.

But at this moment, we were the bait, alone in the sky. The time passed slowly, in time to the beating of rotors overhead. We approached the village of Giong Loc.

Crack, crack, crack—like the crack of a bullwhip, bullets cut through the air, missing the chopper by inches. Robertson yelled to me, "Dammit, that was close." "Too close," I shouted, jerking back from the open door.

We were receiving small-arms fire from a nearby wooded area. The pilot dropped the nose of the Huey and made a steep bank to the right. At the same time, the door gunner on the right opened up with an M-60 machine gun, raining bullets down through the trees, trying to keep Charlie pinned down.

Robertson radioed Ritchie. I pulled the pin on the Willy Peter grenade and tossed it out. The idea was to mark the area where the VC were hiding. The grenade ignited halfway to the canopy of leaves below, leaving a trail of white smoke as it toppled down through the trees.

Things were happening very fast. I took a deep breath to calm myself. Then I radioed the gunships at Hill 42 and sent them the map coordinates pinpointing where I'd thrown the grenade. They raced to Giong Loc, spotted the smoke filtering up from the trees to the west, and started working the area with cannon fire and rockets to keep Charlie's attention. As they arrived on station, we flew like a bat out of hell towards Hill 42.

After linking up with Ritchie's platoon in the troop-carrying Hueys, called slicks, we led them into a small grass clearing just 500 meters from the smoke. We flew in low and fast, with the treetops rushing by just beneath us. I saw the clearing, still partially obscured by a lingering mist.

The choppers dropped down to four feet above the ground. We quickly jumped from the hovering choppers into razor-sharp elephant grass. The ground was uneven, punctuated in places by old craters carved in the floor of the forest by American bombs. The whole maneuver took less than twenty minutes. The slicks returned to get the rest of Delta Company, waiting anxiously at the Cu Chi airstrip.

But there was no time to linger in the small clearing we had used for our LZ. We moved out in the direction of the VC, the gunships swarming above us like angry hornets in hot pursuit. In a matter of seconds we were in dark, dripping woods, the maw of the beast.

■　　■　　■

My job that day, as acting S-3, was to coordinate the use of the aircraft and plan the insertion of Delta into the AO, if and when contact with the enemy was made. When the operation was over, it was my job to coordinate the helicopter extraction of the troops from the AO.

But since eagle flights were a common Wolfhound tactic, I decided to tag along with Delta Company during the entire operation. In less than two weeks, I would be assuming command of Alpha Company. I wanted to learn as much as I could, as soon as I could. There was a lot that I desperately needed to know about Wolfhound tactics—and about myself, under fire.

The area in and around Giong Loc was an active enemy stronghold. As we struggled through the dense underbrush, approaching the area where Charlie had taken his shots at us, we had to step with utmost caution. Everywhere were mines and booby traps. Snipers zeroed in on us, slicing the air from hidden perches in the trees overhead, promising death without warning.

Each encounter with a sniper or a booby trap stalled our advance, giving the elusive VC more time to flee. And as luck would have it, by the time we reached our initial objective, Charlie had vanished. Or he seemed to have vanished—swallowed, perhaps, by the fading mist.

Ritchie put two-man listening posts to his front and rear and on each flank. Then he told his troops to take a break and eat, while we waited for the remainder of Delta Company. Once they joined us, Robertson and three of his platoons would lead a more thorough search of the area, sweeping out from the initial point in a pinwheel-like movement. At the end of the day, I would call for choppers to meet us back at the LZ, to lift everyone out and home.

The break gave me my first opportunity to size up the grunts, the leg infantrymen in Ritchie's platoon. I thought they wouldn't be too different from the men of Alpha, the company that I was going to lead.

Maybe back in their hometowns they hadn't looked anything alike, but war had imposed a certain sameness or commonality. Mustaches were in fashion, but there wasn't much else that was fashionable about them. Many of them were young men, but they all looked old and worn in their jungle fatigues. They were all tired and dirty. They were also quiet men. The effect was of thoughtfulness, reflection, but not serenity. What were they reflecting on? Their eyes jerked nervously, right and left, up and down.

These young men moved like old men, too, slowly and cautiously, not just because they were tired but out of necessity. The anticipation of mines and booby traps was by now as instinctual as breathing. Every step was a conscious acceptance of risk. At the same time, each man carried an enormous amount of the stuff of war, and for some, the weight of their gear often enforced a slow wide-footed walk, like the giant in a fairy tale.

The gear included olive-drab jungle fatigues, canvas and leather jungle boots, and steel helmets with elastic camouflage covers, bleached to a light yellowish brown from the sun. Most wore heavy flak jackets to help protect their upper bodies. Each one had at least two canteens of water. They all carried several fragmentation grenades, a bayonet, and a small shovel-like entrenching tool for digging foxholes. Some had smoke grenades. Many of the men carried machetes.

Most had olive-drab terry cloth towels draped around their necks to wipe the sweat and dirt from their faces. They all had a green plastic poncho liner, which promised some protection from the rain or could be used as a makeshift litter. Many of them carried cans of C-rations in extra socks tied together and hung over their shoulders. In the elastic bands on their helmets, each had stuffed a miscellaneous collection of small and personal stuff: pictures from home, cigarettes, a toothbrush, mosquito lotion, playing cards printed with the ace of spades, and other good luck charms. Everyone had at least one large compress bandage, used to quickly stop bleeding or keep air out of a sucking chest wound.

Most of the grunts carried an M-16 rifle and ten to fifteen magazines of extra ammunition. Some carried M-79 grenade launchers that propelled 40 mm grenades over a hundred yards. Others, larger in stature, hauled the heavy M-60 machine guns with extra belts of ammo draped across their chests. Some had shoulder-fired, light anti-tank weapons (LAWs), and many carried claymore mines, which were placed in front of their foxholes in night defensive positions or used for offense during ambushes. Some carried extra mortar shells. Some of the men carried heavy PRC-25 radios on their backs.

Everyone was bearing a heavy load, the latest tools of war. Yet the lightly equipped VC could easily cut and run, moving quickly through the forest at will. It wasn't surprising that the American GIs, weighed down with their involuntary possessions, should have a hard time staying in contact with such an enemy.

■ ■ ■

My examination of Ritchie's men ended abruptly. A hand holding a grenade shot straight up from the ground, like Jack's beanstalk, twenty yards from me. The hand tossed the grenade toward a group of three GIs sitting off to my right. "Grenade," one of them yelled as he instantly picked it up and hurled it out of range. *Boom!* Had he hesitated for a split second, the grenade would have torn him apart.

At the same time the other two jumped forward and sprayed a magazine of ammo each into what seemed the hard ground where the hand came from. As if by instinct, they threw open a well-camouflaged cover to a VC tunnel and fired several more rounds down into it. It was all over in a matter of seconds—long, life-threatening seconds.

The grunts pulled out three dead VC, riddled with bullet holes and with chunks of their bodies blown off.

"Fuckin' sons of bitches tried to kill us. Did you see that, man? We *wasted* your asses," one of the GIs said as he kicked and spit at each of the dead VC. Then he sat back down and finished his C-ration breakfast of canned peaches and pound cake, staring at the bodies, defiantly, the whole time.

In a matter of seconds, flies were picking at the corpses. Several of the other GIs walked over to the corpses and took pictures. Ritchie called Robertson and reported three enemy KIA, killed in action.

Waste is an ugly term. I would hear it in Vietnam many times from that day on. It was used there as a transitive verb, meaning *to kill*. In Vietnam the grunts wasted the VC and NVA soldiers. Or the VC and NVA wasted us.

To waste someone was to kill him. Somehow it seemed to me that to waste someone was worse than to kill him. Of course it's not. But to me, waste is to kill as pornography is to sex—something way out on the far side of normal, somehow deviant, perverted.

Maybe it was the manner of killing that was different. I had never seen what an M-16 round, or any other bullet for that matter, did to a human body at close range in just a few seconds. I found myself gawking at these small heaps of once-living flesh with a morbid sense of curiosity.

The corpses were dressed only in black shorts and sandals. They were tall for the Vietnamese. Ritchie thought they might be of Cambodian Khmer extraction because of their size. Their eyes were still open except one of the men's—half of his head was gone; he had just one eye open.

Holes where bullets had exited were the size of a fist. Irregular chunks of flesh and bone were torn from arms and legs. One of the VC's shoulders was blown off; just a few shreds of mangled flesh held together the upper arm. The lower arm was gone from the elbow down.

It was a horrible sight. It's burned into my memory. But somehow, at that time, in that place, it didn't seem to bother me. My eyes weren't looking at the dead VC as people, I looked at them as an enemy to be sought out and killed. That's how I was trained, how everyone around me was trained, how infantrymen are trained.

Maybe living through seeing Young's body torn apart in base camp also had something to do with it. That was an image I also had in my head, just as powerful as the one in front of me. I was still angry and bitter, and those emotions insulated me.

Ritchie sent one of his small, thin-framed tunnel rats down

into the tunnel to see what he could find. After only a few seconds the tunnel rat emerged. He had two AK-47 assault rifles and some bandoliers of ammo. He reported that it was a small tunnel, probably for hiding only.

I had my own doubts about how far into the tunnel he had gone, but I know that I wouldn't have gone very far myself. Ritchie shouted, "Fire in the hole," and dropped a fragmentation grenade down into the tunnel. We scattered—*boom.* Then Ritchie told his men to "saddle up and move out."

Robertson had reported the arrival of the rest of Delta Company. The sweep of the area was about to get under way.

As the platoon moved out, several of the grunts put another bullet into each of the corpses as they walked by them, I guess to waste them some more. At the time, I thought it foolish for American soldiers to spend ammo on dead gooks; it might be needed later to save their own lives. But as the weeks and months wore on and I witnessed such events many more times, I changed my opinion. I saw the shooting as a release of pent-up rage. A rage to get even for a buddy that had been killed or wounded. To get even for having to endure the endless life-threatening searching for Charlie. To get even for having to live the life of a grunt in Vietnam.

The rest of the afternoon was spent trying to reestablish contact with the VC while destroying anything that we came upon that could possibly aid them in their guerrilla war against the South Vietnamese. In addition to the three enemy KIA, Delta Company reported four friendly wounded by a booby trap, two AK-47s and 460 rounds of ammo captured, six tunnels destroyed, twenty-seven banana trees (a source of food) cut down, twenty bunkers blown, a cache of eighteen bags of rice (more guerrilla food) dumped into the river, and six POWs (probably farmers) detained for questioning. I was assured by Robertson that it was all justified because we were in a "known VC area." I got the impression that he felt it was a pretty successful day.

I had nothing to judge it against, but it seemed like a pathetic way to be fighting a war. We weren't trying to seize and hold tactically or strategically important terrain, as in other wars. We just tried to find the enemy and then kill or capture him—to generate statistics for higher headquarters. Or so it seemed to me.

■ ■ ■

With the sun low in the sky, we returned to the small grass LZ we had come into that morning. One of Delta's platoons had previously secured the area. The other two established a loose perimeter in the woods around the clearing. I called the 25th Aviation Battalion on the radio to confirm, per my previous request, that we still had six slicks waiting with gunship support to extract Delta Company.

But fate wasn't going to be that kind to us. I was told that only four slicks, and one on-call gunship, could be made available. All the other 25th Division aircraft were tied up supporting units in Tay Ninh Province.

I quickly did the math, which wasn't encouraging. We would need seven lifts of four slicks each to get everyone out. Hueys don't have the passenger capacity of a Boeing 747. They require a four-man crew: a pilot, a copilot, and two door gunners. If you load more than six additional American troops into one, it's dicey getting up and out of a small LZ without clipping trees and crashing.

With each round trip taking twenty minutes, we'd need over two hours, even without holdups or incidents, to get everybody out. Before the last lift, it would be nearly dark. I was nervous about the situation, for sure. But I didn't really have a choice. We had to get the extraction under way.

The thing is, I also had a strange feeling that we were being watched. That Charlie had been following us all day, keeping us in sight, shadowing our every move. Now he could see the pattern of the extraction, he could count the number of men remaining on the LZ. Every twenty minutes that number got smaller. When the odds were heavily in his favor, he would strike.

The first four lifts went without incident. Then things started to happen around the perimeter. Enemy snipers moved into the trees and started firing at us, picking their targets. I radioed the lead chopper pilot and told him that the LZ would be hot for the fifth lift but that we still had enough firepower on the ground to keep the snipers down. After that we would need gunships to help us out.

The fifth lift went fast, with door gunners firing on the way in and out. No one was hit. Now there were only forty-four of us left on the ground. I was the senior officer. Robertson had left on an earlier lift. Since I was responsible for the extraction, I decided that I should go out on the last lift—only after I was sure that no one was left behind.

■   ■   ■

I tightened our irregular perimeter around the small LZ to limit the distance those getting out on the sixth lift would have to run to get to the choppers. I kept all the remaining machine guns and LAWs with my group. We needed them to protect the sixth lift on its way in and out, and to help defend against an attack that I knew would come when only twenty of us were left on the ground.

We hugged the ground inside the old bomb craters. Staying as low as possible, I maneuvered the heavy weapons into positions where they could do the most damage to the attackers. Every time I stuck my head up, bullets zinged by. My mouth was dry, but I was sweating more than I think I ever have, before or since. I took a drink of water from my canteen, hugged the ground some more, and waited.

The whole time I kept thinking about that magazine article I'd read before I got to Vietnam. The one where the author describes a battle in which an infantry unit is annihilated in circumstances much too similar to mine. The VC waited patiently until the numbers greatly favored them; then they attacked.

It was like a premonition. The effect was not to reassure me, it was to scare me out of my wits. Was I about to be overrun? I heard the *dut-dut, dut-dut, dut-dut, dut-dut* of the sixth lift coming in.

The lead gunship came in low, laying down a base of cannon fire along the tree lines to the south and west of the LZ. On the ground, we concentrated our firing to the north and east. The noise was almost unbearable.

The slicks came in fast again with door gunners peppering the woods with M-60 machine-gun fire. They landed, were loaded in less than ten seconds, and lifted off. Two of the choppers took hits but could still fly.

One more lift to go. My dust-clogged rifle jammed and wouldn't fire. I pulled out my .45 caliber pistol and radioed for more gunship support to be diverted to assist us. We were now surrounded by a substantial enemy force that had moved their own automatic weapons into positions where they could fire on us.

I felt very alone and afraid. I was afraid that I was going to die— in that clearing, on that day, and very soon. If only we could hold out for twenty more minutes. I had to get a grip on myself, and fast. At least die like a man. Do something!

It was starting to get dark. I could see what appeared to be bushes moving far to our front as well-camouflaged Charlie crept toward us. The enemy firing picked up. Volley after volley of small-arms fire and repeating bursts of automatic weapons cut through the grass and kicked up the dirt all around us. The acrid smell of gun powder was suffocating.

I passed the word to fix bayonets. The guy to my left got his thumb shot off and the guy to my right had a bullet rip through the top of his helmet, only scratching his head. I felt a hard thud on the small of my back and a warm wetness soaked my buttocks. I reached back—it was water, not blood. A bullet had ripped straight through my canteen.

It was getting darker; visibility was decreasing rapidly. We held our fire so the muzzle flashes of our weapons wouldn't reveal our exact positions in the tall grass and craters that sheltered us.

Fifteen minutes to go. The movement in the bushes got closer, about 200 to 300 meters away on two sides of us, but still near the woods.

I needed artillery support badly, but we had to get the shells in the air very quickly or they might hit the choppers on their way back in. I took a chance and called in the fire mission. I used the point where I originally dropped the Willy Peter for reference and tried to calculate the right adjustment to hit the area in front of us, where most of the firing was coming from.

"Tango Niner, this is Trojan Three. Fire mission."

"Trojan Three, Tango Niner. Go ahead."

"This is Trojan Three. From Willy Peter, drop 600 [meters], right 250 [meters]. Fire for effect." I had no time for a spotter round.

If my map was correct and I had estimated the distances properly, the rounds should fall just inside the wood line. If I made a mistake, the shells could easily blow us out of our craters or fall on some empty patch of jungle. Even if the calculations were correct, there was always the possibility that a round might fall short of the target. The guys around me were convinced they were going to be wasted by our own fire mission. We waited.

My heart was pounding against my chest, pressed tight to the ground. More bullets zinged by, inches over my head. Then *ba-room, ba-room, ba-room*—the artillery shells exploded. I felt shock waves. Shrapnel whistled by. I could hear blood-curdling screams that I hoped were coming from the VC, not my men. Snipers fell from the trees; it looked like one got caught in some branches, swinging upside down like a limp rag doll.

The VC on the ground started moving quickly towards us; they knew if they got closer, we couldn't bring in more artillery without hitting ourselves. We were outnumbered by at least four or five to one.

I said to myself, "God, please get those choppers here before it gets too dark." All around me, men were saying, "We're not getting out, we're not getting out alive."

Then, as though perfectly timed—*dut-dut, dut-dut, dut-dut*—two fully loaded gunships appeared on my horizon. I made contact. We fired four LAWs to mark the enemy positions all around us. I also marked our position with purple smoke. The VC opened up on us, but we stayed low as the gunships did their jobs with cannons and rockets.

The earth all around us was coughing dirt, steel, and probably VC body parts up into the sky. I could see some of the black-clad VC running back to the relative safety of the trees.

Then the slicks came in fast, door gunners blasting away through red-hot gun barrels. We got ready, staying low to the ground so the door gunners could fire over us. Then we ran, sideways and backwards, as fast as we could, firing everything we had at the VC, crouching and dodging craters, scrambling through the elephant grass to the hovering slicks.

Several guys were hit and dragged to the choppers. At the last second, I hesitated and looked around to make sure that nobody was left behind on the LZ. I didn't see anyone.

I threw myself into the last slick headfirst onto the floor just as it lifted off, my legs still dangling down on the outside.

On our way up, red and green tracer rounds whizzed by me, passing straight through the two open doors of the chopper. Had I raised my head, it would have been blown apart. Seconds later—*ping, ping, ping*—the chopper took three hits, one through the Plexiglas canopy, narrowly missing the copilot.

As we rose higher and higher into the darkened sky, I felt like I was in the middle of the grand finale at a 4th of July fireworks display.

■   ■   ■

Once out of small-arms range, the pilot looked back at me and said, "You're lucky to be alive. There were gooks running all over the place. We almost turned back—too much shit coming our way."

He stopped and just gaped for a moment. I don't think either one of us could believe our eyes. The pilot's name was Captain Tim Strum. I had served with him and we had partied together in Gelnhausen. We hadn't seen each other for over a year and a half.

And now he had saved my life, risking his to come in for us through a hail of fire. When we landed, I told him again that I couldn't believe that we bumped into each other the way we did. I hugged him and thanked him for his help. He wished me luck and lifted off again. He was in a hurry to get back to his home base before it got too dark. I never saw him again.

■   ■   ■

I found myself back at base camp, on my feet and headed for the Wolfhound TOC. I was the same man I had been that morning, but also profoundly different. I was intoxicated, high on thoughts of the last hour. Perhaps it was just the rush of getting through it all and feeling that I'd met the test, that I had not disgraced myself in my first real battlefield encounter. But I felt a sense of self-confidence, a narcotic high, even a brief sense of invincibility that I'd never experienced before.

At the LZ, during the battle, I was as scared as I can imagine being and utterly convinced that I was going to die. Yet there was also a deep and visceral excitement. It kept me thinking, sharpened me, made me totally alert. It was if somewhere deep inside me there was an ancient element of my soul, a warrior spirit that lay waiting to be of service, taking control when it sensed my fear, enabling me to fight for my life and those of the men around me.

■ ■ ■

Much has been written about men under fire. The question is often raised, why do they risk their lives, why do they take such enormous chances to reach an objective? It hardly seems rational, even when there is a rational cause to fight for.

The buddy element has often been cited as the primary motivation for a soldier's courage and effectiveness in battle. A man risks his life to save his friends, to avenge them, or to protect them. As a theory, it was developed in the twentieth century and helped to shape Army policies in World War II.

And in fact, it happens often in the infantry; I saw it time and again in Vietnam. But I saw more.

I think most people think of a buddy as a close friend, someone with whom they've shared a lot, where a tight bond has been forged. Yet when Strum brought his choppers in through a wall of fire to save our beleaguered force, he was risking his life for men he didn't know, who weren't his buddies in the traditional sense. Sure he knew me. But when he flew into the LZ to extract us, he didn't know I was there. And he didn't know anybody else.

Chopper pilots did that sort of thing, all over Vietnam, every day. And medics, crawling through heavy enemy fire to treat the wounded, often risked their lives for individuals they hardly knew.

Perhaps the definition for the word buddy needs to be expanded for the purposes of the Vietnam war, even for all wars. A more fitting definition for the word buddy in the context of war is any American soldier in trouble.

Winning Hearts and
Minds

Back at Fort Benning, I had been taught that the mission of the infantry was to close with and destroy the enemy. Yet the real job of the Wolfhounds in Vietnam, and the other units fighting with the 25th Infantry Division, seemed to be different.

Certainly we were trying to hurt the Vietcong units and drive them from their sanctuaries in Long An and Hau Nghia Provinces. But we were also trying to "win the battle for the hearts and minds" of the South Vietnamese inhabitants. After all, the enemy was not across a border or on the other side of some battle front. Many of the villages and hamlets among which we encamped and operated were known to be sympathetic to the Vietcong.

Often the villagers had no choice in the matter. The VC used terror tactics, torture, and murder to assure allegiance to their cause. They were committed to uniting South Vietnam with the Communists in North Vietnam, and they didn't hesitate to impose force and violence on their future fellow countrymen.

The job of the 25th Infantry Division was to destroy the VC and to win the villagers over to our side. Our weapons in this fight were acts of kindness and goodwill, real and substantial humanitarian programs that made a difference in people's lives. The Pentagon's bureaucratic word for the strategy was *pacification*. But the men I knew in the Wolfhounds were not bureaucrats.

They pursued the work of charity as sincerely and passionately as the work of war.

The day after the eagle flight to Giong Loc, I was briefed on the 25th Division's pacification programs, and particularly on Operation Lanakai.

During Lanakai, the 25th liberated the village of Rach Kien, which had been occupied by the VC for many months. After driving the VC from the village, GIs rebuilt and painted the elementary school, which had been closed by the VC during their occupation. The GIs also rebuilt the empty marketplace and provided medical treatment to hundreds of patients. Rach Kien was slowly returning to its earlier days as a local center of commerce.

I was honestly surprised to learn about Lanakai and similar programs by the 25th Division. I hadn't heard of such humanitarian efforts before leaving the States for Vietnam. It was a different side to this strange war, and to the profession of being a soldier. It was nice to learn that there was more to what we were doing here than the stark image of men killing men in the jungle.

■ ■ ■

In a few days, I got a chance to participate in the Wolfhounds' humanitarian programs. I joined a MEDCAP (Medical Civic Action Program) mission. We were headed for the small village of Trung Suc. The mission was supposed to be conducted jointly with the Tiger Division, an ARVN (Army of the Republic of Vietnam) unit.

I left Cu Chi base camp in a Jeep with a young doctor from the 25th Medical Battalion and an interpreter from 25th Division Headquarters. Two other Jeeps, ridden in by four medics and filled with boxes of medical supplies, followed close behind. It was early in the morning, but the air was hot and dusty, as usual.

Both Jeeps were marked with a large Red Cross symbol. We carried very few weapons to protect us if ambushed. I was told that this was to show the villagers that we were on a goodwill mission. We were also informed that the area we were traveling in was relatively safe, at least during daylight hours. But my adrenaline was still high, and I continued to be a little nervous during the thirty-minute drive to Trung Suc. It was impossible to forget the close calls in just a few days during the mortar attack on Cu Chi and the extraction of Delta Company near Giong Loc. VC seemed to be everywhere, why not Trung Suc? This was not a safe part of the world.

When we arrived in Trung Suc, the villagers were gathered in a large group outside a low saffron-colored building. Standing in the center of town, it had solid walls at each end and six large columns on two open-air sides. The roof was red terra cotta with large exposed rafters. The floor was a hard cementlike clay. It seemed as if this large open structure was used as a central marketplace. There were bits of wilted vegetables on the floor and shabby wooden stalls lining the walls. The marketplace had not escaped the effects of war; the walls and columns were pockmarked with damage from bullets and shrapnel.

We found the ARVN Tiger Division troops standing around the building in groups of two or three, looking bored. They were supposed to be providing security. In my judgment, it was something less than tight. But as usual, they were dressed impeccably, in well-tailored jungle fatigues and red berets, the height of military fashion. I began talking to the ARVN troop leader, hoping to improve the security situation.

Outside the building close to a hundred people were lined up, old papasans and mamasans, younger adult females, some children, and a few young men. The word had gone out. The market was about to become a makeshift medical clinic.

Wasting no time, the doctor and the medics went straight to work. One by one, they took each person's temperature and blood pressure. The interpreter helped describe to the doctor and medics what was ailing each patient.

There were patients with swollen insect bites that had become infected. Some had intestinal worms. Others had yellowish pus oozing from boils all over their bodies. Some of the villagers had cuts and bruises on their arms and feet, and some had open holes the color of beef liver that looked like shrapnel wounds. Some had stitches to be removed.

One of the mamasans brought a small black-and-white pig with a shell fragment in its left hind leg. It was also treated and stitched up.

Some of the older patients had illnesses like malaria and yellow fever. Some had illnesses the doctor couldn't identify. A few of the villagers were just curious. And some were probably VC during the night hours, particularly those with the fresh and suspicious-looking open wounds.

None of the peasants showed any visible emotion, at least to me. Yet it seemed by the size and patience of the crowd that they were eager for treatment. All of the sick and injured were treated with great care by the American medics. It took all day. We barely finished in time to get back to Cu Chi before nightfall.

All that day, the well-dressed troops of the Tiger Division watched while we did all the work. They didn't help with the treatment or the management of the villagers. They just stood and looked indifferent. Unfortunately, I often saw the same tendency during joint combat operations.

The MEDCAP mission struck a chord inside of me. When I was in college, studying premedicine, one of my heroes was Doctor Tom Dooley. He was known far and wide for his extraordinary humanitarian work in the 1950s. During his tour of active duty as a doctor in the U.S. Navy, he was stationed off the coast of Vietnam. While there, he experienced the flood of refugees escaping from Communist-held areas in Southeast Asia. Then on leaving the Navy, he decided to stay behind in Indochina, where he dedicated himself to practicing medicine in the remote jungles of Vietnam and Laos. As a freshman in college, I learned of him by happening upon a book, *Deliver Us from Evil,* that he wrote in 1956 describing his experiences as a jungle doctor.

Back then, I often fantasized leading a life like Dooley's after completing medical school. The work at Trung Suc gave me a microscopic glimpse into the daunting challenges Dooley must have faced routinely in his work. It made me feel, if only for that one day, a little like him, a good Samaritan. And it was good to be helping people, not killing them, after the Young tragedy in Cu Chi base camp and the furor and terror of the extraction from Giong Loc. I was on my way to living up to the Wolfhound legend: kind to our friends, ferocious towards our enemies.

■　■　■

The second occasion for me to be a good Samaritan came a few days later. In my Jeep, I led a deuce-and-a-half truck, olive drab with wooden slats for sides, into the small village of Ap Boi. We were on a *Helping-Hands* mission. The truck was filled with clothing, soap, candy, and some other things I can't remember.

Moving through the village, I felt like the Pied Piper of Hamelin. But I was leading the crowd to good fortune, not doom.

All the children rushed to follow us. Many adults joined them. The crowd grew and grew as we slowly moved along the dirt road, lined with banana and palm trees, to the center of town. By the time we stopped, we had an orderly crowd fifteen to twenty people deep circling the truck, everyone with outstretched arms, shouting, "GI numma one, VC numma ten."

Three GIs jumped up into the bed of the Helping-Hands truck and began lifting the small children up one at a time. They picked out colorful shorts and a T-shirt for each child. The enthusiastic soldiers helped each one try the clothes on, gave them some soap and candy, and then helped them down. There were lots of smiles on innocent little faces. I could tell that the GIs were having fun.

The adult villagers waited until all the children were taken care of; then they raised their arms to catch trousers and shirts thrown by the GIs from the truck. It took over three hours to distribute everything.

As before, in Trung Suc, there were South Vietnamese troops standing around, watching impassively.

I mingled with the crowd. Here, too, I felt good about what the Wolfhounds were doing. But I also remember thinking later about the children in Ap Boi, about their terrible situation, and how unfortunate they appeared in comparison to American children. I tried to conceive of what it was like for them, growing up in a country in chaos, with a deadly war raging on all around them. But of course, I couldn't really imagine it. My own childhood had been too safe and protected, in the heartland of America, where towns and cities had not seen the carnage of battle for more than a hundred years.

The trip back to Cu Chi was not without incident. We pulled off the road for a minute to let some tanks and armored personnel carriers from the Fifth Mechanized Infantry pass by. A few feet from my

Jeep, five gigantic gray-brown water buffalo were drinking from a small water hole in an otherwise dry rice paddy. They seemed harmless and indifferent.

Sitting by the side of the road, I was still feeling the glow of the mission in Ap Boi, feeling very proud to be an American soldier. Then suddenly, without warning, one of the water buffalo snorted, charged forward, and attacked, slamming its head and horns into the right rear of my Jeep. The impact pushed the vehicle several feet back onto the road and bent the quarter-inch steel radio antenna mounting bracket. I was nearly thrown out of my seat.

Then he came at us again. Without hesitating, I drew my .45 caliber pistol, chambered a round, and fired when he was just four feet away. I was never much of a pistol shot but luckily hit him in the top of the head. Still, it was a close call. He dropped just one foot away from the Jeep.

I can remember thinking that we had a long way to go in winning the hearts and minds of the Vietnamese water buffalo. In fact, water buffalo turned out to be a constant concern whenever we operated near rice paddies and farmlands. I often saw small children riding on their backs or leading them around by a rope attached to a nose ring, like docile pets. They appeared harmless. But for some reason they attacked GIs often and without warning.

There were many occasions when we moved, with heightened tension, through open rice paddies. All of a sudden to our left or right, we would hear bursts of M-16 rifle fire. Everyone would hit the ground, thinking a firefight was breaking, only to learn that one of Alpha Company's men was protecting himself from an angry water buffalo.

One theory about the beasts was that they didn't like the way we smelled. And another theory: they were hard-core VC.

■   ■   ■

After assuming command of Alpha Company a few days later, my duties kept me in the field. I was unable to participate directly in any more MEDCAP or Helping-Hands efforts, but I think of them often. It troubles me that most Americans don't know that thousands of these missions were completed by men of the 25th Division and by other combat units.

The evidence was in towns and villages all over South Vietnam. Hundreds of one-room tin-roofed schools were built of cinder block, water wells were dug, churches were rebuilt, and sewers were constructed.

It seems to me that when most Americans think of the Vietnam War, they have images in their heads of a GI burning a peasant hootch, of a small child running from a napalm attack, or of the My Lai massacre. What I see in my head is very different.

I see young U.S. soldiers trying to help the people of countless villages; I think of medics treating sickness on MEDCAP missions or GIs handing out soap and candy from the back of a Helping-Hands truck. And I also see American soldiers getting wounded on the battlefield, sometimes while trying to protect innocent villagers caught in the cross fires of war.

Our standing orders when near villages and hamlets were not to fire until fired upon. This placed our lead elements in grave danger near villages or hamlets occupied by the enemy. And at the platoon level, the leaders and the men didn't like the odds. "Sure," said platoon leader Lieutenant Steve Ehart. "Pentagon planners and McNamara's theorists could put a spin on it, but grunts—out in front and in harm's way—never bought it. They knew that he who had the first shot probably had the first kill." Nobody on the ground fighting Charlie liked the odds.

When fired upon from a village, we always opened up first with indirect weapons like the M-79 grenade launcher. The M-79 fires a projectile with a small bursting radius. The arched trajectory doesn't speed dangerously through a village like a high-velocity bullet with a straight trajectory. This tactic gave the villagers time to get down into the bunkers that they all had in their hootches.

We were sometimes attacked by VC that shot at us from behind a human wall of villagers, trying to bait us into firing at them through the innocent bystanders. There were times we took casualties that could have been avoided were we able to open up with all the available firepower.

I remember two Alpha Company soldiers getting wounded by a land mine near Loc Ninh. A peasant woman spoke to me through our interpreter. "Too many Americans are dying. I wish it will end." Then she gave us the names of the local VC elements that planted the mines. Afterwards, she refused the customary reward of a few piasters for information about the enemy.

For years after Vietnam, I would look at American children, including my own, and think of the children in Ap Boi and many other villages. The contrast could not have been more stark. The children I saw in America were surrounded by toys and games advertised on television and bought by their parents: Barbie dolls and Sesame Street, Lego, and Disney items. Toys were the symbols of love and caregiving. Our children were secure and safe, physically and economically. America has been to war often in the twentieth century, but war has not been to America.

I never once saw a child in Vietnam with a manufactured doll or toy, much less a television to watch. The favorite toy seemed to be a large hoop the children themselves made from a flexible branch or vine. A stick was used to steady the hoop and roll it like a wheel through the streets of the village.

There was no such thing as security or safety in these villages. While I saw smiles from time to time on the children's faces, I saw many more tears. Tears caused by the shaking of the ground and the thundering roar from nearby shelling. Tears on seeing a family member being hauled off for questioning. Tears over the loss of their homes. Tears over the loss of their parents.

■ ■ ■

There were two parts to the Wolfhounds' mission in Vietnam. On the one hand, we were risking our lives fighting a ruthless enemy who was determined to impose a totalitarian regime on the people of South Vietnam; on the other, we were helping those people through acts of humanity and charity. Hearts and minds were as important as landing zones and eagle flights.

During my tour in Vietnam I saw American soldiers fight hard to win the battle for the hearts and minds of the Vietnamese people. After I left, the battle continued.

So in the end, did we win them? I like to think that we did, at least some of their hearts and minds. Why else would so many Vietnamese welcome us to their country today? Why do so many embrace the move to a free economy? Why have so many immigrated to the United States, and why do so many more still want to come to live in America?

Believing that we won the battle for their hearts and minds is important to me, even if it can't be proven. It helps me deal with the whole experience. It helps ward off the ghosts.

Taking Command

I could feel the hot rays of the brilliant midday sun penetrate my fatigues, burning my back as though uncovered. It was over 100 degrees, not a cloud in the sky and just a hint of a breeze.

First Sergeant Charles Rutledge was waiting for me. At five-foot-seven, he was about my height, but with his girth he looked as though he'd been chiseled from the trunk of a 100-year-old oak tree. And he was as tough and hard as an old oak. Rutledge had called the troops together in front of Alpha Company's tent barracks. I was about to be introduced as their new company commander. "Teeen hut," he shouted. The troops snapped to attention. Saluting me, Rutledge said, "Sir, the men of Alpha Company." "At ease," I replied.

The men were back in base camp for three days of rest after weeks of fighting in Tay Ninh Province during Operation Junction City. Alpha Company and other Wolfhound units had suffered heavy casualties. It was one of the first large operations of the war fought against hard-core North Vietnamese Army regulars, dug in along the Ho Chi Minh Trail.

The men stood at ease in faded, sweat-drenched jungle fatigues and worn jungle boots. Their feet were placed shoulder-width apart, hands clasped behind their backs. All 103 of them looked directly at me. Take away their uniforms, put them in a mix of civilian clothes, and they might be any crowd of young American males, like you would see at a baseball game between the Yankees and the Red Sox. But there were also things that made them different from most other groups of young men.

The Wolfhounds of Alpha Company were all lean, with faces and arms deeply tanned by Vietnam's tropical sun. Most hadn't shaved for several days. And like so many other infantrymen I'd seen since arriving in Vietnam, they looked older than their years and exhausted. But the most pronounced common characteristic was the leaden look of anguish on their faces and in their eyes. These were the faces of combat infantrymen who had seen death, heard death, smelled death, time and time again, not those of ordinary men doing ordinary things.

■ ■ ■

All of Alpha's troops were waiting to hear what I'd say. They were bound to judge me more quickly and harshly than I would judge them. After all, I was supposed to be their leader.

I was silent for an endless moment, as they stood silently looking back at me. I imagined they all had the same questions in their heads. Who is this new guy? Did he go to West Point? Does he have any experience in-country? Has he seen any combat? Can he lead? Can I count on him? Will he take care of me? Will he do something stupid and get me killed? And perhaps the most critical question, what does "Top" think of him?

Top, short for Top-kick, and First Sergeant Rutledge were one and the same. As Alpha's top-ranking noncommissioned officer, the men referred to him, affectionately, as Top. And having served as the first sergeant with the same Alpha Company in Korea, he was somewhat of a Wolfhound legend.

I read somewhere that no matter what you accomplish in life, your childhood insecurities stay with you. And so it was with me that day, as I stood in front of the men I would lead. It was an excruciating moment. It was impossible not to be conscious of how I looked to them, wearing thick glasses, towered over by many of the men standing in front of me. I'm hardly the type that Hollywood casts as the commanding officer of a tough bunch of warriors. I suspected most of them would have rather been staring into the eyes of a classic John Wayne or Charlton Heston look-alike: tall, hard-eyed, square-

144

jawed, confident, with a naturally commanding presence. Instead, they saw a short, round-faced guy wearing glasses who appeared to be more of an academic than a warrior.

These men of the Wolfhounds had been fighting together, for their individual and collective lives, for a long time. They'd seen their buddies get wounded, some of them killed. The outgoing company commander, leading them during most of Operation Junction City, was a "pineapple," affectionate slang in the 25th Division for a native Hawaiian. Many of the men had served with him in Hawaii and shipped out for Vietnam with him as well. He was liked and respected by everyone. They were baptized by fire together.

As the new kid on the block, what could I possibly say that would make a good first impression? I'd seen some action, had a few close calls, but I was still pretty green. I felt inadequate by comparison to the outgoing company commander and each of my platoon leaders. In fact, I felt inadequate compared to the men of Alpha Company themselves. They had all been through so much more than I—and survived.

I decided that the probability of putting my foot in my mouth was pretty high. It would be best to say very little. Let them judge me later by my actions in the field, not by my words in base camp. So I told them that I had heard of their accomplishments. That I was proud to be a part of Alpha Company and the Wolfhounds. I told them that I was not one for a lot of "chickenshit," the petty bureaucratic stuff that doesn't matter in the field. I'd spend all my time and energies on our mission and on their welfare.

I finished by telling them that I knew they needed rest, and I wasn't going to keep them standing in the hot sun any longer unless someone had a question of general interest.

There was only one question. Rutledge asked, "Sir, were you with Delta Company at Giong Loc last week?"

"Yes, I was," I answered. There were no more questions.

At first, I didn't understand why Rutledge asked his question; he already knew the answer. He and I had talked before calling the company together. During our conversation he told me he had heard about the Giong Loc extraction in base camp. But by asking the question in front of the troops, he was establishing my credibility in an indirect manner. He later told me that he had passed the word around about my performance at Giong Loc and the wounds I received during the mortar attack on base camp. He told the other sergeants in Alpha, knowing that it would give them confidence in me the first time we found ourselves in a tough situation.

■ ■ ■

Just as I was ready to dismiss the company, a young corporal raised his hand. He told me that he had a presentation to make—for the men who had been lightly wounded and sent back to base camp while the company was in the field. I said, "Okay." Then he bent over and picked up a large glass jar, near his right foot, that I'd not noticed earlier.

At first glance, it appeared to contain an assortment of dried prunes submerged in a clear amber-colored liquid. As he got closer to the front of the formation, I could see that the prunes were not prunes.

The jar contained human ears, in formaldehyde, one each cut from a dead VC or NVA soldier during the Junction City operation. There was a loud cheer as the young corporal presented the contents, symbolically, to Alpha's walking wounded—some on crutches, some with arms in slings, and others with various parts of their bodies in bandages.

My mind seemed to stop and race ahead at the same time. I couldn't halt the ritual, it was obviously important to them, and I was anxious for their respect. I was new, I was green, I didn't understand. What kind of unit was I joining? Could I really be a part of this, let alone be proud of it?

Afterwards, I asked Rutledge, who seemed as surprised as I, "What's with the ears?" He said that he didn't know who took them, nor did he condone the practice. He suspected that it was done to avenge Alpha's dead and wounded and also that some of the troops saw it as an effective psychological warfare tactic.

According to the Buddhist religion, as I recall Rutledge's interpretation, if a believer dies missing a body part, he or she will spend eternity searching for it. The believer will never get to Buddhist heaven to be reincarnated. Some of the men believed that cutting an ear off of a dead VC was one way of saying, if you choose to fight against Alpha Company's Wolfhounds, you are doomed in the afterlife.

■   ■   ■

It was hard for me to accept that American soldiers were disfiguring enemy corpses in the name of good tactics. When we played war in the pretend jungle years ago in Willow Run, the Americans were always the good guys, kind to prisoners, passing out candy cigarettes. Then I recalled reading before arriving in Vietnam about VC in the Ia Drang Valley using machetes to hack the genitals off dead GIs. It had sounded horribly savage when I read it. Were we as bad? Maybe I should call the men back into formation and issue my first order as their new commander: "No more ears."

But I couldn't imagine doing that. Somehow it didn't seem like the right thing to do, the best way to start off my first combat command. And, after all, I reasoned, taking ears is not as bad as taking genitals.

I could feel myself being pulled into the combat culture, with its own set of rules, its own logic. In combat, it is correct behavior to blow an enemy's head off when he is still alive and coming at you. It's okay to vaporize the enemy by bombing them at night in their jungle camps when they're still alive and perhaps sleeping. And if it's acceptable to drop napalm on attacking enemy troops and set their living bodies ablaze, how can it be wrong to take a single small ear when they are stone-cold dead? Particularly if it helps the morale of your own soldiers. And especially when the enemy is mutilating our own dead.

Taken out of context, the act of soldiers shooting more bullets into a dead enemy for revenge, as I had seen during the eagle flight with Delta, was deplorable and inhumane to me. The same was true for taking an ear as a souvenir or for psychological warfare. But I saw those acts differently when I was there, in-country, even though I didn't sanction them. The context was that of a foot soldier fighting in a jungle war, each day facing personal traumas and the possibility of his own horrible death. In those circumstances, such behaviors, such deplorable practices, seemed almost acceptable, an outlet—a necessary ritual to keep a man fighting and to stop him from going crazy.

I became the commander of Alpha Company on that hot day in Vietnam. I was about to do what I had trained to do for almost four years—lead an infantry unit in ground combat. And all the training was about being in control, directing my forces, achieving an objective. Taking command.

But I kept thinking that something bigger had happened. Something was taking command of me. A powerful force that I had no control over. Something I didn't like but couldn't escape from or simply reject.

Before I fell asleep, I thought about all the seemingly noble reasons that I decided to be an infantryman, to fight for my country, and perhaps die for my country. And in just the brief period I had been in Vietnam, how I was hit smack in the face with the brutality of combat. I was still prepared to die for my country, but I was not prepared for all that I would witness, for what men do in battle, how they slaughter each other. And many were men like me. They grew up believing in the Sixth Commandment: "Thou shalt not kill" and in the Golden Rule: "Do unto others as you would have others do unto you." But once in combat, they violated both with a vengeance. The will to survive is so strong that, in the end, it is what takes command of men in combat.

■ ■ ■

It has been many years since I fought in Vietnam. Yet I am still haunted by some of my actions after assuming command of Alpha Company. I learned early as a company commander that every soldier in the company watches everything you and your platoon leaders do. Silently or not, in their minds infantry grunts question each command decision, each order. Is it the best for them and their buddies? Is it reckless? Will it endanger their lives unnecessarily?

So we thought of what was best for them, first and foremost. We never wasted helicopters evacuating wounded VC. Someone who wasn't there might ask, why not show compassion, why be need-lessly cruel? But helicopters were often in short supply. The very chopper we used to send back a wounded VC might be needed down the trail minutes later to evacuate a wounded GI—perhaps a GI with both his legs blown off and bleeding to death.

It wasn't war games back in Hohenfels, Germany, and it was hel-icopters, not Jeeps. But I well remembered the lesson Colonel Norvell had taught me when I sacrificed a Jeep, which I would later need to save lives, to send Sandler back to the rear area in Gelnhausen.

When we found a tunnel opening concealed in or near a vil-lager's hootch, we often made the male head of household, if we could find him, go down into it first. He always claimed he didn't know how the tunnel got there, but my platoon leaders and I knew differently. If the opening was booby-trapped, the odds were that he knew how to disarm it, or else he, not one of our men, would be in-jured or killed.

We wouldn't take chances with the lives of our men, and I think they respected each one of us for it. If they didn't, the will to survive might have led one of them to kill me or a platoon leader in a firefight; no one would ever know who did it. Such alleged "fragging" incidents were reported to have happened on several occasions later in the war, in other outfits.

It's easy for me to rationalize that we made the hard decisions that kept more Americans alive at the cost of dead VC and that we had no choice but to do what we did. And that's probably true. But there is more to it; it's more complex.

On many occasions it later turned out that we didn't need the chopper that could have saved a wounded VC. And there were times when papasans may have been hit by booby traps that a GI might have been able to disarm. While fighting in Vietnam, we looked at the enemy as no more than a target. Army training makes it easy to do so.

But later, with the passage of time, I came to see the enemy sol-diers as just like us. They also had loved ones, families, and dreams for the future. Their government and politicians made the war, just as ours had. Yet it was the soldiers themselves, the flesh-and-blood men of the Vietcong and the North Vietnamese Army—just like us Americans—who had to kill and maim other men like themselves, endure incredible hardships, and then suffer long afterwards.

I came to believe that if even one of the enemy died that we could have saved, part of me died with him. So while I came home alive, a big piece of myself, what I think of as my innocence, did not survive the war. It was destroyed during those months after taking command of Alpha Company—lost forever on those narrow trails under the green canopy of the real jungle.

Alpha's Angels

ood sergeants, also known as noncommissioned
officers or NCOs, are the backbone of the Army.
I had always been told that, and I learned it myself, over and over again, prior to and in Vietnam.
Whenever I was unsure of myself or needed the
good counsel of an old pro, there was always someone like
Sergeant Rutledge around to give me a tip or two.

Military effectiveness depends on the chain of command.
At the level of an infantry company, that chain goes from the
company commander, typically a captain, down through the
lieutenant platoon leader, to a platoon sergeant, and then to a
squad leader, also usually a sergeant. It's not unlike the multi-
layered hierarchy of a big Detroit corporation, but much more
permanent and strict. If the private is the equivalent of the ordinary guy welding steel on the assembly line at Willow Run, the
platoon leader is the department manager and the platoon sergeant is the shop foreman.

Sergeants have a special place in the American military tradition. From Sergeant York to Sergeant Bilko and *No Time for
Sergeants,* the NCO is a beloved if contradictory figure: alterna-
tively brave and comic, tough but good-hearted, honest and
simple, yet often scheming. But in fact, most of the sergeants that
I worked with in the United States, Germany, and Panama were
intelligent, dedicated, and highly professional, often with combat
experience in Korea or during World War II. They typically
began as privates and worked their way up the ranks. A good sergeant has an intimate knowledge of the needs and attitudes of

enlisted men and maintains a strong camaraderie, real if sometimes practiced, with the men in their platoon. Young commissioned officers often come and go, but sergeants tend to stick around, career soldiers in the Army for life.

In the end, it's the sergeants who must motivate the troops to perform, to do what's been ordered by the commissioned officers above them in the chain. Particularly in the field and during combat operations, if the NCOs are not on your side or you lose their respect, you get nowhere as an officer.

So one of the first challenges that a new company commander or platoon leader faces is to take the measure of their sergeants and establish good relations. Much of the success that I enjoyed in each of my prior assignments was due to the support of the many outstanding noncommissioned officers with whom I served. I was hoping for the same in Vietnam, where it really counted.

■　■　■

One of things that caught my attention immediately after assuming command of Alpha Company was the age of the platoon sergeants and squad leaders. Many of them were very young, in their late teens and early twenties, and inexperienced by normal standards. And most of them had fewer stripes than authorized for their positions. I was concerned that the shortage of qualified platoon sergeants and squad leaders in the field would place an added pressure on the less-experienced sergeants and young platoon leaders, who were relatively new to combat. And, in fact, it did.

I soon learned that a number of sergeants with more experience had been wounded or killed. But what surprised me most was that several of the older, more senior sergeants in the company had managed to put themselves into jobs handling logistics and resupply. These responsibilities often kept them in base camp and relatively safe by comparison to field operations.

At first, it troubled me that Alpha's MO, its method of operating, kept some of the company's most knowledgeable and savvy noncommissioned officers out of harm's way. I chewed on it over and over from different angles, trying to see it from their point of view. Some of the rear area sergeants were just a few years from retirement. I assumed they wanted to limit their chances of getting killed so close to retiring. Another factor was their age. They were in their late thirties and forties and possibly not in good enough shape to withstand the rigors of field operations in a place like Vietnam. These were certainly understandable concerns. Still, my initial instinct was to order them to the field and replace them in base camp with men with less combat experience. But I decided to wait before making changes to the way the previous commander ran the company. I soon learned that it was the right decision.

If the Army as a whole can be as hidebound and bureaucratic as any mammoth automobile conglomerate, economic realities for an infantry company in the field dictate a more entrepreneurial approach to business. With Rutledge as their leader, Alpha's rear area sergeants were masters at begging, borrowing, bartering, and otherwise scrounging up extra insect repellent, cold beer, soft drinks, candy, and even ice cream to be lifted out to us by helicopter. They also did everything they could to speed the mail to the troops in the field and generally expedite the logistics of daily life for their customers.

It didn't take me long to see how important this function was to the company's mission. The morale and the safety of the troops in the field depend on the timely resupply of every necessity, from food and water to ammunition. The smallest of life's pleasures means a great deal to men who face the possibility of death every day. And it takes ammunition to win battles.

Another of these masters in the art of logistics was a career NCO whom I'll call Ace. Like Rutledge, he was popular and highly respected by everyone in the company. And like many Wolfhound NCOs, he was a deadly card player. He played a lot of high-stakes poker at the noncommissioned officers' club, and Ace was often a big winner. Shortly after taking command of Alpha Company, I was quietly informed about the novel manner in which he used his winnings.

As the story went, he purchased a dilapidated shack in Cu Chi town. It was made from old wood and corrugated metal and stood just outside the main gate of the 25th Division base camp. He wrangled some of the guys from the engineering battalion to clean it up and repair it. Then he scrounged up some meager amenities: a few chairs, some cots, a washtub, a small cooler for beer and ice, and a small transistor radio for music. When he was done, the hut was painted watermelon green. The last touch was a sign on top in large red letters, framed in bright yellow, reading "Alpha's Angels."

After this palatial establishment was completed to his satisfaction, Ace went to Saigon and made a business arrangement with the Flamingo Bar—a place known, at the time, for its classy bar girls and prostitutes.

■　　■　　■

When Alpha Company was in the field, which was most of the time, we periodically rotated each of our platoons back to base camp. That meant that every two or three weeks, the men could look forward to a few days of rest and relief from the paddies, jungles, and swamps of the Wolfhounds' AO.

On those occasions when he knew in advance that a platoon was arriving, Ace contacted the Flamingo Bar. A group of petite girls wearing colorful ao dais would show up at Alpha's Angels, chattering and giggling. One of the battalion's medical staff checked each girl for venereal diseases—she was either cleared for work or sent back to Saigon.

When the troops landed at the air strip, Ace had a deuce-and-a-half transport truck already waiting. The men piled in, dropped off their gear in the company area, and went straight to the shower point. All cleaned up, many of them were soon back in the truck with lifted spirits—on their way to Alpha's Angels for some *Bamh Bamh* beer and *boom-boom,* hooting and howling like true Wolfhounds all the way to town.

Most of the men satisfied their basic need for boom-boom, quick sex, with no questions asked. But others, including some who were married or had sweethearts back home, just talked with the "angels," though it was difficult because of the language barrier. The vocabulary many of the girls relied on was limited and all too direct:

"Yu wan sucki-fucki? Me numma one." Talking or trying to communicate could cost more than other services because it took more time. Some of the men would just hug a girl, swaying back and forth, perhaps thinking of someone back home. I knew of at least one young Wolfhound who became very attached to one of the girls. He told me that he planned to marry her "when the war was over."

The girls at Alpha's Angels were tiny, pretty, well mannered, and enthusiastic about their work. Everybody seemed to have a good time. Ace paid the bill. I don't know what I would have thought of this arrangement back in Willow Run, or even if all of it were true, but in Cu Chi the whole thing made a lot of sense. It was reported that Alpha Company enjoyed the highest morale and the lowest VD rate in the division. I didn't ask any questions.

■   ■   ■

But there is more to the stories about Sergeant Rutledge and Ace. Early in my tenure as Alpha's CO, I was on my first search and destroy operation in the Ho Bo Woods, searching for Charlie. At the end of a day of humpin' the boonies, we established our defensive perimeter. I was struck by the casual way that some of the soldiers in the company appeared as they went about the business of protecting themselves.

The men were tired and it seemed that very few were really digging in deep enough to protect themselves from enemy fire. Most of the fighting positions were no more than small slit trenches scratched into the soil. Some had makeshift roofs, made from olive-green poncho liners supported by small sticks, to keep out the rain. To me, the positions looked much too shallow to provide even modest cover for someone lying in the prone position. I agonized about what I should do or say to the men. I was still a little low on self-confidence.

I thought to myself, These guys have been through a hell of a lot of combat; they must know what they are doing. I just got here. I'll look like a by-the-book jerk if I run around telling my platoon leaders and sergeants to dig in better. Who am I to tell a bunch of combat vets how to save their own lives? So, I didn't. Though anxious and uneasy, I figured that I would wait for a while and watch to see if they would dig deeper positions that offered more protection.

Later that afternoon, Rutledge called me on the radio. He suggested that he and Ace fly out on the next available chopper "to see how things were going." Half an hour later, they arrived. We walked the perimeter and checked each of the positions. Rutledge and Ace chatted briefly with some of the platoon sergeants. I could tell they didn't like what they saw, nor did I. Then Rutledge called me aside, discreetly.

"Sir, if Charlie hits you tonight a lot of these guys are going to die, and for no good reason. You've got to make them dig in deeper, no matter how tired they are. Be sure you and the platoon leaders personally check the entire perimeter. Don't assume that each of the platoon sergeants and squad leaders is always going to do what's in his best interest."

I could tell that both Rutledge and Ace were concerned about each and every one of us. They left on the next chopper that went out. I was more than a little ashamed of myself for not acting more quickly, and more decisively, on my own.

Then I called the platoon leaders together and instructed them to get all of their troops to dig in as deep as possible. Charlie didn't hit us that night. But every night thereafter the platoon leaders and I personally made sure that the men were well dug in.

We suffered relatively few casualties during my watch as Alpha's CO. That alone says a great deal about the quality of my platoon leaders and their platoon sergeants and squad leaders. But there would have been many more casualties were it not for career sergeants like Rutledge and Ace. They knew how to fight a war—on and off the battlefield. I'm grateful for what I learned from them and others like them.

Searching for Charlie

P op smoke, pop smoke, and fast," I shouted. Two F-100 Super Sabre jets, black against the blazing sun, were roaring down on us. They were in attack formation. These were U.S. planes and therefore on our side. But we could spot bombs, still fixed to the underside of their wings. I was sure the pilots couldn't see us at the speed they were flying. And I had an ominous feeling that these two jet jockeys were about to dump their loads. This was something they often did in certain uninhabited areas after a mission. But this time it was going to be on our heads, unbeknown to them.

Panic stricken, we threw ourselves into nearby bomb craters. Several of us tossed orange smoke grenades to mark our positions. Someone yelled, "What the hell are they doing?" Someone else moaned, "Oh, no!" I hit the ground with a thud.

The jets roared by, gaining altitude in a steep climb. But they had left behind a deadly gift. Four bombs were descending rapidly, heading straight at us.

I pressed my whole body down, face against the earth. I wriggled from head to toe and dug hopelessly with my hands and feet into the loose dirt. My heart pounded in my chest, my stomach tightened. I shut my eyes, held my breath, and thought, I'm finished.

Then explosions—*boom, boom, boom, boom.* Dirt shot up to the sky. Hot razor-sharp bomb fragments whistled by in every direction. Suffocating smoke filled my lungs, mingled with the acrid smell of cordite.

Gradually another smell replaced it: the stink of death. After the dirt settled, I opened my eyes. A few feet in front of me, I saw an image I'll never forget—a jagged chunk of human skull.

Attached to the skull was thick black hair, matted and mixed with congealed blood and decayed brains. Nearby, I also saw a leg and a lower torso with entrails oozing out. They were covered with ants, apparently feasting.

In the first flash of panic and disgust I assumed they were the grotesque remains from one of my own men, torn apart by the F-100's bombs. But the odor of decay told me that they were from a person or persons who had died some time ago. The saliva dried in my mouth. I thought, God, that could've been me. I pulled quickly back and away from the horrid sight.

I jumped up and looked around. I radioed my platoon leaders, checking on casualties. It seemed like a miracle; it *was* a miracle. Not one of our men was killed, or even hurt, though deadly shrapnel from the bombs had filled the air all around us.

The craters had saved us. There were huge holes in the forest floor, six feet deep, dug the previous night by bombs even more crudely powerful than those we had just survived. A bombing mission, code-named *Arc Light,* by a flight of the massive and ancient B-52 warplanes had pounded the area where we were standing. The gruesome remains I still smelled were probably casualties of Arc Light.

But without those holes scooped out of the earth, we would have been on open ground, exposed with no protection. Like stalks of grain ready for threshing, many of us would have been cut to shreds. We would have been a collection of bloody parts, with ants waiting to feast on us.

So I cursed the F-100s, but I couldn't completely blame them. Today, Alpha Company was operating close to, but not inside, a free-fire zone. There were several such zones near the Wolfhound Area of Operations, where our planes often dumped unused bombs before returning to their home bases. Landing with bombs still attached can be very dangerous. I assumed that the F-100 pilots had spotted the extensive ground damage and crater field we were moving through.

Thinking the devastation marked a free-fire zone, and not seeing us, they had let their own bombs fly.

My mission today was bloody enough, without being the target of friendly fire. I was supposed to lead Alpha Company through the Arc Light target area and count the number of enemy casualties.

But counting enemy bodies after a B-52 strike was a sick joke, conceived by bureaucrats sitting in air-conditioned offices. All we ever found were small pieces of bloodied flesh and fragmented body parts, scattered on the ground or embedded in splintered trees. How many living human beings these fragments represented was anybody's guess. It was a gruesome task, like so many others we faced while searching for Charlie.

■　■　■

In most American wars, the enemy is easy to find. There is a front, a line on the map, that defines the two sides in the battle. They are over the next hill or on the other side of a stone fence or in that bunker up the beach. It's simple to recognize them. They wear red uniforms or brown uniforms or gray uniforms with funny helmets.

But in Vietnam, we spent a lot of our time looking for the enemy. He didn't announce himself, he was hard to recognize, and there was no line on the map. We searched by moving slowly, day after day, through endless boondocks: swamps, rice paddies, jungles, hamlets, and small villages. They were called search and destroy operations. To me and other Wolfhounds, it was *humpin' the boonies.*

Humpin' was an arduous and violent way of life, peculiar to the infantrymen in Vietnam. And after taking command of Alpha Company, I was constantly in the field humpin' the boonies—searching for Charlie.

We started each operation with a helicopter air assault or eagle flight into an AO. Most of the time we landed in the Plain of Reeds, Ho Bo Woods, War Zone C, or the Iron Triangle. On many occasions the LZs were hot and we had to fight our way off them and into the surrounding jungle.

But the LZs were often cold, Charlie was somewhere else, and we could walk off. Then we began searching for Charlie. And we searched. And we searched.

It wasn't a stroll in the woods. My troops hauled a lot of heavy gear, their backs and shoulders aching from the loads. We all popped salt pills and malaria pills. We greased ourselves with insect repellent to gain some relief from the flying fauna. We picked leeches from our bodies. Our feet oozed pus from jungle rot. Most of the time we were filthy. And tired. We all wanted to go home. But we searched for Charlie.

We carried our earthly possessions with us. I had a .45 caliber pistol, extra ammunition, a map case, maps, grease pencils for marking on the maps, a bayonet, radio codes, three canteens of water, extra eyeglasses, a compass, a flashlight with a night filter, and lots of fragmentation and smoke grenades—and a small picture of my wife and two infant children.

I also kept wooden end-filters from Dutch Master cigarillos with me—I chewed on one all the time to calm my nerves, though I was never a smoker. It was important that I always sounded calm on the radio when talking with my platoon leaders or higher headquarters, no matter how I felt.

Sometimes I carried a twelve-gauge Remington pump shotgun. Others in my command group also preferred shotguns. They were good for close-in work. And mine didn't jam when I was in a tough situation, like my M-16 during the extraction of Delta Company near Giong Loc.

While we were searching for Charlie, it was always steaming hot or monsoon wet. The terrain was as much an enemy as the VC or NVA. We moved through impenetrable vegetation, hacking our way through vines, brush, and tangled brambles—with thorns that shredded our jungle fatigues and slashed our skin. We slogged through rice paddies, rivers, streams, and swamps, sometimes sinking to our armpits or even all the way under. And we searched and searched.

Some of Alpha's newer grunts, not yet acclimated to the hot weather, suffered heatstroke or heat exhaustion. We had to bring in helicopters to fly them back to base camp. On a few occasions someone would fake exhaustion, not wanting to keep humpin' and perhaps die a horrible death. We told the fakers to get up and keep going or we would leave them behind, all alone in the jungle. It angered them. Some were furious. But it's amazing how fast they got back up.

We had to make an example of the fakers. We had no choice; all eyes were on us. Others would have used the same trickery to get back to the relative safety of base camp. And we had to keep searching for Charlie.

Snipers, harassing fire, mines, and booby traps slowed us all down, killed some, and wounded many others. Sometimes friendly forces fired on us by mistake, like the F-100s did. And one time in Alpha Company, during the chaos of combat with men scattered, disoriented, and afraid, some of our own men fired on each other by mistake. None of us wanted to die so far from home, killed by a friend. But we searched and we searched.

Sometimes, we found places where Charlie had been and things that he had left behind. Out of policy, we destroyed those things. We destroyed Charlie's bunkers and weapons caches, his bags of rice, his banana trees, and his tunnels. When we found them, we destroyed his jungle camps, schools, and field hospitals. And we kept searching for Charlie.

Occasionally, we found Charlie. But it was usually when and where he wanted us to. Then we fought him in small violent clashes or firefights that often ended as quickly as they started. Once in a while, there were real battles, ferocious pitched battles that lasted hours or days.

Paradoxically, when we did finally come close enough to the enemy to grapple with him, the first thing we attempted was to withdraw. Whenever possible, we pulled away from close engagement with Charlie, and my platoon leaders or I would then call in the full fury of the U.S. military on his head: artillery, gunships, and air strikes. Sometimes even naval guns on ships in the South China Sea would join in, lofting giant shells that sailed for miles, high over the jungle, to land with devastating force on the enemy below. We did everything we could to avoid American casualties.

Only after we hit Charlie with everything we had did we move in for the final assault. Then we would see men die, abruptly and quickly. Or we listened to men die slowly in pain, sometimes screaming for a mother or wife. Or we would watch men get their bodies blown apart and still live.

Afterwards, we cleaned up. We brought in dustoff helicopters to evacuate our own casualties. We carefully counted VC bodies. We radioed the body count to higher headquarters. The troop helicopters arrived. We packed up, loaded up, and went humpin' for Charlie again. Searching for Charlie, back in the boonies, in the same AO or in another AO.

■　■　■

While waddling through leech-filled muck and fighting jungle rot, it was easy to imagine the people who gave us the orders sitting comfortably back at base camp. But we knew they were watching our progress eagerly. When we counted VC bodies, I think our count was often inflated by those above us before they passed it up the line, doubtless out of enthusiasm. Often, when we actually found and engaged with Charlie, the higher-ups would suddenly get excited, even overzealous. Senior commanders and staff officers from brigade headquarters, two levels up the chain of command from Alpha Company, would fly into the area. Even officers from division headquarters would make an appearance. They circled high above the battle in their helicopters and watched. The choppers made great seats for spectators, noisy but safely out of harm's way.

One day, a member in good standing of the top brass cut in on my radio frequency to tell me how to fight the battle. I guess he wanted to feel like a part of the action. Of course, he couldn't see all that was going on way down on the ground. The vegetation was too thick.

I'm sure he meant well. But if I had followed his orders, a lot of Wolfhound blood would be on my hands.

The battle was near Duc Hoa. My first platoon, commanded by Lieutenant Doug Colliander, was caught between two well-camouflaged bunkers near a large canal. Pinned down in dense underbrush and tall grass by heavy machine-gun fire, no one could move.

The bursts from the machine guns were so intense that the bullets were cutting paths through the grass like a lawn mower.

Lieutenant Steve Ehart was maneuvering the third platoon to take the machine guns out.

The brigade officer who cut in on my radio frequency saw a lone VC fighter trying to cross a small stream 200 meters behind the machine guns. He couldn't see the well-camouflaged guns. Nor could he see the rest of the enemy force we were up against.

In a nasty tone, he directed me to order the first platoon to get up, chase after the running VC, and take him prisoner. I ignored the order. There was no way that I was going to order my men to get up and run through the killing fields of the two machine guns.

Then, still high above the action, the officer got back on the radio and said, "Alpha Six, you get your troops after that gook now or I'll relieve you of your command and put someone down there who can obey orders! Over."

I snapped back sharply, "Tracer Four, Alpha Six, if I go after that gook, I'll kill my men. We're pinned down. Now please get off my frequency so I can talk to Alpha Three-Six, out." Alpha Three-Six was the radio call sign for Lieutenant Ehart with the third platoon.

Happily, Tracer Four shut up. We returned to our business, infantry business on the ground and under fire. In due time, we achieved our objectives. We neutralized the machine guns, completely routed the enemy force, killed beaucoup VC, captured several enemy weapons, and took only a few friendly casualties, none killed. The would-be prisoner got away. So what!

I never heard from that officer again. I think it was in part because my battalion commander, code name Trojan Six, who later awarded me the Silver Star for that day, must have gone to bat for me and told the meddling officer how out of line he was. Trojan Six, like many senior Wolfhound officers, was a courageous leader who spent a lot of time on the ground facing danger with his troops, not as an onlooker from the sky.

On July 9, seven days after the action near Duc Hoa, I was wounded near Zulu and taken by a dustoff medevac helicopter from the field back to the 12th Evacuation Hospital at Cu Chi base camp.

■　■　■

We weren't always alone in the woods, humpin' the boonies, searching for Charlie. We often brought along a variety of friends, collaborators, and guests.

Engineers and demolition experts would go humpin' with us, and they were always welcome. When we needed to get helicopters in to evacuate our casualties or for resupply, engineers cleared away trees and other vegetation to make a landing zone. The engineers helped us destroy VC tunnel networks, bunkers, mines, and booby traps. When we found our own dud artillery shells and dud bombs that hadn't exploded, the demolition experts destroyed them. We didn't want Charlie to use our own explosive ordnance to make deadly booby traps.

And thanks to the engineers and demolition experts, we sometimes managed to make hot meals in the boonies. They always brought along plenty of C-4 plastic explosive. With a fuse and blasting cap, the right amount of C-4 was strong enough to blow up a 500-pound bomb, enemy bunkers, even a reinforced concrete bridge. But it was also great for heating C rations. We could light a piece the size of a marble with a match. It burned hot enough, without exploding, to warm up a can of beans and franks or other goodies.

We nearly always had scout dogs and tracker dogs from the 25th Division's canine units with us when we humped. They were beautiful German shepherds, good at sniffing out booby traps and tracking the VC.

We also used the dogs and their handlers when interrogating prisoners. Traditional forms of questioning often failed to bring results when hard-core VC or NVA prisoners were interrogated. So we would bring in one of the shepherds.

The dogs weren't naturally vicious. They only listened to their handlers' commands. But they were big. When standing on their back legs, the dogs were as tall as the average VC, about five feet. No matter how stubborn the prisoner, a killer dog up on its hind legs growling and poised for the attack, with his sharp teeth inches from the prisoner's face, always worked. It seemed to the prisoner that the only restraint on the dog was his handler's leash. I often wondered myself what would have happened if the handler had lost control of his dog when questioning a prisoner. It never occurred while I was commanding Alpha Company. Though I have to say, there were many times I wanted to see it happen to some of the prisoners.

One of our scout dogs, Chief, was a favorite. He had saved the lives of many of us by locating mines and booby traps before anyone tripped them. On one horrible day in the Ho Bo Woods, Chief was killed by a mine. It was like losing one of Alpha's soldiers. He may have been a dog, but we all saw him as one of us, a true Wolfhound, ferocious towards enemies but kind to his friends.

Sometimes members of the press and war correspondents went humpin' with us. They were a scruffy lot. Most of the time, they kept to themselves and tried not to get in anyone's way. They always seemed to be sitting under a tree smoking and writing in little notebooks. I'm not sure what they wrote. They didn't tell me; I didn't ask. I was too busy—searching for Charlie.

Of course, they never asked me anything. I thought that was odd. After all, I was in charge of the humpin'. You'd think they'd want to know what was going on, what our objective was, what plan or strategy we were following, how we felt about our jobs. But perhaps they didn't need another point of view besides their own.

The gentlemen of the press displayed varying amounts of courage. When the shit started to fly, some hit the rear and got out of the way fast. I wonder how accurate their war stories were. But some reporters stayed up front, close to the action. I think their stories were perhaps closer to the truth.

On many occasions, our battalion chaplain, a tall sandy-haired captain named Tucker, also went humpin' with us. He wanted to be with us—and we all wanted him there—if and when someone needed last rites. But when he flew out to join us in the field, we always had mixed feelings. We were comforted by his presence but worried about what it meant. Did someone higher up somehow know that we were going to need Tucker's comforting services? Of course, we always did.

Tucker himself seemed to think he was invincible. Many of us wanted to believe it, too. It meant that someone above was watching over him, protecting him. Maybe that someone would protect us, too. When I joined Alpha Company, I was told that Tucker had once been hit with a bullet, probably a stray shot from a distance. But the prayer book he carried in the shirt pocket of his jungle fatigues stopped the bullet before it pierced his skin. Thereafter, he carried the frayed book, complete with the wedged-in bullet, on his steel helmet right next to his insect repellent.

On some missions, searching for Charlie, we were accompanied by soldiers from the South Vietnamese Army (ARVN). We always dreaded it. We couldn't rely on them when the chips were down, and I resented the way they treated prisoners and VC suspects. Many times we had to pull them away from kicking and torturing prisoners during questioning.

On one occasion, I was leading Alpha Company as the right-flank American unit during a river assault crossing at a large horseshoe bend on the Oriental River southwest of Saigon. On my right was an ARVN unit. Our mission was to cross the river in River Assault Group (RAG) boats and destroy VC units that were dug in on the other side of the river.

The RAG boats were armored cracker boxes, with flat vertical sides. They were very easy for the VC to knock out with a rocket. So it was extremely important that the ARVN unit stay in line with Alpha as we attacked across the river, suppressing rocket fire from the opposite bank.

We loaded the boats in mangrove swamps on the near side of the river, while artillery and air strikes kept the VC down on the other side. We began to move towards the VC position. There was 300 meters of water to cross. When we reached the halfway mark, we opened fire, peppering the far side with .50 caliber machine guns mounted on the boats. After 200 meters, we called for a halt in the artillery fire.

At this point, it was critical that the ARVN troops coordinate their machine-gun fire with Alpha Company's right flank. We should both be hitting the far riverbank as hard as possible, forcing the VC to keep their heads down. That was the plan we had agreed upon.

We started to receive incoming fire from the VC. I looked to my right, and I couldn't believe my eyes. The ARVN boats were doing a

180-degree turn. They were making a run back to the safety of the riverbank we had just departed from.

This cowardly act meant that my right flank was completely open. Without the covering machine-gun fire, a VC rocket team was able to move into position. They fired and almost took out an Alpha Company RAG boat to my far right. I was furious. I wanted to call in artillery fire on the ARVN troops as they cowered in the bushes behind us, just watching the VC trying to chew us up.

Talking to other officers, I learned that my experience wasn't unique. The ARVN had the reputation of being halfhearted and unreliable, more interested in dressing well, with snappy, pressed uniforms, than in actually winning their war. The South Vietnamese government didn't even completely mobilize their forces until the Tet Offensive of 1968, after I had left Vietnam.

From that day on, I did everything I could to avoid ARVN troops. I hated them. Here we were, American soldiers risking our lives for their country, while they hid in the bushes. I was afraid of what I would do if the ARVN ever pulled a stunt like that again.

■   ■   ■

When we searched for Charlie, usually my biggest fear wasn't being betrayed by ARVN troops or even bombed by my own Air Force. It was getting lost. I worried about it constantly. I think my platoon leaders did also. Not knowing exactly where you are is the worst possible situation to be faced with. It can cost lives, needlessly, during a firefight, on patrol, or when just moving through an AO. When you call for artillery or an air strike on a given set of map coordinates, you better not be standing on them. Or you'll be blown to bits.

Unlike commanders of today, who have satellite-driven global positioning systems (GPS), we had to rely on maps and a compass. And we were relatively good with them. But it was still difficult to maintain a sense of direction. Moving all day through tangles of underbrush and endless swamps, with no easily identifiable landmarks to use as reference points, made it easy to get disoriented. Even open paddy lands, where the same few features are repeated again and again, could be fatally confusing.

Sometimes, the only way we could establish or pinpoint our location was to ask the artillery to fire two white phosphorus spotter rounds into two separate areas, positions that I knew we were not near. Then we took compass readings to the white smoke rising from each explosion, added 180 degrees to each one, and marked the back azimuths on our maps. The two lines intersected at our exact location.

Helicopter "spots" from above were also used frequently by me and my platoon leaders to pinpoint our location. After marking our own position with colored smoke, a well-timed request to someone 1,000 feet above in a helicopter put us back on the right track. Fortunately for us, Trojan Six was often there when we needed him.

One time when we were out humpin', I used this technique and learned we were 1,500 meters inside Cambodia, a big no-no at the time. The border between Cambodia and Vietnam was shown on my map as a dotted red line going through the Plain of Reeds. The border wasn't marked in any way on the ground—no river, no fence, nothing. And we sure didn't see any dotted red lines in the wet muck as we chased Charlie across the border.

We moved back into South Vietnam as fast as we could. It would be many years before President Richard Nixon ordered U.S. ground troops to attack VC safe havens in Cambodia, before students protesting his actions at Kent State University in Ohio would be accidentally killed by National Guard troops.

■　■　■

Charlie seldom launched full-scale attacks against us when we were humpin' the boonies. During the day, he hid and watched as we moved. But he wasn't frightened or passive. He wounded or killed us with snipers, mines, and booby traps. As we advanced, he would often spray us with harassing fire and then, after a brief exchange, flee into dense undergrowth.

But at night, when we were exhausted from humpin' all day, he mortared us, probed our positions, and sometimes attacked. Afterwards he dragged away his dead and wounded. Then he would simply disappear into the darkness to fight again another day. It was classic hit-and-run guerrilla tactics, on Charlie's terms, not ours.

At the end of each day of humpin', we established a night defensive perimeter to protect against an enemy assault. We used the clock system to organize our perimeter, generally in the shape of an irregular circle. Our direction of travel was always designated as 12 o'clock. One platoon occupied the perimeter from 12 o'clock to 4 o'clock, another from 4 o'clock to 8 o'clock, and another from 8 o'clock to 12 o'clock. We were authorized four platoons in Alpha but had only the equivalent of three in the field most of the time. Many times I had only two with me.

At the center of the clock, I put my command post. From there, I could react quickly no matter which direction we were hit from and communicate effectively with each of my platoon leaders.

It was an approach to defense as old as war itself. Each time we set up our positions, I was reminded of the Western movies I watched as a child. At night, the pioneers would circle the wagons, with a fire in the center, against the threat of Indians attacking from the darkness outside.

Inside our circle of wagons, we dug foxholes and set up claymore mines in front of them. When the perimeter was initially secure, resupply helicopters flew in with fresh supplies. They brought in ammunition, water, and food. Usually the food consisted of yet more C rations, but sometimes the helicopters brought manna from heaven, hot meals in large, olive-drab thermos containers.

Sometimes they delivered rolls of concertina wire that we placed around the perimeter in front of the foxholes. With the wire in place, we positioned trip flares in front of it to provide early warning against someone trying to sneak up on us. Bales of sandbags were dropped in so we could fill them with dirt from the foxholes and use them to strengthen our fighting positions.

Sometimes, the helicopters dropped a big orange sack. It contained something we all waited for with desperate anticipation—the mail. I received letters about every two weeks.

Getting mail was more important than getting food or getting sleep. A letter was heaven, no letter was hell. I can't describe the sorrow that consumed me on those occasions when I saw letters passed out but didn't get one. Letters from home, from mothers and fathers, sisters and brothers, girlfriends and wives, friends, and sometimes from people you had never even met, any kind of letter kept us going. Letters gave us a reason to want to get through it all. A reason to watch where we stepped and a reason to get down when the shooting started. A reason to try to stay human in a savage place.

I often sent letters home from the field, as postcards, written on the three-by-six-inch brown cardboard tops of C ration boxes. It just wasn't possible to carry letter paper with me. And stamps weren't required. All I did was write "free postage" where a stamp would normally be placed.

But I had trouble with that word "free." It wasn't really free, I always thought. We were paying with our blood, our innocence, and maybe our lives.

On some days, within our defensive perimeters, Chaplain Tucker conducted nondenominational church services. He used a makeshift altar draped in a black cloth. On it he placed a small white cross that he carried in his backpack.

With Tucker's help, we prayed for fallen comrades. We prayed for them and asked God to protect us. Afterwards, we were quiet for a minute or so with our own thoughts. Then we went back to the business of preparing to kill or get killed.

It was all so incongruous. Sometimes surreal. For me, always sad.

■   ■   ■

In establishing our defensive perimeters, we selected good positions, with interlocking fields of fire for our machine guns. And we selected the ideal site for my CP. But we positioned the weapons and the CP elsewhere until it got dark.

The problem was that villagers and farmers watched our every move. Mamasans moved back and forth through our lines selling Coca-Cola. And sometimes the mamasans worked for Charlie.

They would mark our positions on their bellies and breasts

with charcoal. When he was available, we always asked Tucker to check the mamasans over before they left our lines. We asked a man of God, rather than a young rifleman, so there would be no hint of abuse, in case the mamasan was on our side.

The mamasans were always chewing betel nuts, their teeth stained black from the betel nut juice. Some of the mamasans marked a path to a key defensive position by discreetly spitting the dark red betel nut juice on the ground in a line leading from our positions out into the jungle. When Charlie attacked, his sappers followed the juice stains, like Hansel and Gretel's bread crumbs, straight to their objective.

That's why we moved the CP and machine guns again under the cover of darkness. If we were lucky, we fooled the VC. If we were even luckier, we stopped them by blowing them apart with claymore mines, set along the path we had guessed they would follow. If we weren't lucky, they could blow us apart with their satchel charges full of dynamite.

One night early in my tour as Alpha's CO and after humpin' all day in a heavy monsoon rain, I moved my CP into a villager's small hootch near a hamlet that was presumed to be friendly. We established our perimeter in an area generally around the hootch. I should have known better.

The mamasan shared her chicken and rice with me and my command group, then she retired for the night. At about two in the morning she got up from the straw mat on the dirt floor where she was sleeping. She lit a candle and placed it in the window opening. Then she quickly crawled down into the bomb shelter that every hootch in Vietnam seemed to have.

Within seconds we were under heavy mortar and machine-gun fire. Bullets put out the candle and shattered one of our radios before we neutralized the enemy position with artillery fire.

This mamasan was definitely VC. That's the way it was. We never really knew whom we could trust when we were out humpin'. And I learned where not to put my CP.

■　■　■

One of the most important things we did when establishing our night positions was to plan and mark defensive concentrations for artillery support. We called them *Defcons*. By preregistering six to eight Defcons, I was able to quickly get very accurate fire support during an enemy attack.

Lieutenant Petre and I picked, with the help of our platoon leaders, the areas around the perimeter where the enemy was likely to mass for an attack. After we marked them on our maps, Petre radioed in the map coordinates to the artillery battery supporting us.

The battery fired several marker rounds for confirmation. When the shells hit the target, Petre told them to mark the gun settings as Defcon One, Defcon Two, and so on.

Each Defcon became a critical reference point for directing the artillery support when Alpha was under attack. On my command or that of one of our platoon leaders, Petre was able to make abbreviated radio transmissions like "Fire mission: Defcon One. Fire." Or "Fire mission: Defcon One. Right one hundred [meters], down two hundred [meters]. Fire." Since the target areas were preregistered, we always got the rounds flying sooner and more accurately than would otherwise be possible, particularly during the intensity of combat.

I also used the Defcons to direct harassing and interdiction shelling, called H&I, throughout the night. At irregular intervals all night long, Petre called in H&I fire missions around our perimeter. This made it extremely dangerous for Charlie to try to sneak up on us. He never knew when or where the next volley of death-delivering shells might arrive.

We did everything we could to keep a wall of steel between us and any would-be attackers.

■　　■　　■

Artillery was not all we used to guard against a surprise attack. We also put three- or four-man listening posts (LPs) in several locations all around us for early warning. Having more than two men in each LP helped assure that, on a rotational basis, at least two were awake while one or two tried to sleep.

We placed the LPs outside the barbed wire between the troops in the foxholes on the perimeter and the Defcons. Then we established simple radio codes that could be sent by clicking the handset rather than speaking. This enabled the listening posts to signal us without being heard. One click every fifteen minutes might signal that all was well. Three clicks on the radio might mean that the men in the listening post thought they saw or heard something moving toward them. Two clicks could mean that they were ready to be replaced and return to the perimeter.

Signals at regular intervals were essential. We had to know that the men at the listening posts had not fallen asleep or had not been silently killed. In some 25th Division units, there were occasions when Charlie had sneaked up on soldiers manning listening posts and lobbed a grenade at them or slit their throats without making a sound.

And we had effective techniques, including simple passwords, for getting the men back through our lines before an attack, quickly and safely, without being shot by our own men.

It was scary duty for the guys in the listening posts. They were out in the jungle at night, many meters in front of friendly lines, and all alone. Even with the many precautions, it was an extremely dangerous assignment. There was always the possibility that an artillery round would fall short. Or an enemy attack could be mounted quickly and with such ferocity that an LP would be overrun before the troops there could return to our lines. And there was also the possibility that a new recruit might panic in the dark and unknowingly shoot one of our men coming back into the perimeter from a listening post.

In spite of the danger, our platoon leaders never had a Wolfhound complain or refuse to do LP duty when it was his turn.

On all nights we established ambushes along likely enemy routes that led towards our perimeter or sent out night reconnaissance patrols. For each of these operations we blackened our faces and taped anything loose—our dog tags, weapon slings, and trouser legs—so that we could move silently and undetected to our objective. Often the only means of navigation for these operations was a kind of jungle dead reckoning. We used a compass, and two men counted paces to our objective. We used the average of the two counts for accuracy. If we were off by a few yards, it could be deadly.

On some patrols we also used our noses for navigation. As we got to within a kilometer of a VC camp we could often smell *nouc mam* in the still night air. *Nouc mam* is a pungent condiment sauce made from rotting fish that the Vietnamese use on just about everything they eat. There were several occasions where, in the black of night, we would have gone past our objective had we not been able to smell our way to it.

The nights often seemed very long. When daylight arrived, we pulled in our ambushes, patrols, and listening posts. Then we started humpin' again. And we searched and we searched for Charlie.

■　■　■

Humpin' was tiring and there was never much time for sleep. There were days when it was boring, uneventful, just routine. But mostly humpin' the boonies was full of risks, pain, exhaustion, adrenaline charges during the fighting, and always the blood. Always the fear.

There were no battle fronts or lines on the map or territory won or lost. We moved through terrain the enemy knew much better than we did. Mines, booby traps, punji pits, snipers, enemy ambushes, and enemy informers were everywhere. Both the friendlies and the enemy wore black pajamas, the typical peasant garb. We couldn't tell who was on our side. If someone was shooting at us we assumed he or she was VC. And in time our attitude was that if a Vietnamese was wearing black and was dead or running away from us, he or she had to be VC.

One of the hardest things to accept about searching for Charlie was going back to the same places, humpin' again and again and then again. It created a very real morale problem for my platoon leaders and their grunts: "Oh! Great, sir. We're going back to the Ho Bo Woods again. Can't we Arc Light or Rome plow them to clear away the thick vegetation and then occupy the area? We'll take fewer casualties." It was tough for me to order my men back into the same areas —where we knew Charlie would be waiting—over and over again. But I had my orders.

Every minute of every day that we humped, we faced danger and possible death. Wounds or death could come at any time and in many ways. And its messenger may not be a hardened VC guerrilla fighter or North Vietnamese regular. It could just as well be a rifle-carrying or booby-trap-making young woman, mamasan, young boy, or papasan.

It was even rumored that some Americans were killed by mamasans and children with electronically detonated explosives tied to their bodies. We had to protect ourselves against such a possibility, but I never saw it happen.

■　■　■

Humpin' revealed many contrasts and incongruities that seemed to be so much a part of the war in Vietnam: A small child riding on the back of a water buffalo as tanks, trucks, and artillery pieces roll by. Steaming hot days and frigid nights. American troops pinned down in battle, while South Vietnamese soldiers in clean tailored uniforms, seemingly oblivious to the action, have lunch in nearby cafes. Infantrymen searching for Charlie, while support troops in civvies party it up in citylike base camps with air conditioning, theaters, and even swimming pools. Beautiful, peaceful-looking, and almost mesmerizing terrain exploding with gunfire, leaving dead and dismembered bodies as enemy calling cards. Mamasans on bicycles selling Coca-Cola. Troops slogging through mirrored rice paddies, as a young girl wearing an ao dai and conical straw hat frolics on a dike, silhouetted by a blazing sun. U.S. troops killing and dying for a cause deemed hopeless by many Americans.

12th Evac

I was still dazed when the Medevac chopper that plucked me from Zulu arrived at Cu Chi base camp. We landed next to the 12th Medical Evacuation Hospital, known as the 12th Evac. Litter bearers rushed me to the triage tent. In triage, the medical staff has the task of sorting battlefield casualties into three groups. It's a difficult task and emotionally draining for the doctors and nurses.

The first group is for soldiers with mortal wounds, like massive head, chest, or abdominal injuries. Still hanging on, they will die soon. Nothing can be done to save them. Nurses and Red Cross workers make them as comfortable as possible. Chaplains are available to administer last rites. But the surgical staff, besieged with critical cases, cannot waste time on them.

Soldiers in the second group have wounds that are life threatening, but there is hope for survival. Time is of the essence. Life or death depends on how quickly they are treated. They must be attended to immediately, before anyone else. Doctors and nurses work painstakingly with this group to save lives and to prevent the amputation of legs, arms, hands, and feet as often as possible.

The third group is for individuals with injuries that are not life threatening. They are stabilized, cleaned up, made comfortable, and left to wait their turn for further treatment. I assume that I was in this group, but I don't really know.

I didn't regain full consciousness, bouncing along on a litter and still with a morphine buzz in my head, until I was moved from triage. I'm not sure how long I was there.

When I passed between the tent flaps on my way out of triage, I saw a black sky. It was night. I tried to focus on the silhouette of someone walking alongside my litter, holding a plasma bottle overhead. A rubber tube was running down to a needle taped to my arm.

I assume that I went straight from triage into surgery, though at the time I had no clear idea of what was going on or where I was being taken. All I could make out was a montage of blurred images: olive-green canvas, wounded soldiers, bloodied bandages, medical paraphernalia, and people rushing all around.

I felt no relief or comfort. Instead I was angry at myself, cursing because I was injured, unable to be with my troops, to do my job. Where were Petre, Alverez, and Washington? I felt isolated and confused.

Then I saw her. It was a nurse holding the plasma bottle. Her brown hair was tied up and tucked under a cap, revealing a round freckled face. She appeared to be in her midtwenties but looked exhausted and careworn. I noticed blood splattered on her uniform. I hadn't seen an American girl for a long time; she seemed exotic, a memory. I wanted to touch her, to see if she was for real. Was I dreaming? I thought, Oh, please hold me. I reached out to her.

She tried to calm me down. She said, "Captain Brewer, you've done your job. Please don't move; you'll hurt yourself."

Suddenly, I was lifted up. My nose was filled with the strong odor of antiseptic. Overhead a blinding circular light framed three people wearing green surgical masks. They peered down at me. Shutting my eyes from the glare, I felt something smooth and cool on my face, over my nose.

Someone said, "Try to relax and breathe normally." I took a breath or two and drifted off, unconscious once again.

■　■　■

When I woke up, I was in a Quonset hut recovery ward, lying on my back. I was strapped down in a litter-bed that had clean sheets and a pillow. Still completely disoriented, mumbling under the influence of the anesthesia, I was sick to my stomach and nauseated.

My lower right leg and foot were heavily bandaged. They were elevated well above the mattress and secured so that I couldn't move them. I had a morbid curiosity about my wound. But there was nothing I could do to examine it. I lay back and looked around me.

The first thing I noticed was the patient to my right. He was a thin young man, perhaps eighteen or nineteen, with blond hair and a mustache. He had a terrified look in his eyes, as if he had his feet caught in a railroad track with a train rushing towards him.

He was thrashing his arms wildly about, swatting at the air in front his face, screaming, "Get them away, get them away, please get them away."

A young nurse in jungle fatigues whispered to me. "He's hallucinating again from a heavy dose of Demerol, a strong painkiller. It makes him see imaginary swarms of large insects."

I later learned that he was very seriously wounded in both legs and his abdomen by a Chinese Communist claymore mine. The staff estimated that the probability of his keeping his legs was no better than fifty-fifty.

The nurse spoke to me quietly, soothingly. She told me that I had been out of surgery for about an hour. A doctor would see me as soon as possible to talk to me about my wounds. She loosened the straps securing me to the bed. "We used these as a precaution to prevent you from hurting yourself when coming out of the anesthesia."

She showed me a small green cotton bag with a drawstring. This was my personal valuables bag. I was to keep it with me at all times. It contained my wallet, watch, eyeglasses, a few Military Pay Certificates, my dog tags, and three iron grenade fragments. These were souvenirs of the VC hand grenade that had put me there, pieces removed from my leg and ankle during surgery.

After tying my valuables bag to my bedpost, the nurse twisted me partially over on my side, opened the flap in my gown, and gave me a big shot of penicillin in the butt. Then she handed me a small paper cup of water to drink, fixed my pillow, smiled at me, and turned to the patient next to me. He was still screaming.

After settling him down, she returned to tell me that if I had to urinate or move my bowels I should call for a nurse to help me with a bedpan. I asked her if she could try to find out what happened to Petre, Alverez, and Washington. She said she would, then she left.

I dozed, on and off, for several hours. Whenever I was awake, I marveled at the clean sheets and pillow. I had spent months sleeping in filth, dirt, mud, and slime. Clean sheets made me feel safe, closer to the world, and closer to home.

In fact, the war suddenly seemed far away, for me and for wounded soldiers lying in beds, row on row, all around me. There was even one of the enemy, a VC captured near Zulu, lying with us. He was just another man lying between clean sheets. The horrible conflict seemed distant and in the past tense. It wasn't, as I was about to learn.

■ ■ ■

At about four in the morning I awakened to sounds I had come to know all too well. It was the explosive *splat, splat, splat* of incoming mortar rounds.

Just as I turned to the kid in the next bed to see if he had heard the same thing, a crimson-orange blast ripped open the metal roof in the far corner and lit up the Quonset hut.

The VC were mortaring Cu Chi base camp and mortar rounds and shrapnel were raining down all around the hospital. I couldn't believe it. I thought, Oh, shit, I've made it through all that I have, and now this.

With no way to seek protective cover, I was sure that I was going to get killed. I waited, my eyes staring up, to be blown apart. The two nurses on night duty shouted, "Mortars, incoming mortars," and quickly proceeded from bed to bed, with total disregard for their own safety, aiding the wounded and helpless soldiers.

One of the nurses assisted those that could be moved by helping them get under their beds, where their mattresses offered some protection from flying pieces of shrapnel. The other nurse placed mattresses on top of patients, like me, who could not be moved quickly from their beds. After assuring that all of us were protected, and only then, the two nurses crawled under my bed.

The mortar attack lasted for only a few more minutes. We didn't sustain any more direct hits, though shrapnel pierced through the walls of the recovery ward in several locations. Glass was broken and several mattresses torn, but nobody was hit.

I have never forgotten the selfless, caring, and undaunted courage displayed by the two nurses. It rivaled the best of the best that I had seen displayed by men in combat.

■　■　■

Later that morning after the mortar attack, a doctor came by to talk to me. He loomed over my bed, tall and thin. He had bags under his eyes and a stubble beard. He had probably been working all night.

He began by announcing the Army's verdict. "Congratulations, Captain Brewer. No more fighting for you. You'll be going to Japan." The medical verdict came next. "We have to do some skin grafts to close your wounds, and we don't do that sort of work in Vietnam. The nurses here will be changing the dressings on your wounds to protect them from infection until you leave." The open wounds weren't the only legacy of the grenade. He told me that the fragments he removed had damaged my Achilles tendon and crushed some of the bones in my ankle.

I asked the doctor if he knew when I would leave. I also wanted to know how long I would be in Japan and what would happen to me afterwards.

"You'll be leaving soon," he said. "Your stay in Japan will depend on how fast your wounds heal. Since you won't be able to walk for several months, you'll probably be sent from the hospital in Japan to a duty station in Japan, Okinawa, or Korea, maybe even the U.S., to finish your tour of duty." He smiled and wished me good luck.

I saw Colonel Richards, my brigade commander, walking down the row of wounded. He stopped at my bed and shook my hand, thanking me for all I had done. I learned from him that Alverez and

Washington had minor flesh wounds and would be out of action for only a few days. Petre's were a little worse, but he would not have to be evacuated.

I felt bad, guilty, knowing that they would be returning to the field, where they would have another chance to get killed. Why was I the lucky one getting out?

I felt especially bad about Petre's wound. The very night before we made the air assault into LZ Zulu, Petre and I were sitting together in a foxhole looking up at the stars. After a long while, he broke the silence by saying, "If I keep staying close to you, Brewer, I'm going to get hit." It's as though he had a premonition.

Richards also told me that Bravo Company saw heavy fighting during the night and that First Lieutenant Mike Tarantola, who had assumed command of Alpha Company when I became wounded, was doing well under difficult circumstances. He was Alpha's executive officer. Much of his time in-country, up till then, had been spent on company administration in base camp. I was relieved to learn that Alpha was holding its own under his leadership and that he was okay.

Later that same morning, a medic told me that Captain Jones, another Wolfhound, had died in the Quonset hut next to mine. He had suffered a small bullet wound to the abdomen.

His death hit me hard. I had difficulty accepting it. He was a peer of mine. I saw him often at battalion briefings and on joint operations. I had a lot of respect for him and his leadership skills. He always seemed like a larger-than-life hero to me, the image of a warrior, well over six feet with a muscular build, square-jawed, handsome, and full of self-confidence.

Men with wounds that seemed much more serious than his, with parts of their bodies blown away, had often lived. How could a man like Jones die of a small hole in his belly? His death reminded me once again how vulnerable we all were to fate and random chance. Where you get hit in combat and whether you live or die is just a matter of luck.

I was eager to leave for Japan.

■　■　■

After lunch, two litter bearers showed up with no notice. They carefully slid me from my bed onto a litter. One of them untied my small bag of valuables from the bedpost, secured it to my left wrist, and rested it on my stomach.

They carried me out of the recovery ward and placed me in a small truck. I learned that I was going to Vung Tau, on the coast of the South China Sea, for a brief layover before Japan. The truck drove to the base helipad, where a chopper was waiting. Its overhead rotors were revving up for the takeoff. With my litter strapped to the side of the chopper, I was airborne in a matter of seconds.

It was still less than twenty-four hours since I'd been wounded. It felt odd, completely surreal. For months it seemed like I had been in constant motion, jumping from helicopters, running and fighting, leading men in combat, their lives in my hands. Now I was flat on my back, totally helpless. I needed assistance to relieve myself. And like a piece of freight, I was completely at the mercy of those transporting me.

Strapped to the outside of the small helicopter, I had an excellent view of our flight. After about forty-five minutes in the air, the chopper banked and started its descent. I caught a glance of the white sandy beach along the coast of the South China Sea, with whitecaps lapping up against the shoreline. It looked idyllic, like a picture postcard of a tropical island. I thought, This can't be Vietnam. Where are the steaming jungles, the endless paddies, the mud and dark?

The surreal feeling continued. When the chopper landed at Vung Tau, I saw a bunch of men and women in shorts and bush hats, tanned and healthy. Was this a resort of some kind? It turned out that Australian forces fighting in Vietnam were headquartered there. To my eye, trained in the crucible of combat, it all seemed too casual.

Soon I was flat on my back in another hospital bed, complete with the clean sheets that I had come to covet. A small plastic radio was playing an American song, evidently a hit because it was repeated frequently. It was "Monday, Monday" by the Mamas and the Papas, a song that, even today, makes me think of Vung Tau.

Litter bearers were placing Lieutenant Jack Barto, a Green Beret with a nasty wound in his left leg, in the bed across from me. I would get to know him very well. He became my constant companion during my evacuation from Vietnam and during long hospital stays in Japan and Valley Forge, Pennsylvania.

All of us in the ward were in the same situation. Our injuries required treatment that was not available in Vietnam. Vung Tau was a staging area for us on our way to Japan. We were simply in transit together.

We were happy to have come so far.

■　■　■

I have two vivid memories of my stay in Vung Tau. The first concerned news I heard about a member of Alpha Company, a PFC (private first class) we all called BC, for body count.

As I've said, body count was what the war in Vietnam was all about. After every battle or firefight, we had to count the bodies of the enemy killed and report the number up the line. It was dangerous work because the bodies were often booby-trapped. BC always volunteered to do it. He was insistent. It seemed important for him to take the risk. I don't know why. He was a small man in a company of big soldiers, and the reason may have been self-esteem.

On the second day of my stay in Vung Tau, I learned that BC had been seriously wounded by a booby-trapped VC corpse. He was struggling for his life—and his limbs. I was devastated. I knew the odds were against him. I left for Japan the next day and never did learn of his fate.

The second overriding memory of Vung Tau is of the constant pain we all experienced. We had all been operated on, but our wounds were still open. This was a common practice for battlefield injuries, where there is a high risk of infection. The safest way to prevent infection is to allow the wound to drain for several days.

Wounds sustained in combat are dirty. When a bullet or piece of shrapnel tears into flesh, it carries with it tiny particles of a soldier's dirty clothing, equipment, or other contaminants. In my case, those were small pieces of leather from my combat boots, cotton fibers from my socks and jungle fatigues, and minute particles of soil. Letting the wound stay open for several days enables the foreign matter to seep out or come to the surface.

While open, the wounds are treated with antiseptic and dressed with bandages to keep out new germs. It's important to change the dressings on a frequent and regular basis.

But at Vung Tau, the dressings sometimes weren't changed frequently enough. Old bandages would stick like glue to large areas of torn flesh, open tissue, and congealed blood. It's difficult to describe the pain when a dressing is peeled off after sticking to a large open wound. I think it's something like being skinned alive, very slowly. It was terrible. And my open wounds were not nearly as large as some of the other soldiers' in the ward. I don't know how they were able to withstand the torture.

■   ■   ■

After two days in the hospital at Vung Tau, I was loaded onto a plane bound for Yokohama, Japan. Lieutenant Barto went on the same plane.

First we were packed into an army-green bus with a large red cross painted on its side. It was specially designed to carry individuals on litters for short distances. We were stacked on shelves, three high, one above the other on each side of the bus. We were a strange kind of freight.

The bus drove to the airfield, where a C-119 transport plane was waiting. These were gigantic cargo aircraft, their massive presence accentuated by the camouflage pattern painted on their sides. C-119s flew regularly into Vietnam loaded with heavy cargo like tanks, trucks, and munitions. After unloading material for the war, Air Force ground crews quickly transformed the planes into flying hospitals, carrying the wounded away from the war.

As they were moving us from the bus to the rear loading ramp of the plane, I was surprised to spot a large group of soldiers who didn't seem injured. They were able to walk onto the plane under their own power. I didn't get it. Were they all slackers? One of the Red Cross "Doughnut Dollies" later told me that half of the soldiers going to Japan did not have wounds received by hostile fire. Many of them had illnesses that required special treatment, such as hepatitis or malaria.

Some had back or other stress-related injuries. Some had self-inflicted wounds, and an alarming number had mental disorders.

I didn't know what to think about it. Looking at my companions, all wounded in combat, knowing what they had suffered, I found it difficult to reconcile how soldiers could be evacuated for any lesser reason.

We waited on the tarmac. It took a long time to load the plane. When our turn came, Air Force medical staff secured our litters to shelflike brackets that lined the inside of the C-119's fuselage. Barto was below me. It was like being in a long row of narrow bunk beds. My feet faced the rear of the plane, and I could see down the length of the interior. The cargo ramp and upper door began to slowly come together and close. Looking out, I got my last glimpse of Vietnam.

In the distance, I saw dark green mountains and an azure-blue sky. It looked cool, serene, and peaceful—very different from the Vietnam I had known. In the foreground, I saw aviation equipment and personnel rushing about, purposeful and earnest, and a stack of coffins sitting on the tarmac. This was a reminder of my Vietnam: dead soldiers waiting for their plane home, the legacy of a heated conflict under the green canopy of the far-off jungle. It seemed like there were two countries, two different realities.

I thought of the hell I had been through and of the Wolfhounds I was leaving behind. I thought about the nurses and the other medical personnel in the 12th Evac, their dedication and their professionalism.

But I thought especially about the two nurses that risked their lives protecting us during the mortar attack on Cu Chi.

I was on my way out. They were still there, each day facing the carnage of war, working hard to save lives and give men hope, with caring hearts and sometimes holding back tears.

I wondered if I would ever see them again. I wanted to say so much.

Yokohama

T he bullet had smashed into his right shin, shattering both the tibia and fibula. It tore through and exited his calf muscle, leaving his lower leg and foot dangling by bloodied shreds of flesh and razor-sharp bone splinters.

Jack Barto's wound was not uncommon. VC snipers in bunkers or tunnel openings, well concealed in the jungle foliage, often aimed first at the legs of GIs. Their intent was to wound. They knew that at least one or two other GIs would rush to the aid of a fallen buddy. Then, with more exposed targets, the sniper carefully aimed for the heads before squeezing the trigger again and again, this time to kill. Barto had escaped death only by getting thrown into a deep ravine as his leg was blown out from under him.

During the long flight to Yokohama, Japan, with my stretcher right above his, I got to know Barto a little better. He had been with me during my brief stays at the 12th Evac and at the hospital in Vung Tau, but we were both groggy from painkillers. Now, more awake, we could talk.

He looked like he was in his late twenties. I didn't ask. He had a straight nose, pointed jaw, crew-cut brown hair, and penetrating dark eyes. There was a positive aura about him most of the time. He managed to seem confident and self-assured while flat on his back strapped to a litter, a considerable achievement. He was a Green Beret, and he did fit the stereotype: rugged, tough-minded, gung-ho. But there was a gloomy side to Barto that often surfaced when he talked of his experiences in the field.

Sometimes when his eyes met mine, it seemed like he was looking through and beyond me, to a time and place I had never witnessed.

The Green Berets are members of the Army's elite Special Forces unit. Formed in the early sixties at JFK's request, the Special Forces unit consists of highly motivated and highly trained personnel assigned to antiguerrilla warfare and other specialized counterinsurgency operations all over the world. Like Navy Seals, they display some of the highest esprit de corps in the armed services. In Vietnam, they served as military advisers to the ARVN. They were often attached to local militia units like the Regional and Provincial Forces, referred to disparagingly as "Ruff-Puffs" because of their ineffectiveness. Green Berets also led the tough Montagnard tribesmen from Vietnam's strategic Central Highlands on clandestine operations deep into enemy territory.

Barto, a career soldier, was midway through his second tour of duty in Vietnam when he was hit by the sniper's round, fired at very close range. He was in severe pain and he knew that he might lose his leg, but he somehow managed to exercise an uncommon sense of humor. On the way to Japan, he kept our spirits high with joke after joke and with his relentless teasing of the nurses and the Doughnut Dollies. I think it was his way of avoiding too much thought. He had a lot to think about after two tours in the jungle— and an uncertain future.

He wasn't married and didn't speak of relatives or friends. Like some other Green Berets I've known, he seemed to see the Army as both career and family. I don't remember him talking of anything in his life outside the military or of anything he was looking forward to back in the States. This contributed, I think, to the grave concern he showed over the severity of his wounds. If he lost a leg, his old career would never be the same. He had nothing else he was trained to do. He would have to start his life all over.

■   ■   ■

When we landed in Yokohama, it was back into litter-carrying buses for the short trip to our new home at Camp Zuma. We were tucked into beds in yet another hospital ward. Barto and I ended up, once again, directly across from one another. Maybe it was fate.

When I was still out humpin' the boonies with Alpha Company, I had planned to take my one-week rest and relaxation (R&R) leave in Japan. It was one of the preferred destinations for R&R, which all of the soldiers fighting in Vietnam were eligible for after six months in-country. But I had dreamed of a week of night after night on the town in Tokyo, not lying on my back in a hospital bed in Yokohama.

Barto and I were part of a group being prepped for our next surgical procedure. First the nurses took our temperature and blood pressure. Then came the thing we dreaded most. They changed our blood-soaked dressings, now a day old and stuck to our flesh. The nurses were as careful as they could be, but it was hell as usual. We all suffered our separate agonies together, as stubborn dressings were slowly peeled off our unforgiving wounds.

At last I was free of the bandages and dressings, though my leg was supported by a large splint. The nurse asked me if I had seen my injury.

"No," I said, "I wasn't in any hurry and haven't been able to with all the bandages on."

She propped me up with a pillow and twisted my lower leg and foot inward until I could see.

"There," she said, "It's not too bad. We'll have you dancing in a few months."

I looked with a mixture of dread and intense curiosity. I was surprised to see that most of the inside of my right ankle and heel, an area roughly two inches by three inches, was torn open and that I had several smaller holes on the inside of my lower leg, just above the ankle bone. There was a small half-inch bridge of skin separating the two halves of the larger wound, which was bloody and raw, like a piece of meat. I could see bone, and the pearly white chord of my Achilles tendon.

I felt a little queasy and lay back down. The nurse gently applied antiseptic and put on a temporary dressing. A doctor was on his way to have a look at my injury.

It's not that it was pretty, but I remembered many of the guys with injuries much worse than mine. I thought about all those who had died or would die in the field or in the wards of Vietnam. I felt guilty again for getting off so easily. In effect, I had what during World War II was called *a million-dollar wound.* It was serious enough to get me home, but not so bad as to cause severe physical problems later in my life.

After a short wait and another shot of penicillin in the butt, a young doctor came by to look me over. He planned to repair my wounds the next morning. Some would be stitched together with wire stitches. For the opening that was too large to sew up, he would remove a thin layer of skin from my right thigh and graft it over the opening. Then I would have a cast with a window in it to provide access to the injured area. This would keep my leg in the correct position for the graft to take hold and for the bone fractures to mend.

A similar scene was replayed time and again throughout the day, as each patient was carefully walked through what was going to happen to him in surgery. I listened when I could, took some pain pills, and tried to get some sleep.

■　　■　　■

The next morning, I awoke after surgery. During my unconsciousness, I had been moved to still another hospital ward. I was a little woozy. I looked around the room. Most of the other patients appeared to be more permanently established. Their skin had a ghostlike pallor, as if they had lived indoors for some time. I didn't see anyone I knew from the pre-op area. Across from me, a bed was empty.

My leg was elevated in a heavy cast that held my knee and foot turned to the right so that the inside of my ankle was facing the ceiling. I was very uncomfortable. A nurse told me that it was necessary to prevent blood from flowing down and knocking the skin graft off.

The patient in the bed next to me had his entire face and head bandaged except for small openings for his mouth and nose, though I couldn't see either of them. Most of the other patients that I could see were in casts and heavily bandaged, some like Egyptian mummies. The atmosphere was hushed and eerie. Radios were playing music or news softly. Several nurses moved from patient to patient, adjusting intravenous drips, giving medicines, and trying to comfort the soldiers. Aides were helping some of the guys use their bedpans.

Gone were the olive-drab surroundings I had become so accustomed to. Everything was white with shades of gray. The pace was slow, almost like a dream, quite unlike the rushing around in all the prior wards I had been in. For the first time in many months, I had nothing much to do but think. I thought about what had happened to me.

In less than four full days, I had been wounded in Tan My, lifted out of the bush, operated on and then mortared in Cu Chi, flown to Vung Tau, shipped to Yokohama, and operated on a second time and was now resting over a thousand miles from the war. In those few days, my world had shifted kaleidoscopically, again and again. And through the whole strange trip, I couldn't help admiring the efficiency of the Army's medical evacuation process. It was hard to believe this was the same hurry-up-and-wait Army that I had first gotten to know back at Fort Benning.

I wondered who they would put in the empty bed across from me and what his story would be. By midafternoon I knew. It was Barto again. He was operated on after me, and as luck would have it, he ended up in the last empty bed in my ward. His left leg was thankfully still there. It was elevated and contained in a cast all the way up to his groin. He was still under the influence of the anesthesia.

When he came out from under, he too was surprised to see who was across from him. We later concluded that there were two good Army reasons for us going through the evacuation pipeline together, one medical and one bureaucratic: the nature of our wounds and our last names starting with the same letter of the alphabet.

■　■　■

I was in the hospital in Yokohama for almost two months. It was a very emotional time for me, one that I will never forget. As an infantry commander in the field, I had to hide my feelings when we took casualties. I couldn't let it shake me or get the best of me. It was important to the morale and the welfare of the Wolfhounds in Alpha Company for me to be in charge of my emotions. I had to stay tough and focus on our mission and the welfare of those still able to fight. Their lives depended on it. So did mine.

But it was different lying in a hospital looking at the carnage of war. All day long, I was witness to what few of the politicians that send men to war ever see. I didn't have to build walls between my feelings and my responsibilities. So feelings took over.

There was the young, twenty-two-year-old, Rob Whitehall, who had recently graduated from architecture school in Chicago. The right side of his face, his right arm and shoulder, and half the right side of his torso were blown away. VC sappers tossed a satchel charge of dynamite into the armored personnel carrier he was in. He reacted quickly and picked it up to throw it outside and around the opening of the armor-plated carrier. It exploded just as he let it fly. He had saved the lives of the others in the carrier, and his own, but a career in architecture was no longer in his dreams.

And Tim Roberson, the eighteen-year-old boy with the bandaged face in the bed next to me. Thinking his foxhole was about to be overrun, he pulled the pin on a Willy Peter hand grenade and hurled it towards the advancing VC. It hit a tree and bounced back, exploding just a few feet in front of the foxhole, covering him with burning white phosphorous that sticks to flesh and devours it faster than hydrochloric acid. Both his eyes were burned out of their sockets, and his arms and hands had burns that in spots had eaten all the way to the bone. On several occasions I helped Roberson by writing, as he dictated, letters to his girlfriend and by reading her letters to him.

Bobby Michaels, only nineteen years old, stepped on an antitank mine. They never found his legs, his testicles were gone, and he had to urinate and defecate through tubes connected to a sack attached to his bed. He would be a vegetable for the rest of his life.

Then there was Smitty. He had two holes in his back as big around as grapefruit. When his dressings were changed, you could see his lungs pumping, in and out, against the damaged muscles in his back.

There were many others. The human tragedy was appalling. I talked with men and boys that thought they would have been better off if they had died. Sometimes, when thinking about what their lives in the future might be like, I found it hard not to agree with them.

■ ■ ■

I tried to pass the time by reading and listening to the radio whenever I could. It was depressing. I learned of the Six-Day War fought between Israel and its Arab neighbors, which had taken place in June, while I was still fighting in the jungles of Vietnam. I didn't pay much attention to the outside world back then. Now, on learning about the way Israel unleashed everything it had to win a war in just six days, I was angry. The United States was the strongest nation on Earth. Compared to the forces Israel had faced, North Vietnam was numerically and technologically weak. Why weren't we able to accomplish in Vietnam what Israel had accomplished?

As an Army officer, I could understand the difference in the two wars. The Israelis fought a conventional war, in open desert terrain, against an enemy who was easy to find. We were fighting an unconventional war, in the jungle, against guerrilla fighters who could be found only when they allowed it. But it bothered me that so many Americans were dying in a "limited war" with "limited objectives," as the Vietnam conflict was often described by our leaders.

I learned of the riots that took place in Newark on July 11, while I was in the hospital in Vung Tau. Over twenty people were killed. I listened to the radio in Yokohama in late July during the riots in Detroit, where over forty people died. Federal troops had to be sent in to calm things down.

In early August, I was permitted out of bed for the first time. A nurse's aide helped me into a wheelchair. It had an extension for my leg, still in a cast, to rest on. The aide wheeled me outside into the sunlight to get some fresh air. I found myself with several other patients, all wearing our light-blue hospital gowns, in a small courtyard.

A steel chain-link fence surrounded the hospital. On the other side, a crowd of angry Japanese with fists in the air peered through and shouted, "Americans go home. GIs go home. No more nukes." It was an ugly scene. I had not done anything to these people. I quickly asked to be wheeled back to the ward, where I learned that a U.S. nuclear submarine had tied up in Yokohama harbor and the Japanese were demonstrating to get it out.

I had trouble making sense of it all. Why weren't we fighting to win in Vietnam? What were so many soldiers paying the supreme sacrifice for, if not to win? What was happening at home? Some of the riots in America had caused more casualties than most of the firefights I had experienced in Vietnam. And how could Japan, a nation we had helped rebuild after a war it had started, be treating us so poorly?

The America I was hearing about now seemed very different than the America I had left. I wondered what it would be like when I finally returned. I felt caught in a no man's land, suspended between realities. I thought I'd understood the war I was fighting, and now I didn't. I wasn't sure I would understand the country I was going home to.

■　■　■

But Yokohama was not all bad. As the time passed, each of us was getting better and getting closer to going home. New patients arrived daily to take the place of departing patients. We swapped war stories and talked of family. The nurses were professional and caring and they tended to our every need—well, most of our needs. The doctors were dedicated, thorough, and friendly. They took the time to answer all our questions and keep us informed of our progress. Red Cross workers helped by bringing books and magazines. They sometimes played cards or other games with us. Patients that could be rolled over received weekly back massages from Japanese masseuses—no geishas, only short, barrel-shaped elderly women.

Each weekday around midmorning the physical therapist, Mary Sweeny, visited our ward. Her visit was the highlight of the day. Lying in bed for a prolonged period with no significant exercise causes muscles to atrophy. In just a few days on my back, my own muscles, particularly in the legs, began to shrink and turn to flab. It was important that we do some form of exercise. It was Mary's job to make it happen.

Mary was a lonely soldier's dream come true. Pretty, with a petite and sexy figure, she had red hair, green eyes, a beguiling smile, and a generous manner. She made us horny. She always entered the ward at the far end, pushing a small, stainless steel cart with shelves holding her equipment. She spent about ten minutes with each patient. At her urging, we lifted small weights, pulled on thick elastic bands, or squeezed devices that helped develop our arms, hands, and wrists. Afterwards, she recorded the progress on each patient's record.

Each day she made us do a little more than the day before. For some, in the beginning, it was all she could do to get them to lift their arm or leg five or ten times. When anybody advanced to a new level, Mary rang a small bell and we all cheered. For those with casts, she reached under the cast and asked them to "make a muscle," always praising them when she could feel the muscle she was touching get hard.

Unknowingly, she had set herself up for Barto. And he was always up to form, teasing her. His leg cast reached nearly to the top of his thigh. So Mary had to reach under his cast at his groin to see if he was tightening his thigh muscle.

Each day, Mary made her way from bed to bed towards him. As she approached, he shouted out, "Miss Mary, Miss Mary, come feel my muscle. Please feel it, pleeeeez feel it. It's getting hard just thinking about you."

Mary always smiled and blushed but never lost her composure. In time she started replying, "Pleeeeeze, Jack, pleeeeeze don't let it get soft; I'll get there as soon as I can." The rest of us howled with each exchange, while letting our own imaginations run wild. We often chimed in with digs of our own. I suppose that today it would be considered sexual harassment. In 1967, in an Army hospital in Yokohama, it brought joy to a bunch of shot-up GIs from Vietnam.

We all fell in love with Mary. It was good medicine.

■　　■　　■

Our destinations after Yokohama were pretty much in the hands of our individual doctors. Many factors came into play when deciding

195

where to send us. Most critical were the nature of our wounds and the length of time remaining in our tour of duty. During my stay, no one from the ward returned to Vietnam. The wounds were just too serious.

Some, but not many, were shipped to new duty stations in the Far East like Okinawa, Korea, Guam, or bases in Japan, where they were placed on light duty. Others went to specialized treatment facilities like the Army Burn Center at Fort Sam Houston, Texas. Most went to veterans hospitals in the United States, like Great Lakes in Chicago, Walter Reed in Washington, D.C., or Valley Forge in Pennsylvania.

In early September, when my wounds had healed sufficiently to allow a move to a new hospital, my doctor met with me. He told me that he was considering keeping me in Yokohama until I could move around on crutches—probably for another month. Then he planned to send me to an Army base in Okinawa and place me on light duty. There I would finish the four months remaining in my overseas assignment.

My doctor was a straight shooter who wasn't too impressed with administrative bullshit. And he was very approachable. So I told him my story. How I had been selectively retained on active duty. That I had a civilian job waiting for me in a company that manufactured, among other things, products used in the medical industry like artificial heart valves and hydrocephalic shunts. How much I wanted to return to a hospital in the States. How important it was for me to get on with my life.

I went on to tell the doctor that as soon as I could get around on crutches, I planned to go to Washington, D.C. There I would personally plead my case for a speedy discharge from active duty. Since my wounds prevented me from doing what I was trained to do, kill people in the jungle, I thought the Army would accept my request. The doctor said he would do what he could do to help me.

When I finally received my orders, they were for the Army Hospital in Valley Forge. They were signed by my doctor. He had come through for me.

And Barto, of course, asked if he could go along.

The author (radio call sign Alpha Six) with glasses removed for the picture, somewhere in the Iron Triangle, May 1967.

Captain Frank Maki (killed by enemy fire in 1971), ROTC instructor at Eastern Michigan University, mentor, and friend of the author's.
(Photo courtesy Mrs. Gay McCormick, Captain Maki's surviving spouse)

Lieutenant Steve Ehart (Alpha Three-Six) calling for a situation report with the help of his radio operator, Specialist Thomas McGilvray, Jr.
(Photo courtesy Sergeant Alfred "Luke" Serna)

Army Chaplain Tucker (left) with the prayer book that stopped a bullet that may have taken his life, sitting with Alpha Company medic Specialist Bert Hale, who bandaged the author near LZ Zulu before his dustoff helicopter arrived.

Second Lieutenant Calvin Neptune, a few days before he was torn apart by shrapnel from a Vietcong mortar round. (Photo courtesy retired Colonel Calvin Neptune)

Officer's quarters in Cu Chi base camp. The damaged one to the far left was occupied, briefly, by the author prior to the mortar attack on Cu Chi base camp described in the chapter titled "Why?"

The street leading from the 25th Infantry Division's base camp area into Cu Chi town.

■ Children standing outside the dentist "office" in Cu Chi town.

Typical South Vietnamese village elder, like the one who one night advised the author not to attack local Vietcong units because the position of the stars in the sky was not right for victory.

Mamasans cleaning up after a Vietcong mortar round damaged the Wolfhound Tactical Operations Center in Cu Chi base camp.

Wolfhound troops on a Helping-Hands mission in the village of Ap Boi.

The L-19 Bird Dog used to direct tactical air strikes in support of Wolfhound units.

Photographs

■ First Sergeant Charles Rutledge (aka Top), Alpha Company's highest ranking noncommissioned officer and Wolfhound legend.
(Photo courtesy Platoon Sergeant Gary Pearse)

■ Sergeant Alfred "Luke" Serna, who served three years in Vietnam, with Staff Sergeant Gary Pearse, platoon sergeant with Alpha Company's third platoon.
(Photo courtesy of Sergeant Alfred "Luke" Serna)

The author (second from the left) with some of Alpha Company's troops during a search and destroy operation in the Ho Bo Woods.

| *Part Four* |

On with Life

Going Home

At the appointed time, a squad of orderlies appeared to pack Barto, me, and several others into wheelchairs. They rolled us out of the ward to the rear of the hospital complex.

The sky was clear, with a few puffy white clouds rolling by. In the bright sun, we looked pallid and unhealthy. Our Vietnam suntans had long since vanished. We were wearing blue hospital pajamas, the only clothes we had left. Small groups of Japanese demonstrators, like those we'd previously seen protesting U.S. nuclear submarines, hovered just outside the hospital gate waving signs reading "Americans Go Home."

Miss Mary and several nurses ran out to say good-bye. Mary gave us each a big hug, the first most of us had received in a long time. She reminded us to do our exercises. Barto asked her if she would "pleeeeeze" feel his muscle one last time. Amidst many hoots and laughs, our much-anticipated journey home was about to begin.

I felt more ambivalent than I had expected. I had grown attached to some of the patients in Yokohama and to some of the hospital staff, and I knew that I would probably never see them again. I still felt a pang of guilt for leaving friends in Vietnam behind, fighting a deadly war, including Alpha Company and the soldiers I had served with. And I fretted over what I was hearing about things back in the States, all the turbulence, all the marching and shouting. What was it going to be like when I got home, a soldier from a controversial war?

Right now, we weren't even soldiers; we were just cargo. The orderlies laid us out on stretchers, loaded us on a bus, and stacked us one over another. They drove us to a U.S. Air Force facility near Tokyo, where they unloaded and reloaded us into another C-119 cargo plane. Once again, stretchers were tied to racks along the sides and middle of the plane's boxcarlike fuselage.

But we were delicate cargo, handled with care. Some of the guys had portable intravenous bottles hooked up to them. Some were in partial- or full-body casts. Barto still had a cast running from his hip to his foot. Mine had been removed three days earlier and replaced with a heavily bandaged splint running from my knee to the bottom of my foot. I had to be careful when moving around, but I was in better shape than many soldiers on the plane.

Other than our injuries, there was not much to distinguish one piece of human cargo from another. We each had a small green valuables bag, a large yellow envelope with medical records, and a small tag on the left ankle, if the left ankle was available.

The tag showed our destination, for me Valley Forge, and listed the medications we required during the trip. I tied the green bag to my wrist and stuffed the envelope under my back.

Not all of us were loaded on stretchers. Some walked into the plane with assistance, others under their own steam. One very hostile-looking guy sported a more distinctive wardrobe than the rest of us. He was dressed in a straight jacket. He kept jerking his head to the left, again and again, every second or two. I think he repeated this for the entire trip. I don't know for sure.

Soon after we lifted off, I fell asleep and stayed that way across the cold reaches of the North Pacific. I didn't wake up until just before we landed in Alaska. On touching down, I heaved a big sigh of relief—I was back in the United States.

I remember three things about the trip from Japan to Alaska. First was my impression that many of the soldiers going home had emotional disorders and accidental injuries, rather than combat wounds. Second was my continuing awe at how dauntingly efficient, smooth, and seamless the Army's medical treatment and evacuation systems were. It seemed that everything had been thought of, every exception and contingency planned for, every step planned and executed flawlessly from the hour I was lifted out of the jungle to the moment I arrived on U.S. soil. Not everything the Army tried to do was done this well.

And I remember how good it felt when the Red Cross workers came out in the middle of the Alaskan night to administer large doses of friendliness and caring. They boarded the plane and moved down the aisles to greet us. "Welcome to America!" a pert little Doughnut Dolly said as she handed me a steaming cup of hot coffee and a chocolate-covered doughnut. "You're in Anchorage, Alaska."

"Pinch me, I think I'm dreaming," I replied. And she did, with a big smile, ever so softly on my nose. Across from me, Barto yelled out, "Don't pinch me, I'll take a kiss." Her face turned pink as she responded, "I'd love to kiss you, Lieutenant Barto, but it's against the rules. Anyway, you'll be home soon and I bet you have someone there who is waiting to give you a big kiss." Barto was silent.

We stayed on the plane in Anchorage while it was serviced and refueled. Soon after the flight landed, a new pilot and crew came aboard. They had us airborne again in less than an hour. Our destination was McGuire Air Force Base in New Jersey, on the Fort Dix Military Reservation.

Prior to liftoff, one of the outgoing crew members told me that it was necessary for the safety of the flight to change pilots after eight hours, though the plane could keep going "round the clock if necessary." I was happy we had a fresh pilot. And I sure wanted to get home safely. But changing pilots after eight hours seemed a stark contrast with the realities of being a combat infantrymen, where I saw equipment fail much more often than men. I recalled the many times that I and others with me had to lead Alpha Company in combat for twenty-four to forty-eight, even seventy-two, hours with little or no sleep. Was our judgment or our reaction time impaired?

With just one flight remaining in the long journey home from Vietnam, I prayed that the plane, bouncing all over the sky and groaning from aerodynamic stress, would make it to McGuire. I couldn't get back to sleep. I was just too excited about going home.

■　■　■

It was an overcast day, with a slight chill in the air, when we landed at McGuire AFB. More Doughnut Dollies came aboard with treats for us, while a long convoy of olive-drab buses waited for us on the tarmac. Then it was into the stretcher-bearing buses one more time. We were on our way to downtown Fort Dix for some administrative processing before leaving for the Army hospital at Valley Forge.

The trip to Valley Forge took well over two hours, and I savored every minute of it. The trees on the rolling hills of eastern Pennsylvania were already showing, in mid-September, a hint of their autumn palettes. It had been a long time since I had seen the American countryside, and there were many times in Vietnam when I thought I would never see it again. But I was back. And all of it, even the heavy auto and truck traffic on the New Jersey Turnpike, was like a beautiful dream coming true.

When we finally arrived at Valley Forge Hospital, my own memories of the war were beginning to seem a little unreal, to fade with the abrupt shifts from one environment to another. But I was constantly being pulled back to Vietnam by the sight and sound and presence of the severely wounded soldiers all around me.

Just to move through the hospital on the way to our rooms was a stark experience, sobering and gut-wrenching. Young men with no arms and no legs sat in wheelchairs, mere stumps of their former selves. Young men with artificial legs struggled to walk, sometimes falling in a heap, like a puppet with its strings cut. Young men with artificial hands and arms were learning to eat without assistance, slopping food and drink like infants learning to take a first meal. Blind young men tried to move without crashing into furniture, walls, and doors. And young men with tubes drooping from their abdomens carried plastic bags filled with urine or feces.

Many of these were young men who would never work again. Young men unable to make love, ever. Young men never to be fathers or grandfathers. Young men staring ahead, hopeless. Young men who would grow old and die in an Army hospital. Young men, each one of them, who had been called by their nation to go fight a war, who had gone and returned to this.

■　■　■

In Valley Forge, of course, Barto and I ended up together again. This time it was in a semiprivate room with only two beds. I didn't think that it was possible in an Army hospital. I had seen only large wards full of patients. But Barto sweet-talked one of the nurses into it. He told her that I might need some privacy when Kathy visited me on the following day.

Before the nurse agreed, he told her, "I will be honored to stand guard for the happy occasion. And besides, as horny as Captain Brewer is, if he can't have his little woman, he'll be chasing you around on his crutches. He hasn't had any in almost a year."

"Oh, shut up," the nurse said as she led us to our room, blushing all the way. Barto was a pro at making the ladies blush.

I didn't have to wait long for the conjugal visit. Early in the morning, on the day after I arrived, Kathy flew from Ypsilanti to Philadelphia. She was met there by members of the Fisher family, relatives of my brother-in-law, Parvin Russell. They lived less than a half-hour drive from the hospital. They were kind enough to open their home to Kathy and give her the use of a car while she visited me. She drove to the hospital that afternoon.

The door to my room opened. She stood there in a bold pink cotton dress, white pumps, and hair bleached a light blond. I was shocked. Her hair had been its natural color, dark brown, when I last saw her.

She hesitated in the doorway. She said she was surprised to see that I was still in one piece. Then she hugged me.

I think she assumed that my wounds were more severe. I didn't have much that was eloquent to say. I quickly introduced her to Barto, who had already called for a wheelchair and a nurse to help him out of the room. On his way out he winked at me and said, "Have fun and take your time. I've got guard duty."

The door shut behind him. After months of uncertainty, I was alone at last with my wife. And the rest of that visit is history.

After a few days at Valley Forge, I was able to move around fairly well on crutches. I was told that I was permitted to take a thirty-day convalescence leave. I could go home to Michigan and wait on orders for my next assignment. Only six months remained before my extended period of service would end, in March of 1968.

So I walked out of that last hospital, on two legs and two crutches. Barto and I said our emotional good-byes. This time there was no way he could invite himself along. I was on my own.

■　■　■

I was home at last. I should have been relaxed and comfortable, but instead I was restless and on edge. I felt caught between the military service I wanted to leave behind and a new civilian career I was late in starting. I told myself I was eager to get on with my life.

But initially, it was difficult for me to relate to people. I saw everyone in a new and different way. I had been to war; they had not. What else can be said?

Surviving ground combat in a war changes everything. I had faced death time and again. And I knew what real fear—saliva-stopping, heart-pounding, breath-sucking fear—was all about. I thought, How could they ever know the true value of life without facing death and escaping it? I imagined that there was no way we could truly understand each other. They had no idea what I had experienced. And they probably never would. They could only try to imagine. But why should they? I wasn't looking for sympathy. I wanted to forget.

I saw other people's interests, like buying a new car or a new piece of furniture, changing jobs, planning a vacation, or watching the big game on television, as shallow and irrelevant. During group discussions with family and friends, I had difficulty focusing my attention. My mind kept wandering. I might as well have been alone with my thoughts.

Often I was preoccupied with the joy of just being home and alive. Everything else paled by comparison. But at other times, in reverie, I longed to be back with my Wolfhounds, back in the action where the fear of death made living so real. Looking back on that period when I first arrived home, I'm sure that others saw me as distant and self-absorbed.

I wasn't the only one that had changed during my stay in Vietnam. Kathy had also changed. Midway during my tour in Vietnam, she wrote me saying that she intended to get a job. I pleaded in a return letter that she should stay home with our two children. I argued that Caroline and Suzanne were already without a father at home. They might suffer if left with a sitter all day long; they needed all the love they could possibly get.

She didn't take the job. She also stopped writing to me on a regular basis. The few brief letters she did send were different than previous letters, almost detached. I couldn't understand why she didn't write more often. Mail was so important to me. In the field, it was my lifeline to humanity. When I wrote to Kathy, I kept begging for return letters. Very few came.

Then with me back home, she kept referring, over and over, to the job incident. She was very critical of me wanting her to stay home, claiming that I didn't care about her or her needs. She said that it was difficult for her not knowing if I was going to return, that she needed something to help her pass the time. I tried hard to understand and make amends. But she harbored a strong resentment. And I nursed a deep hurt over the lack of letters. As time passed, our shaky relationship deteriorated. For some unknown reason, neither of us could forgive the other.

After hosting several days of visits from family and friends, I called Dow Corning. I wanted to learn the status of the job I had been offered in June of 1966, before I was retained on active duty. As promised, the company had a position for me as soon as I could start, whenever that would be.

I was still driven by restlessness. I couldn't just kick back and let things unfold, sit through the thirty-day leave, then go for another six months to some dead-end Army assignment. I wanted to get on with life, move forward, begin my new job. So I decided to go to the Department of the Army's Office of Personnel Administration (OPA) in Washington, D.C., to plead my case for immediate discharge from the Army.

I got in the car and headed for Washington. I wasn't cargo on a stretcher anymore, I was driving the bus myself. Because of my wounds, I could use only my left leg and foot when driving. So for the entire trip I rested my right leg on the hump in the floorboard, forward of the front seat. I operated the accelerator and the brake with my left foot. Luckily, the car had an automatic transmission, so there was no manual clutch. I didn't have an extra foot to manipulate it.

All went well until I found myself daydreaming on the Pennsylvania Turnpike west of Philadelphia. Unconsciously, I pushed the pedal to the floor and picked up more and more speed. A police siren intruded on my dream. I was the first of five cars pulled over at a well-concealed radar trap; I was going almost eighty miles an hour.

As the state trooper, robust and handsomely uniformed, approached the car with ticket pad in hand, I grabbed the jacket to my uniform lying on the seat next to me and squeezed into it. I grabbed my crutches and wriggled out of the car. I stood, unsteady, as he approached me.

The trooper was pleasant looking and professional in all respects. I didn't know what to expect his judgment to be. But I figured that if he knew that I was a wounded vet, he might be somewhat forgiving and go light on the ticket.

When he saw the crutches and the combat decorations on my jacket, he asked me if I had been in Vietnam. I told him the reason for my trip to Washington. He looked at me a moment and said: "Given all you've been through, Captain Brewer, it wouldn't be patriotic for me to give you a ticket, but take it easy from here on, understand?" I heaved a silent sigh of relief and asked him about the other cars he'd pulled over. The trooper shrugged. "I can't give them a ticket, if I don't give you one. It's everyone's lucky day."

When I pulled forward to get back on the highway, he yelled, "Thanks, Captain Brewer, for what you did for us over there in Vietnam. I hope it goes well for you in D.C.!"

■　■　■

In a room at the Office of Personnel Administration, I sat across from a couple of earnest but deskbound Army officers. After a few pleasantries, I started the meeting by summarizing the written resignation that I had prepared in accordance with applicable Army regulations. Then the officers tried very hard to get me to reconsider my request for discharge. They argued that as a young captain and a decorated combat veteran, I could look forward to a "rich and rewarding career in the Army."

Just what I didn't want. They also offered, on behalf of the Army, to pay my way through graduate school and to give me a command of my choice when I completed the course of study, perhaps with the 82nd or 101st Airborne Division.

I told them that I was committed to leaving the service. And that my doctor's best estimate was that it would take three to four more months for my wounds to heal sufficiently for me to perform any job in my "military occupational specialty"—combat infantryman. By then, there would be only two months until my discharge. I asked them to consider my service record and the extra time I had served when they made their final decision. I tried not to plead with them, but it probably looked like I did. I left feeling that they were sympathetic to my cause.

When I arrived back at home, I saw that the canvas duffel bag I'd taken to Vietnam had arrived via parcel post from Valley Forge. Apparently it had followed me, like a loyal canine, each step of the way from hospital to hospital during my long journey home. As soon as First Sergeant Rutledge learned that I wouldn't be returning to Alpha Company, he had packed it up and forwarded it to me.

Inside, I found two pairs of my jungle fatigues, some socks and underwear, and the summer tan uniform I was wearing when I arrived in Vietnam. Rutledge had also included the damaged boot I had on my right foot when I was wounded near Zulu. It had several holes in it from the grenade fragments that injured me and was stained with my blood. And last was a special package. It contained snapshots sent to me by some of Alpha's troops, two enemy propaganda leaflets, and a Vietcong flag captured in Tan My shortly after I was evacuated from the field.

It meant a lot to me for the troops to want me to have the flag. The upper half of the flag is red, the lower half is blue, and there is a large yellow star in the middle. It may have belonged to the VC unit that wounded me. It hangs on the wall in my den, not far from the desk where I am writing now.

A week later I received a set of orders directing that I be discharged as soon as arrangements could be made for me to accept a commission in the Army Reserve on inactive status. I called Barto in Valley Forge to bring him up to date. He said he was happy for me. He still didn't know when he would be released from the hospital or what lay ahead for him. "Until I hear," he said, "I will be spending all of my time chasing nurses."

■　　■　　■

On Wednesday, October 4, 1967, at the Valley Forge Army Hospital, I was honorably discharged from active duty, after four years and four months "of Honest and Faithful Service." A 40 percent disability pension was granted to me for wounds received in action. I had done my job and I was proud of it. My hometown was proud of me, too. Several days later our local newspaper, the *Ypsilanti Press,* ran an article with the title "Decorated Officer Home from Viet[nam]." It was a year when most Americans still supported the war.

But I was saying good-bye in my own mind to the Army and to Vietnam. From now on they would be behind me. Everything seemed to be falling into place. My life was going to start again. The nightmares that haunt me to this day were yet to come.

Back in Civvies

O n a rain-soaked Saturday afternoon, just a few
days after my discharge from the Army, I drove
north on Highway 23 from Ypsilanti to Flint,
Michigan. Dark, low-hanging clouds crowded
the horizon all around me. The landscape was
wide and flat. From Flint, a broad swath of interstate highway,
four smooth lanes across, took me toward Saginaw and Bay City.
Then I headed west on Highway 10 to Midland, where my new
job was waiting.

I had spent the morning shopping at Sears Roebuck for
civvies, civilian clothes. It was a new experience. My adult,
postcollege, life had all been in the Army, and formal dress in the
American military was a style apart. Now all of my purchases,
still in shopping bags, were in the trunk of my blue Volkswagen.
My new wardrobe included a gray pinstriped suit, a dark-blue
suit, five white cotton shirts with button-down collars, a pair of
wing-tip shoes, and three diagonally striped ties in bright colors.
It wasn't a closet full of Armani, but it would do for Dow Corning. I vowed never to wear anything even remotely like Army
green again—not olive drab or military khaki.

Abruptly, the sun broke through the threatening clouds.
Rays of golden light slanted down along the highway, as though
lighting a path to my new future. I can remember at that moment feeling very pleased with myself. I was speeding closer and
closer to a new home, a new phase in my life. It seemed like I
had done a lot already in a short span of years. I had graduated
from college, was married, had fathered two children, had

survived Vietnam, and was about to start my first civilian job with a large, world-class company. I had met all the challenges that had been thrown at me, as tough and terrifying as some of them had been. Now I was in calm water. It would be smooth sailing from here on. Or so I thought.

I rolled into Midland and parked in the center of town. I knew nobody and had nowhere to stay, so that was the first order of business. I found the local newspaper and went straight to the "Rooms for Rent" column.

There wasn't a lot of choice, but by late afternoon the same day, I had found an inexpensive room in a boardinghouse. The white Victorian house, which was rather large, had a wraparound porch with fancy latticework and a wide green yard. The landlady was everybody's image of the perfect grandmother. And the place was only a few minutes' drive from where I would be working, in Dow Corning's headquarters building.

The boardinghouse wasn't a permanent situation. After a few months of serious scrimping and saving, I'd have enough for a larger place. Then I planned to bring my family to Midland and settle them down. In the meantime, I'd commute back and forth on the weekends between Midland and Ypsilanti.

I paid the landlady for the first week's rent, unloaded the car, and unpacked my clothes in the small bare room. The bed sagged a little with age and squeaked when I sat on it. A throw rug decorated the worn wooden floor, clean and shiny. I went out for a short walk around Midland to see the sights and loosen up the knotted muscles from the long drive. I didn't go far or fast. The fact was, I still needed a cane for support. I can remember feeling very self-conscious about my cane, as passersby glanced at me. I imagined that I looked odd, that they weren't accustomed to seeing a young man with a limp and a cane. I wondered what they thought.

Back at the boardinghouse, a pot of warm coffee and a plate of cookies was waiting for me. The landlady struck me as very lonely. She'd lost her husband during the Korean conflict. Maybe that's why she took a special interest in me. On Sunday, she made breakfast, lunch, and dinner for me, while she told stories of her husband and her two sons, each of whom had somehow managed, to her great joy, to avoid military service.

■   ■   ■

On Monday morning, I dressed in my new blue suit, a white shirt, and a tie. The tie was striped in blue, gold, and maroon. I admired myself in the mirror, feeling smug, smooth, and corporate. I grabbed my cane and went downstairs to the kitchen. On the table a bowl, a box of Cheerios, a quart of milk, and a pot of coffee were waiting.

As I drove off to work, there were butterflies in my stomach, like the first day of high school, like my first date, like the day I took command of Alpha Company. I was eager and apprehensive, nervous but determined. Most of all, I was worried about making a good first impression.

As I rolled through the gates of Dow Corning and Dow Chemical, it was like arriving at Fort Benning years ago. I was entering a world apart, becoming part of a vast organization larger than any individual. I remember being awestruck, feeling like an ant in a human metropolis, tiny and insignificant compared to the huge, complex structures towering over me.

Instead of office buildings I was surrounded by distillation towers and tall refractory stacks, with bright golden flames shooting skyward. Smokestacks sent gray plumes of smoke rising slowly into the upper atmosphere, generating a dense haze that covered the landscape. Railroad tank cars waiting to be filled were positioned on rail spurs adjacent to the chemical processing plants. There were endless fields of interconnected pipes, zigging at right angles from tower to tower, punctuated by huge circular valve handles. And there were scattered fields of large white storage tanks, holding chemicals that had just arrived for processing, chemicals that had already been processed, or chemicals between stages of processing. The smell in the air might have been the legendary stench of hell; it seemed to combine the worst effects of sulfur, methane, and ammonia.

At the main gate to Dow Corning's Midland Plant, I asked the guard for directions to the Personnel Office. On my way there, I had time to wonder how I would do here, whether I would survive and prosper. This was like landing in a foreign country or maybe on a different planet, unlike any place I had ever lived or worked. It was a long way from the jungles of Vietnam or the cornfields surrounding Willow Run.

■　■　■

At the Personnel Office, I was introduced around and then sat down to a long discussion with Bob Bott. Bob was one of the candidates to be my boss. Early into our talk, he asked if I would like to help the company implement a new computerized information system for the Personnel Department. The idea was to store information on college recruits and employees, facts about their education, skills, interests, performance ratings, and career preferences. When this Employee Information System (EIS) was completed, the company would have a sophisticated tool to help manage the career development of each individual employee. He offered me the job of project manager.

I was awestruck for the second time that day. Computerized information systems, though common today, were forward thinking and very rare in the late sixties. And I didn't know a thing about computers, information technology, or private industry's concept of personnel management, now referred to as human resources management. It was an abyss of ignorance that I didn't bother to hide from Bob. "Wow, I've never even seen a computer. I don't know the first thing about designing a system for one," I told him.

My complete lack of knowledge didn't seem to faze him. "There aren't many people who've built what we envision," he replied. "Dow Corning will send you to whatever training you need." He shrugged and smiled. "It's really up to you."

In retrospect, the choice was obvious, but it wasn't an easy decision to make, not at the time. What if the project failed? What if I couldn't learn enough to do the job well? "Can I think about it for a day?" I asked.

"Absolutely, Tom. Take your time," Bob said. "We think it's an excellent chance for you to get in on the ground floor with computers. But if you would rather do something else, we can talk about several other opportunities. We have openings that we think you would be right for, in both Personnel and Industrial Sales." I finished the day filling out employment forms, getting my picture taken for my badge, attending an orientation about company policy, and taking a tour of the company's headquarters.

The tour included Dow Corning's computer room. Back then, in the digital Stone Age, computers required huge, specially constructed and air-conditioned rooms, with raised floors for wiring. Compared to today's computers, these were dinosaurs, massive, power hungry, and ponderously slow. And I was suitably intimidated. The technology was alien, complex, with whirring tape machines and flashing lights that signified nothing to me.

It was overwhelming. I had spent all my time in the military dealing with real people, human beings, face to face. In Vietnam, while searching for Charlie and under fire, the one skill I could count on was my understanding of the people I commanded, their strengths and weaknesses, the things that motivated them. I questioned my suitability for a job where all I had to count on was a heartless hunk of metal and wire.

But that evening, I kept thinking about it. I thought particularly about Bob Bott's comment about the future, when he talked about the ground-floor opportunity in computers. In fact, my general confidence was shakier than I liked to admit. I had been away from college for over four years and didn't have any hard civilian skills. I would have to start at the bottom in any area, learn the ropes, get used to new kinds of people and new ways of operating. Corporate America wasn't an LZ in Alpha Company's AO.

If the company had the confidence that I could succeed in computers, maybe I should be confident, too. I thought, Why not give it my best shot?

The following day, I told Bob that I would take on the challenge of developing the new system. I didn't know it at the time, but it was a decision that set the stage for a career in the computer industry that lasted thirty years.

■   ■   ■

As an Army officer, I was always on the job. There were very few off hours. I was accustomed to working long days and weekends. And so it was in my civvies. I worked hard at my new job. It was nothing for me to work twelve- to fifteen-hour days, pull an occasional all-nighter, and work weekends when necessary. The schedule for developing the new system was ambitious, and I was learning my job as I was doing it, which took extra hours as well.

This was a time when the use of computers in industry was still very new. Trial and error was usually how things got done, and that meant that everything took more time than expected. There is no such thing as regular hours when you are doing something that has never been done before. And it seemed the more hours I worked, the happier I was.

When Kathy and the children finally joined me in Midland, she questioned why I worked so hard, why I couldn't spend more time with them. They were very sincere and reasonable questions. After all, I had been away for nearly a year, in Panama and Vietnam and then in the hospital. She had expected that I would have more time for the family when I returned; so did I. But I tried to explain that it was my first real job, that I had to do well in an area I knew little about, and that our futures depended on it.

For a while we were okay. Kristin and Stacey, our twin daughters, arrived in August of 1968. Now we had four beautiful little girls. I did everything I could to spend more time at home and stay on schedule at work. But in time, the relationship between Kathy and me began to fracture, revealing old fault lines that would later break us apart.

No matter how preoccupied I was with my job and family, the war in Vietnam refused to go away. By early 1968, the enemy had launched its devastating Tet Offensive; the war in Vietnam had become a heated national debate. Hawks raged against doves, students against the establishment, police against students, children against parents, brother against brother, and wife against husband. As the number of American troops in Vietnam grew to well over 500,000, the American public's support for the war dwindled, and more and more people joined the antiwar movement.

On several occasions, I and others from Dow Corning's Personnel Department went to university campuses to recruit graduating seniors for the company. We found groups of students demonstrating against the use of napalm in Vietnam. They thought that we were from Dow Chemical, one of the parent companies of Dow Corning. They picketed the recruiting offices and often barred our entry. But it was Dow Chemical, not Dow Corning, that produced napalm for the military. From then on we recruiters had to carry an official written statement. It described our relationship to Dow Chemical and showed that the company's production of napalm represented only a fractional percentage of the company's sales and an even smaller contribution to profits.

I found it ironic and disturbing. In Vietnam, there were battles where, as infantry troop commanders, we had no alternative but to use napalm to save American lives. Now this? The pride I felt about my service in Vietnam began to unravel. I tried to throw myself wholeheartedly into my work, which took intense concentration and long hours. It helped me shut out the war.

Working long hours also helped distract me from other events that I had trouble accepting. Martin Luther King Jr. was assassinated in April 1968. Two months later, presidential candidate Robert F. Kennedy was shot and killed. I had been eager to get home from the war, but it seemed that another war was raging right here at home. Not only over our policies in Vietnam but also over civil rights. In spite of King's philosophy of nonviolence, many African Americans were frustrated with the lack of significant progress in civil rights. Splinter groups were openly promoting violence. Cities were burning. I kept thinking, What have I come back to?

■　　■　　■

By early 1969, my work developing the Employee Information System was completed. The system was up and running, one of the first of its kind. Mission accomplished. I was offered a promotion that required a move to a Dow Corning plant near Louisville, Kentucky. I accepted and spent the next eighteen months in Elizabethtown, Kentucky (E'town), as the plant manager's labor relations representative.

At the E'town plant, we produced some of the high-performance, space-age materials required by the historic Apollo 11 project, humanity's first trip to the moon. And on July 20, 1969, all of us at the plant were very proud. On that historic day, when Neil Armstrong, the first man on the moon, stepped onto the lunar surface, he was wearing a life-support system that included materials made at our plant. And many of the advanced materials used on the giant Saturn 5 rocket that took him to the moon were also produced at the E'town plant.

I remember watching the Apollo 11 mission on television with tremendous hope and enthusiasm. We had put a man on the moon. We were now winning the race to outer space, conquering new frontiers that had seemed impossible when I was a boy. But at the same time, I kept thinking about one of the great contradictions of the times, to my mind. America had the skill and resources to get men to the moon and back, but we still couldn't get our soldiers out of Southeast Asia. Each night on television, I watched commentary on the great achievements we were making in outer space. Then minutes later, the television screen was filled with images of GIs mired down in the jungles and swamps of Vietnam. It was hard to reconcile; it was more than disheartening. Two years had passed since I left Vietnam. Though politicians said otherwise, there was no end in sight to the war—American soldiers were still humpin' the boonies, counting bodies, searching for Charlie.

Several months after the moon shot, the nation was stunned by the discovery of the My Lai massacre that had occurred the previous year in Vietnam. In March of 1968, an American army officer, First Lieutenant William Calley, led his platoon into My Lai, a village suspected of being a Vietcong stronghold. It was reported that for several days before, his platoon had suffered heavy casualties near the village. As Calley entered the small hamlet, he told his troops to herd the villagers, most of them women and small children, into a large drainage ditch. Then he ordered his men to shoot. Several hundred were killed instantly or left to die in and around the ditch. Several of the children were reportedly shot as they tried to run away. Pictures of the slaughtered villagers were shown time and again on television and in the press.

Suddenly, the moon shot and the race to explore outer space meant little to me. And for the first time in my life, though I presumed from my own experience that My Lai was an aberration, I was almost ashamed to be a Vietnam veteran.

As I continued my work at E'town, the polarization of America over the issue of Vietnam grew dramatically. Campus demonstrations, sometimes characterized by bombings and arson, and clashes with the police became more and more violent. ROTC facilities, libraries, and other buildings on many campuses were ransacked and torched.

In May of 1970, students at Kent State University, demonstrating against Nixon's decision to send U.S. troops into Cambodia, were met by the Ohio National Guard. In the melee that followed, several students were accidentally shot and killed. The tragedy unleashed more protests against the war, and then more protests, and still more. It seemed that the country was in the early stages of a campus-by-campus conflagration, the meltdown of a generation.

■　■　■

During the spring of 1970, while I was still with Dow Corning, I was invited on several occasions to speak at the American Management Association's meetings in New York. The topic: the systems development work I had done when I was in Midland. At one of the meetings, I met the president of Information Science Inc., a small privately held software development company. At the time there were few such companies around. The president was intrigued with the work I had done; it fitted in well with his company's mission. After courting me for several months, he invited me to join his company. It was small, only thirty employees, but growing fast. He offered me a position as a project manager with the responsibility for developing systems, for other corporations, similar to the EIS at Dow Corning. It seemed like an easy transition to a position that would be full of promise.

My work at E'town was winding down and I was about to be transferred back to Dow Corning's headquarters in Midland. Kathy was very disappointed about the impending transfer. She hated Midland.

In truth, it wasn't much of a town; it didn't even have a movie theater. Kathy was eager to try the East Coast.

I thought that moving to the New York City area would have a positive impact on our relationship. I also looked forward to the freedom of working in an environment that was free of big company bureaucracy. Though I liked what I was doing and I respected Dow Corning, I accepted the offer to join Information Science. In July of 1970, we moved to New City, New York, a rural town turning into suburbia, just one hour north of New York City.

The war still dominated the news. People talked of it constantly. In the twelve to eighteen months that followed, it seemed to me that the press worked hard at suggesting that My Lai was representative of America's conduct of the Vietnam War. A growing number of veterans were themselves actively protesting the war in demonstrations all over the country. Ordinary soldiers returning from the war were scorned, allegedly spit at, and often treated like lepers. On those occasions when circumstances led me to tell people that I had served in Vietnam, I typically received two responses. The sensitive people changed the topic or excused themselves. Others asked, in a manner expressive of loathing, "How could you do such a thing?"

It never failed to shock and disturb me. As a young boy growing up near Willow Run, I assumed that if I ever had to fight in a war, I would be taking my place in a long line of patriot-soldiers, like the men who had served in World War II and Korea. They were soldiers who had fought for America, on the side of freedom, and returned home to the cheers of its people. And though I was initially welcomed home and treated as a hero, I was beginning to ask myself an uncomfortable question. For me, it was a nerve-shattering question: was I a patriot, a hero? Or had I participated in something shameful, futile, and misguided, a darker side of our nation's history? I wanted the answer to the second question to be no: finally and unequivocally. But evidence to the contrary was growing, day by day.

■　　■　　■

Yes, I was back in civvies. By now, I had been home from Vietnam and out of the Army for over three years. But somehow the war wouldn't go away. It was all around me; it was still with me. I couldn't get it out of my thoughts. I had difficulty being happy about anything. I felt more and more alone and emotionally isolated from others.

In the ensuing years, the emotional turmoil I experienced would be one factor in destroying my already shaky marriage to Kathy. And it would nearly destroy me.

The Aftermath

You . . . are . . . a . . . sick . . . human . . . being." Kathy's words hit me hard as she slammed the door in my face and left the house, outraged.

All of her guests had left the house a few minutes earlier after watching me escort one of them, with some force, to the front door. It was late on a Friday night in November. I had just returned from La Guardia Airport in New York City after an exhausting week-long business trip. Just five months earlier I had begun my job with Information Science, hoping that the move to New York would help close the fissures in our relationship. Instead it was coming apart.

That night I walked into a scene that was becoming more and more common in my house. Kathy and her friends were gathered in the living room with a jug of Gallo wine, deriding President Nixon and the Vietnam War. They talked with contempt of those, like me, who had fought in the war. It didn't matter that I was there, listening.

I asked them to change the topic. Instead they attacked with their standard barrage of personal insults: "Don't you believe in free speech?" "Maybe if you didn't wear a suit and tie you could understand our position more." "Grow a beard and relax, Tom. Don't be so uptight."

And from Kathy: "This is my home, too, and my friends can talk about anything they want to when they're visiting me. If you don't like it, maybe you should leave; you're hardly ever here anyway."

Finally her friend Pratt, someone who considered himself

a philosophical genius and general know-it-all, shouted out, "Why don't you drop some napalm on us?" I lost it, and out the door he went. The rest of the acrimonious crew filed out, and Kathy last of all, with her final withering comment.

Alone, I walked around the house. It looked as if a Midwest tornado had visited us. Stuff was strewn helter-skelter everywhere—several days of dirty dishes in the sink, empty wine jug and goblets in the living room, and two feet of dirty laundry on the family room floor.

I could taste the anger boiling up inside of me. Whenever I saw the house like that, I assumed Kathy had left it in disarray to spite me. Maybe it was my military training, but I've always been a stickler for orderliness. Later in my life, I was able to see things differently. With four small children, the oldest only six, it was difficult for her or anyone in those circumstances to stay ahead of the mess. And I wasn't around to help. My new job, which was meant to help with our relationship, kept me always on the road.

Now I could hear the children crying in their beds. I tried to comfort them. I knew it would be another Mr. Mom weekend. I would try to make up for time lost with the children, clean the house, and wash the clothes. I expected that Kathy would return late on Sunday, as often happened. She'd give me her *I hate you* look, we wouldn't talk, and I would be off to work again early on Monday for another week of traveling. Another week of trying to act like a normal happily married man.

When the children settled down that night, I tried to sleep but couldn't. A feeling of hopelessness consumed me. After thrashing about in bed for hours, I climbed to the attic. I found my 9 mm pistol, an old souvenir from Gelnhausen, and a magazine half-filled with bullets. I pushed the magazine into the pistol grip. Damn you, I'll show you, I said to myself as I jammed it up, thinking of Kathy and her friends. At the time they seemed like the enemy in Vietnam: setting mines and booby traps, surrounding me, attacking, then running away to their tunnels. Charlie was still trying to destroy me and all that I stood for.

Back in the kitchen, I grabbed a bottle of Dewar's White Label Scotch and went out onto the back deck. I sat there with my bare back against the cold gray cedar siding on the house, looking out over the back lawn, silvery and blanketed with a new autumn frost. The pistol lay between my outstretched legs. I thought seriously that everybody would be better off without me.

With each gulp of scotch, I felt not better but worse. With each gulp, I became more depressed. I started slamming the back of my head against the side of the house. *Bam.* "Why doesn't anyone understand my feelings about the war?" *Bam.* "Was I part of an evil war?" *Bam.* "Did I have to kill?" *Bam.* "Why does my own wife support her friends at my expense?" *Bam.* "Why don't I have friends on my side?" *Bam.* "Why am I working so hard—to come home to this?" *Bam.* "Perhaps I am a sick human being." *Bam, bam.*

I reached down for the pistol, chambered a round, and put the pistol to my head; the cold steel barrel numbed my right temple. "I want peace. This will be easy; take a deep breath and then just one quick squeeze on the trigger. I won't hear it, I won't feel it, do it," I said to myself.

"Count down from five and pull the trigger; do it, do it," I pleaded. Another two gulps of the scotch." *Bam.* "Five . . . four . . . three . . . two . . ."

Just as I was ready to pull the trigger, my father's words came to me. I heard him preaching about how difficult life can be. He would say that no matter how bad things become, you can get through them if you search for the good in your experiences.

How his preaching voice found its way into my whiskey-soaked brain, I'll never know. But it did, and it saved me that night. I lowered the pistol from my head and stood up.

My first thoughts were of the children. I stumbled into the house and looked in on them. They were sound asleep. Looking down at their little cherubic faces, I thought, Oh, God, how could I have almost left them without a father? Then I worked my way towards the bedroom. *Thud.* Blackness and oblivion.

Early the following morning, I awoke lying in the hall, leaden with guilt, both my head and heart aching. I was filled with disgust—disgust at myself. How could I have survived Vietnam and made it home, only to let myself get so out of control, get so pathetic, become so much what I didn't want to be?

God must have also been looking out for me that night. With the alcohol in my bloodstream, I had no control. A small twitch of the finger would have discharged the pistol. It was a miracle that I didn't do it, on purpose or by accident. On my back porch in a New York autumn, I came as close to death as I ever had in the jungles of Vietnam.

■ ■ ■

In fact, Vietnam had never really left me, not for long. For the first year after leaving the Army, I was nearly at peace with myself. But late in 1968 that changed, abruptly. A torrent of vivid flashbacks and horrid nightmares came crashing down on me.

I don't know if there was a specific incident that triggered them, but there was no lack of reminders of the war that year or the next. We were all bombarded by images of Vietnam in magazines and newspapers and on everybody's television screen. Campuses across the nation were in turmoil. It seemed that protesting the war had become a national pastime. It was the *in thing* to do. People were passionate about it. Everywhere I went, the pros and cons of the war were being debated, often in violent terms.

In 1970, when we moved to New York, Kathy grew very close to a group of friends who were politically far to the left of my own conservative bent. Given the amount of traveling I was doing, she probably spent more time with them than with me. In my presence, they often spoke out against the Vietnam War and against those who fought it. It had a devastating effect on me, but that didn't seem to moderate their comments. I wanted to write it off, blaming it on the impressive amount of wine they occasionally consumed. But they frequently made the same withering comments when they were stone sober. I don't know if they were intentionally attempting to provoke me. I do know that there was no way they could understand how sensitive I was about the subject and how wounded their comments left me.

It was a bitter and emotional conflict between two perspectives on the war, two realities. One reality was the one portrayed by the antiwar movement, my wife and her friends, and much of the media. The other reality was the one I knew, based on my own experience, firsthand and intensely personal. There seemed to be no way to resolve the conflict.

I couldn't just shrug and forget it. The issues were too deeply etched in my character. I grew up believing that it was honorable to fight for my country when called to do so. I'd answered the call and had some terrible experiences. I was trying to put them behind me. But now I felt betrayed by the country I had served, including my own wife. Of all the people in the world, I needed her understanding, not her scorn.

I began to question my involvement in the war. And I began to nurse a burning resentment towards Kathy, one that swelled inside of me, one that would never go away. I told myself that to survive emotionally, I would have to leave her at some point. I resolved in my mind to do it when the children were older. Until then I would put up a good front. But in spite of that resolve, I was sinking into an emotional abyss.

There were times during the 1970s, like that Friday night in November, that the strain was almost unbearable. A dark storm of undercurrents would run through me, leaving my emotions and self-confidence, even my will to live, shattered. I was visiting a psychiatrist, who worked with me to find a perspective on my situation and experiences, but the basic conflict did not go away.

There were even times when I had fantasies of going back to Willow Run, to talk with or visit my old high school sweetheart, Beverly Pink. Not because I still had romantic feelings for her, said my psychiatrist, but because I needed to erase the war, psychologically—by escaping back in time to a more innocent life, to a place and period when things were simpler and clearer.

By the late 1970s, the grip of the war was lessened. My own strong will to survive, to avoid becoming a victim, helped. And in 1978 I married a loving second wife, Penny, who provided understanding and common sense. I was better. But not at total peace.

In fact, I doubt that will ever happen. Flashbacks and horrible nightmares, though more rare, still occur. Strangely, when I started writing this book, I expected my memories to be stimulated and the nightmares to worsen. But instead, the process has helped quiet them.

■　■　■

Still, I see flashback visions of Zulu and Tan My every day as I shower and dry the still-tender pink scars from my wounds. Sometimes when I walk through the fields and woods near my home in Connecticut or Penny's family retreat in Pennsylvania, I'm thrown back to the stinking paddies and rotting jungles of War Zone C. On a clear night, with stars poking through the black, I return to long nights in the Ho Bo Woods, wondering if I'll be alive in the morning. On dark wet nights, I see ambushes and feel Charlie sneaking up on me.

My heart skips a beat and my chest tightens at an unexpected loud noise. The *dut-dut, dut-dut, dut-dut, dut-dut* of a helicopter takes me back to eagle flights and Giong Loc. On seeing a crippled Vietnam veteran or the Vietnam Veterans Memorial, I see men strewn about on battlefields and still feel guilty. I came home, when so many men did not.

When I hear politicians promoting war as a means to support our national interests, I see veterans hospitals. I want to force the warmongers to spend just one day at one of the hospitals, where they can witness, firsthand, the carnage of their decisions.

Ever since I was a small child, I dreamed of going hunting in Africa. My father and I often talked about such a trip, but he didn't have the means to fulfill the dream. In 1994, I sold the company I had started some years earlier with Penny. I finally had the time and the money. I took our fourteen-year-old son, Topher, on safari in Tanzania.

I hadn't shot a rifle at anything since Vietnam. When I came home from the war, I gave away all of the hunting rifles that I had used while growing up in Michigan. So when we began planning our safari to Africa, I had to purchase several guns appropriate to a safari. Topher and I took the guns to a nearby shooting range to do some target practice. When I looked down the barrel and through the sights of my rifle, focusing on the circular target 100 yards away, I suddenly saw Charlie shooting back at me. I pulled back and looked away. I was shaken. I tried to get the feeling under control. But every time I bent over the rifle, the feeling came rushing back again.

When we got to Africa and joined our professional hunter and his crew, the feeling got worse. They wore green military-style uniforms, similar to my jungle fatigues in Vietnam. I found myself carrying rifles and stalking dangerous animals in the Miombo forests and tall grass of the East African plains. It was humpin' the boonies all over again. The visions revisited me. An adventure that I had looked forward to since I was a small child was stained with bloody flashbacks of the war.

■   ■   ■

In one of the recurring nightmares that I have, the sky is dark and the flickering, pale-yellow glow from parachute flares is illuminating the woods where I crouch. Hordes of raging demons are rushing me from all sides. I'm surrounded, blood gushing like a waterfall from my stomach. I think I'm going to die. The demons are colored black and green, nearly naked, malnourished and covered with dripping swamp filth. Large wartlike tumors protrude from grotesquely disfigured bodies. Some have half a skull and one eye hanging out, others only one leg and shreds of flesh hanging from where the missing leg once was. Some have heads but no faces; some have large holes in their torsos with maggots and flies busy at work in thick red ooze. Some are carrying, by the hair, the bloody heads of what appear to be Americans. They scream and shout, "You die, you die. . . ."

Wave after wave of the angry demons rush me with knives and swords. I fight for my life, striking out at them, my arms flailing. As I fight, a lifeless yellow-gray face with a flat nose and protruding chin is watching. It's the face that belonged to the first Vietcong I killed. He's still wearing the same blank stare as when he died in a bamboo thicket, just a few yards in front of me. The dream ends as the face, a mask of death, moves closer and closer. It presses against my own face, nose to nose, eyeball to eyeball. I awake thrashing about, gasping for breath.

I'm no dream analyst, but I think the nightmare's origin stems, in part, from the tremendous guilt that I feel for taking someone's life, even in a war.

I don't think it was a natural thing for me. Despite the war games we played as children in Willow Run, or because of them, when I was growing up I wanted to be a doctor and save lives. Yet with that same sense of idealism, I believed in our country's need to defend itself, to protect our friends and values. So I believed in the Vietnam War, and reason told me that in war the logic is kill or be killed. So was killing a result of my ideals?

Every day I live with knowing that I consciously chose a life path that led to that situation, to the necessity to kill. Many soldiers fighting in Vietnam had no such choice. But when I graduated from college, I had the option of selecting the branch of the Army I would serve in. I could easily have selected a branch that didn't engage in direct face-to-face combat with the enemy. Instead, I chose the infantry for what I thought, at the time, were good reasons. I even lied on my physical exam so I could fight. How responsible does that make me?

There are no words that I know to explain what I experienced when witnessing someone's life leave him at my doing, as I watched. Time stopped for a split second and the sight of death, instant and permanent, was seared into my memory. It has never gone away. At the time it lay dormant, as I went on with the ugly business of leading an infantry company in combat. But for over thirty years since then, it occasionally returns, in my dreams, to haunt me.

■　■　■

In the second nightmare, the little details vary, but the theme remains the same. Sheets of monsoon rain are pouring down. I'm being attacked by human waves of enemy soldiers in the green uniforms and helmets of the NVA. They are coming at me from off in the distance. They get closer and closer. I'm all alone. I can't find any of the weapons that I need to defend myself. I look desperately for my rifle, pistol, hand grenades, or bayonet, but I can't find them. As the attackers get progressively nearer to me, I keep searching all around, splashing in mud puddles, frantically looking for something, anything, to use against the enemy.

Close to panicking, I find my rifle, but it jams and won't fire. The attackers get closer; I try to fix the rifle, get it to fire. It doesn't. I keep trying. I'm breathing hard, my heart is pounding in my chest. The soldiers get closer. I throw the rifle down and start pumping my arms as a bird flaps its wings in flight. I pump and pump. The attackers close in on me. I pump and pump and pump, until my arms feel like they're going to fall out of their sockets. I'm exhausted. The attackers get closer, almost on top of me. I'm afraid that I'm going to die at any moment.

I pump my arms again, rapidly. My shoulders ache. Then just as the attackers reach me, I lift slowly upward and fly over them like a large human bird. I flap my arms even harder to get up and over the trees. I have to duck several times to avoid hitting some of the branches. The dream ends with my arms tiring. I spin down and crash in the bushes. The rain pelts me. Blood seeps out of me like I'm a sieve, forming a pool of red all around me. I see an orange flash and wake up finding it hard to breathe.

If I look for antecedents in the real world for this nightmare, I remember three separate events. The first was during a firefight in the dry season, soon after I assumed command of Alpha Company. I flew into a hot landing zone; the air was filled with VC bullets. My rifle jammed because of heavy dust kicked up by the choppers. I thought I was going to be overrun. Fear was magnified by an intense feeling of vulnerability, under fire without a weapon or any means of fighting back.

The second incident was the mortar attack on Cu Chi base camp when Lieutenant Young was hit and ripped to shreds. I kept waiting, terror stricken, for the VC to charge while I frantically raced around looking for ways to defend myself.

The third incident was at Landing Zone Zulu after I had been wounded near Tan My. Rain was beginning to fall. I lay on the ground, my leg opened up by a grenade, waiting to be evacuated by helicopter. Again, I can remember an overpowering sense of helplessness, unable to fight, unable to run or hide, unable to do my job as Alpha Company's leader, just waiting for that chopper to lift me up and out of harm's way.

■　■　■

I'm still hurt and bewildered over what I believe to be distorted reporting about the war. Why is it that America saw little, if any, television footage or news reports on the humanitarian efforts of its soldiers? Why don't more people know of our efforts aimed at winning the hearts and minds of the South Vietnamese people?

Why do so many people think that GIs ran around burning down peasant villages. As I recall it was a court-martial offense in Wolfhound outfits to wantonly set fire to a thatched hootch or hurt a civilian. The indiscriminate burning of villages was not tolerated in my outfit. In fact, we took great care to avoid placing civilians in harm's way. After all, it was our mission. How else could we hope to pacify an area? Random destruction and brutal acts towards civilians didn't make sense.

Why is it that most Americans don't know about the thousands of GIs who lost their lives or were wounded trying to protect Vietnamese civilians? The picture painted by some in the media and entertainment industry of the American soldier in Vietnam as a drug-addicted loser, running around indiscriminately killing civilians, is to me a travesty. Drugs may have been in Vietnam, perhaps in rear areas, but I never saw Wolfhound grunts using them. They had to stay alert to stay alive.

The My Lai massacre of 1968, where hundreds of Vietnamese villagers were slaughtered by a deranged group of U.S. soldiers, is an aberration in ten years of war, not the reality. I'm sure that there may have been some other, less-publicized, atrocities of a smaller scale in such a long war, as in all wars. But during the entire time I served in one of the most highly contested areas in Vietnam, I saw no incidents that lend credence to the unjust stereotype that some have promoted. The soldiers I served with were brave men fighting far from home under difficult circumstances. Yes, they were tough when it came to fighting the enemy. But they were kind and gentle, often at great peril, towards the Vietnamese civilians.

Why, in contrast to My Lai, aren't more Americans aware of the Vietcong terror squads that routinely murdered civilians sympathetic to the South Vietnamese government? Why don't more know about the thousands of civilians and government officials who were systematically murdered by the VC and NVA during the Tet Offensive?

The emotional baggage I carry regarding the media and the war had a tremendous impact on my reaction to the Iranian hostage crisis. In late 1979, as you may remember, a group of Iranian revolutionaries seized the American embassy in Teheran and took a group of embassy workers hostage. When they were finally released in January 1981, the American government, the media, and people everywhere in this country welcomed them home as heroes. Their homecoming was a major media event lasting, as I recall, for days.

I watched and I wept. My tears were not tears of joy, as they should have been, for the hostages who had certainly been through a terrible ordeal. My tears were tears of hurt and of rage over the complete lack of a comparable welcoming home for the nearly three-million servicemen and women who had served in Vietnam. We were hostages, too, of our country's own politics.

I had a similar reaction at the end of the Gulf War in 1991, when the country welcomed home, as heroes, soldiers who had fought in Kuwait and Iraq. They had won a very short, almost casualty-free war. It was a clean fight in the open desert where all the technology worked, a conflict-by-consensus where doubts and controversy and politics were set aside.

Both the embassy hostages and the Gulf War veterans deserved to be welcomed home as heroes. I believed it then, and I still do. But no matter how much I tried, I couldn't see these two media events for what they were, on their own merits. I saw them as a great injustice to the Vietnam veteran. It was rubbing salt in wounds that would never heal.

■　■　■

Today, people viewing my life from the outside may think that my life is nearly ideal. Indeed, I have a loving wife, six great children, a wonderful grandchild, a successful career, and relatively good health. Yet every day, amidst the stuff of this outwardly successful life, I ward off the inner ghosts of Vietnam, fighting hard to keep them beneath the surface; to keep them from consuming me, perhaps even destroying me.

When I hear the *Star Spangled Banner* or see the flag on the

Fourth of July or watch the parade go by on Memorial Day, I choke up and can't hold back the tears. I need to feel good about my war, but it is so hard. Sometimes I feel sad and all alone, carrying an invisible burden that I can't talk about. Sometimes I hurt and weep in utter despair, and I don't even know why. And sometimes, I drink too much.

I want people to say they care that I, that America, fought and shed blood on the side of right, that we did the things we did for a good cause. But I know of few that do. And how can they? How can people really say they care about events and feelings they don't understand? After all, these are things that even I can't understand.

But somehow, like many other soldiers and nurses who carry the physical and mental scars of ground combat in Vietnam, I manage to keep going forward in my life. As a child, I was part of a generation taught by our parents and teachers to believe in God, family, and country. Some of us were also taught that, no matter how bad things might get, we were to keep faith in ourselves. We had to "search for the good" in all things.

Reflections
for My Children

That year, 1967, when I fought in Vietnam, the world was a very different place than it is today. It takes an effort of imagination to remember how different it really was. How do I explain it to my children? To their generation, the sixties are cultural nostalgia, hippies, and Woodstock and the Mamas and the Papas.

In 1967, the Cold War was raging. Humanity was polarized between two ideologies: Communism and democracy. East-West tensions were at the boiling point. The global arms race had shifted into high gear. Red China had recently tested an H-bomb. Nuclear submarines stalked each other beneath the oceans, loaded with city-destroying missiles. The ominous threat of a nuclear war and the total annihilation of humankind loomed large on the horizon.

That year, 1967, as in many prior years, the USSR and Red China were funneling military aid to the North Vietnamese. In turn, they were trying to overthrow the South Vietnamese government, which was anti-Communism. As a consequence, since the mid-1950s, three American presidents from both parties—Dwight D. Eisenhower, John F. Kennedy, and Lyndon B. Johnson —had provided progressively larger amounts of military aid to support South Vietnam.

Each president had repeatedly and publicly stated that the United States must take a stand against Communism in Vietnam.

If we didn't, they reasoned, all of Southeast Asia and many other countries in that region of the world would eventually fall to the Communists. The Philippines, Indonesia, even New Zealand and Australia would be in danger.

By 1967, U.S. combat troops had been in Vietnam for almost two years. Americans weren't the only ones fighting against the VC and NVA. Several of our allies, including Australia, New Zealand, the Philippines, South Korea, and Thailand, had also sent troops to help the South Vietnamese. On the home front, demonstrations against the war were taking place, increasingly strident, but most Americans still agreed with our objectives and supported the war. So did I. And many of us held that it was better to fight the Communists in Asia than on American soil.

American strategies for fighting the Vietnam War were driven, in part, by fear. We feared that the Russians or the Chinese might enter the war. Many of our nation's leaders believed that if either of the Communist superpowers participated directly in the conflict, an all-out nuclear war was highly probable. So instead of provoking them by committing a massive force aimed at early decisive victory, as we did later in the Persian Gulf, our apparent strategy in 1967 was to fight a limited war of gradual escalation.

I might have to explain to my children, because we are rapidly forgetting, what a threat Russia and China appeared to be, and were, in 1967. Russia was by far the largest country in the world in terms of land mass and resources. China was the largest in terms of human population. They both had massive standing armies and huge arsenals of conventional and nuclear weapons. They both had expressed the willingness to use those resources to enforce the spread of Communism around the world. Their political systems seemed robust, disciplined, effective in undermining weaker nations. Democracy sometimes seemed fragile by comparison. Nobody expected Communism to crumble as it did in the 1990s.

But in Vietnam, the doctrine of a limited war resulted in a protracted yet bloody conflict lasting many years. Like the French, who had previously fought against the Communists in Vietnam, American citizens grew weary of the war. The issue of Vietnam became a feeding frenzy for the liberal press and broadcast media. It eventually tore much of the nation apart and became one of the defining events, along with civil rights, of the "Sixties Generation."

Some say that we fought in Vietnam with "one arm tied behind our backs." I agree. Not only were the resources committed to the war insufficient for early victory, but as an officer in the United States Army, I was told that we were guests in a host country, South Vietnam, and that it was the South Vietnamese people's war. We were in Vietnam to help them win it. So we had to get the proper approvals from South Vietnamese officials before launching certain operations.

Many times, we would have intelligence reports indicating the location of enemy troops. But before we could attack, we had to get the okay from the regional, district, and even village leaders in the area. Some of the local leaders were sympathetic to the Vietcong. They tipped them off, and the VC would vanish. When we did get approval from officials sympathetic to our cause, it often took too long. We lost the element of surprise.

One night the men of Alpha Company were preparing to attack a VC camp in War Zone C. We had obtained the approval of the local village chief, a very superstitious elder. But just as I was about to give the order to move out, he stopped me. Looking up to the sky, he pointed to the stars. Through an interpreter, he said the stars told him not to attack. They were not in the right position for victory. I had no choice, given my orders from higher headquarters, but to obey the stars. How could anyone help South Vietnam achieve a rapid victory, fighting like that?

At the strategic level we also fought with one arm behind our backs. We assured North Vietnam that we would not invade in an attempt to win the war. And though it was often reported that we dropped more bombs in North Vietnam than were dropped on Europe in all of World War II, we avoided the very targets that might have helped destroy North Vietnam's will to continue fighting in the south. In another type of American war, like the one in the Persian Gulf or the one in Kosovo, we would have attacked North Vietnam's Red River dikes and flooded major crop-producing areas of the country and bombed its major ports and harbors, like Haiphong.

Finally, in response to intense public pressure in the early 1970s, President Nixon, the fourth president to be directly involved with the war, began to withdraw our troops. By 1973, America had turned the fighting over to the ill-prepared South Vietnamese Army. To put the best face on our withdrawal, we pretended they were ready to fight their own battles. Then Congress voted against any further military aid for South Vietnam, even though the Russians and Chinese continued to support North Vietnam and the Vietcong. Despite our official propaganda, ARVN soldiers weren't capable of defending the country against the disciplined NVA, liberally supplied with weapons and tanks. Within a year, the defense began to crumble. The South Vietnamese government controlled less and less of the country. In 1975, ten years after the first American combat troops landed in Vietnam and seven years after I was wounded there, Saigon fell to the Communists. In the rush to evacuate the U.S. embassy and the remaining Americans in the country, a few Vietnamese who had worked with or married Americans were saved. But the great majority of our supporters in Vietnam were not. In the weeks and months following the defeat of the South Vietnamese Army, thousands of South Vietnamese civilians were massacred by NVA troops and the VC. Many more were sent to "reeducation programs." Hundreds of thousands fled the country to save themselves and seek freedom elsewhere, including the United States.

Therefore, it is often said that we lost the war. The Vietnam conflict is often considered unique in the long list of American wars for a number of reasons. It is cited as the longest American war. Historians note that it was the only war without broad-based popular support. But most of all, it is called the only war that America has ever lost.

I do not agree that we lost the war. The American people just got tired of it. The war was splitting us apart. We couldn't see a clear-cut victory on the horizon anytime soon, and we didn't want to suffer more casualties.

We didn't lose the war in Vietnam. In fact, what I believe we did was abandon a besieged ally in time of need. Without our support, the South Vietnamese lost their war in a short period of time. It was their war from the start. Their war to win or lose.

When the war finally ended, over 58,000 Americans had been killed, hundreds of thousands had been wounded, and over 2,000 were missing in action. Many people still ask why? Why did we waste so many lives?

■ ■ ■

In 1967, when I first arrived in South Vietnam and saw for myself what the Communists were doing, I became convinced that our cause was a just cause. We were helping a small nation, an ally, fight Communist aggression. We were fighting a brutal enemy, who waged a sustained campaign of terror and murder aimed at unarmed civilians who supported the South Vietnamese government. We provided nonmilitary aid and support to help civilians in their daily life. It seemed to be a just cause, even if the South Vietnamese government was somewhat corrupt, even if one of the reasons for participating was to promote America's own strategic self-interest. I think that most of the soldiers alongside me in 1967 also believed that we were fighting for a just cause. And after all these years, I still believe that we tried hard to do the right thing. We just botched the job.

The values of many of the men who served with me during that year were shaped, in part, by growing up in the harmonious post–World War II fifties. America had led the Free World to victory in World War II and then helped our former enemies of Japan and Germany rebuild their war-torn countries. We grew up believing that America was a nation both invincible and generous, a nation that fought on the side of right for the good of all peoples throughout the world. We believed that we owed it to our country to fight, and perhaps give our lives, for the democratic freedoms that America stood for. That is why we became soldiers and went to war.

But it was different for the soldiers who fought later in Vietnam, over the next five years after I was evacuated. Increasingly, they had experienced the escalating divisiveness over the war even before they left the home front for Vietnam. They saw frequent, sometimes violent, protests against the war. They had watched some of the war on television. They heard the voices of many who were attempting to

247

disrupt our war efforts. Their view of the war became something very different from ours, and that made the war itself into a different war.

Morale and military discipline suffered. The Army almost came unglued. It was reported that some soldiers refused to attack the enemy when ordered to do so by their commanding officers. Other stories said that some officers were killed by their own men, victims of fragging incidents. It's often cited that an alarming number of the men who came home from Vietnam suffered severe emotional setbacks, particularly the soldiers who had seen combat.

When I first came home, in 1967, I had the approval of my family and community. And as I've said, I was able to suppress my memories of the war and turn to more positive things. Then the increasing public debates over the war and the constant stream of violent images in the media uncovered the trauma. The debate reached into my home, into my family. It was only then that the emotional toll of the war began to threaten my well-being.

Certainly soldiers who have fought in other American wars have had nightmares and terrible memories. But there is something crucial about the support of family and community in dealing with those memories and with the consciousness of having fought, faced death, and killed other human beings. A nation, a society, sends out its young people to defend itself. When they come back, they need help in being proud of what they have done. And they need to be able to talk about it, to be validated, and to be able to put it behind them. If the trauma of Vietnam is different than that of other American wars, it may be not because the combat itself was different but because the welcome home contained little pride and great amounts of condemnation.

■　■　■

I've read a lot of military history before and since 1967. Perhaps the combat in Vietnam was different than other American wars. Watching the Persian Gulf and Kosovo wars on television—choreographed symphonies of cruise missiles and smart bombs with video cameras—it would be hard to recognize combat as I knew it.

Looking back to when I graduated from college and selected the infantry as the branch of the Army to serve in, I see myself as naive, perhaps even foolish. I could have selected any of the other branches in the Army. I now wonder if I was trying to prove something to myself after the disappointment of not getting into medical school. Was I making a statement to my father, who had not served in World War II? Did my ROTC instructors in college intentionally brainwash me by promoting the infantry, the vaunted queen of battle, over the other branches of the Army? Was I unknowingly misled by veterans who never talked about the realities of combat? Did I make an emotional decision, rather than a rational one? Perhaps I should have avoided combat altogether and paid more attention to my religious teachings and to the Sixth Commandment, "Thou shalt not kill."

Killing, for the sake of killing, is not usually the objective of soldiers in combat. During World War II the primary objective for an infantry unit was to advance on the enemy to seize and hold territory. Success was measured by the hills, bridges, towns, and cities that were taken from the enemy and liberated. Killing was often necessary but as the means to the end, not the end in itself. If you could obtain your objective without killing, all the better.

It was very different in Vietnam. For an infantry commander in Vietnam, high body count was a major objective. It's what the firefights and battles were all about. Translated from bureaucratic jargon, that meant killing as many VC or NVA as possible. It was a "war of attrition." We fought to kill the enemy, seldom to capture or recapture territory. The only terrain we held for very long consisted of large base camps, like high-tech frontier forts or cowboy camps, scattered around the country. We rode out from these forts, riding helicopters, not horses, to raid and kill and then return. It was a good day when we killed more of them than they killed of us.

When you spend your time killing, even to avoid being killed, the line between right and wrong becomes blurred. Perhaps it even disappears. What's wrong in one set of circumstances seems right in another and vice versa. Do you use that much-needed helicopter to evacuate a wounded enemy soldier, or do you leave him behind to die in the jungle—in pain? Do you put him out of his misery? What's right? Wrong? There are no easy answers. You find yourself rationalizing decisions that you never thought you would be faced with, ever. Then you must live with your actions long after the war is over, when from near forgetfulness they return to haunt you.

The old war movies that my friends and I watched when we were growing up, silver images on a black-and-white screen, were very different than the war movies during and after Vietnam. The old movies romanticized war. They often portrayed combat as the hero's path to glory. Everything was simple and sanitized. There were no raw scenes depicting the blood and carnage of combat in gory Technicolor. Presidents and generals seldom made mistakes, and the cause was always just.

I think my friends and I were more innocent, relatively speaking, than kids are today. Certainly the level of graphic violence in media was much lower. There was no need for a movie rating system that labels a movie as restricted. And there was nothing at all to compare with the ultraviolent computer games of the 1990s, Doom and Quake and their competitors, rewarding teenage fanatics with bloody scenes of mayhem and dismemberment. The first time I witnessed anything remotely like the horror of war, I was right in the midst of it.

I don't know for sure what difference it would have made if I had somehow been given a preview of what combat was really like before I started on the path that led to Vietnam. Would ROTC or military training have repelled me? Would I have tried to avoid military service? Would I have served in the military but not in the infantry? Would I have been somehow better prepared emotionally? Would I have fewer of the recurring nightmares that plague me? Or would I have been simply more blasé, less human, less susceptible to the aftermath, more accepting of the violence? Would I suffer less—or perhaps more? I don't know the answer to any of these questions.

What I do know is that I was shaken to the core by what I experienced. Real war is much more horrible than a movie can ever imitate, and combat is no romantic path to glory. I pray that the movies my children and grandchildren watch, and also the books they read and the speeches they listen to, turn them against war and that they never experience it firsthand.

■   ■   ■

As I was writing this, violent turmoil on a global scale continued to prevail. An international terrorist, Osama bin Laden, bombed U.S. embassies in Kenya and Tanzania and declared war on all Americans throughout the world. We responded with missile attacks on his terrorist bases in Afghanistan. Saddam Hussein threw United Nations arms inspectors out of Iraq so that the country's war machine could continue to produce weapons of mass destruction undetected. India and Pakistan faced each other in a standoff over the testing of nuclear weapons and the status of Kashmir. Our old enemy, the North Koreans, tested long-range missiles capable of carrying nuclear warheads to Japan. The Israelis and the Palestinians were still killing each other as they continued their search for a "lasting peace." Warring factions in several African nations engaged in open genocide. Some world leaders feared that fanatical terrorist groups would soon gain possession of nuclear missiles. The Russian economy was so depressed that many feared a resurgence of Communism.

In Yugoslavia, Serbian forces, led by Slobodan Milosevic, slaughtered ethnic Albanian civilians in the breakaway province of Kosovo, as part of an ongoing campaign of "ethnic cleansing." In retaliation, NATO forces bombed Serbia and Kosovo around the clock, while hundreds of thousands of refugees fled to neighboring countries. The refugee problem was worse than any since World War II. When the bombs stopped falling, NATO peacekeeping forces moved into Kosovo, only to find themselves impotent onlookers as Serbs and Albanians, hellbent on retribution, continued to slaughter each other.

Another protracted Vietnam-like conflict, this time in the Balkans, may still be in the offing. And as the world moved into the new millennium, Russian forces fighting rebel forces, using World War II tactics, reduced much of the Chechen capital of Grozny to massive piles of rubble.

The list goes on and on—hatred and violence are ever present.

The Cold War is over, it is said, but the world is as dangerous as when I was growing up, perhaps even more so. And I don't think things will be much better five, ten, fifteen, or even twenty-five years from now. There have been periods of relative peace in history, when human beings have been tempted to think that human nature has changed and permanent peace is at hand. So far, for thousands of years, that hope has proved false.

I fear that my own progeny may one day face some of the hard decisions that I once did regarding military service. If and when it happens, I can't counsel them on whether they should serve or not serve in the armed forces. That's a decision that each one must make, based on his or her own unique past and individual values. Each one's sense of duty.

Given what I know of war, I hope that my children serve America and the world, but as pacifists, committed to nonviolence and unwilling to bear arms. But if any one of them is inducted into the military or is a volunteer I pray that he or she can avoid combat.

In modern warfare, the battles are fought by relatively few. Most of the individuals in uniform are serving in combat support positions. These are assignments where one can fulfill a patriotic duty in time of war, with a high probability of not participating directly in the fighting—and the face-to-face killing. Many opportunities exist in support areas that focus on intelligence gathering, information systems, communications, medical services, logistics, equipment repair and maintenance, legal services, staffing, and administration, among many others. These are jobs that are every bit as essential to winning a war as is winning battles. And they are also jobs where much can be learned, like technical and professional skills, team building, and leadership, that may serve an individual well, long after one has left the service.

■　■　■

It's very easy to rationalize violence and killing on behalf of some greater good or cause. Individuals, nations, and even some religions have been doing it for centuries. But it takes personal courage of the highest order to honor, at all costs, the Sixth Commandment. I didn't have that courage. Or, more accurately, I didn't even think about it. I was too intoxicated with patriotism.

There is no glory in killing, even when bloodshed may be necessary to protect our freedoms and way of life. I say this to each of my children and also to their children: If you experience ground combat and survive, you will never come home from the war—the war will come home with you.

For me to have killed, even in a war, has meant living my own life threaded with a cancer of ghosts, hungry for my soul. Searching for the good helps keep the cancer in remission, but I still know that it's there, waiting to devour me—if ever I drop my guard.

Searching for the Good

As a young Midwestern boy growing up in the fifties, I looked to my father to teach me how to do things, and he worked hard at it. He played ball with me and taught me to be a good sport. We enjoyed hunting and fishing together. He taught me how to use my fists to defend myself from bullies. He showed me how to use a hammer and a saw and how to paint the things I built, to take pride in them. He taught me how to plant vegetables in our garden and to nurture them until the harvest. He showed me how to care for the hogs, chickens, and ducks we raised. I learned how to chop and stack wood. He often said, "You can tell a lot about a man by the way he stacks his wood."

Like others who grew up during the Great Depression, my father also preached the importance of hard work and self-discipline. And he stressed that no matter what the task or job, I should do my best, even if I didn't enjoy what I was doing. When I completed a chore like cutting the grass, cleaning the pigpens, or painting a fence, he always took the time to show me how I could do a better job.

Now, many years later, I know that much of what I learned from my father shaped my course. It determined who I am and what I am. His teachings served me well in the Army, even though he had never been in the armed forces himself. But perhaps the most important thing he taught me was how to deal

with life when it gets hard: "Life is difficult and full of trials and tribu-
lations, and no matter how bad things get, always *search for the good*
in your experiences and use what you find to help block out the bad."

Searching for Charlie in Vietnam and living with the aftermath is
about as bad as it gets for me. So I spend a lot of my time searching
for the good in that war and that experience. While this may seem futile, even masochistic to some, finding the good helps me cope with
all the bad. It helps me keep the ghosts away.

■　■　■

When I search for the good in the Vietnam War, I still see American soldiers risking their lives while trying to win the hearts and
minds of the South Vietnamese people. I remember brave young
Wolfhounds on those MEDCAP missions, treating the sick and injured
peasants in remote jungle villages, giving shots, applying medications,
dressing open sores. I see soldiers on the Helping-Hands missions distributing food and clothing to little children. I remember the GIs who
rebuilt schools, churches, roads, and water sources in villages ravaged
by years of war. I see the smiles of Vietnamese children when I gave
them small valentine cards sent to me in a package from home.

I see selfless Wolfhounds dashing through volleys of enemy gunfire to grab a child and rush him or her to cover. And I remember that
old mamasan who showed me where the VC had placed mines. I also
see Army doctors and nurses working tirelessly at the 12th Evac trying
to save the lives of young men fighting a war far from home.

When looking for the good, I recall why I served in the Army—
to protect the American way of life, as had many before me, and to
help our allies defend themselves against Communist aggression. I
think of the many Vietnamese boat people who fled the Communists
at the end of the war and came to America in search of freedom and
opportunity.

I consider the good impact the Vietnam War has had on many of
our policymakers. Since the war, on many occasions they have been
more cautious about committing American ground troops to do battle on foreign soil.

I owe my continual gratitude for the small pleasures and comforts of life to my tour of duty in Vietnam. In the field, we often endured conditions that were extremely unpleasant. We went days without washing, shaving, or brushing teeth. During the dry season, our sweat-stained jungle fatigues got washed only when we walked through a river or stream. During the monsoon, the downpour rinsed the mud and sweat off us and our fatigues while we were wearing them. Sometimes we went days with little or no sleep at all. When I did sleep, I was often crunched down in a tiny foxhole or makeshift CP bunker with a radio handset propped against my ear. I even learned to catch a few winks standing up in swamp water or leaning against rice paddy dikes. We had oozing sores all over our bodies from mosquitoes, ants, bugs, leeches, thorns, and brambles. We seldom took a step without thinking it could be our last.

As a result, and after all these years, I still find intense pleasure in things I took completely for granted before Vietnam. A warm soap-sudsy shower, fluffy clean clothes, a good night's rest in a soft bed, and a whisker-free chin are still coveted luxuries. I don't have to eat fine cuisine to be happy. Home-cooked anything is better than C rations in the field. The chirping of birds, a babbling brook, and the rustling of leaves in the woods are as symphonies to me. The quiet before dawn: a closeness to God. And at sunrise, a reminder of a new day that I'm still alive. Like individuals with a life-threatening illness, I don't take much in life for granted anymore, even life itself. Each day that I'm alive, even the days punctuated with pain, I try to remember to thank God for the day and, corny as it sounds, to hug those I love.

■ ■ ■

People sometimes say to me: "It must have been terrible to get wounded in Vietnam." I tell them that it's one of the best things that ever happened to me. It brought me home from the war alive. It even gave me a successful career. As far-fetched as it may at first seem, I credit serving in Vietnam and being wounded with getting me in on the ground floor of the computer industry.

In May of 1966, on my return from Gelnhausen, Dow Corning

offered me a position in Industrial Sales or Professional Personnel. The offer came one week before I was retained on active duty. If I had been released from active duty at that time, I would have taken one of those typical entry-level positions. It wasn't until September 1967 that the company created the EIS project manager position that I accepted when I finally began work. This was well over a year after the May 1966 offer and just a few weeks before my return from Vietnam. It was the only systems development position in the Personnel Department. To meet internal objectives, the company needed to fill the position by the end of October 1967. Then I showed up, just at the right time.

Had I not been wounded in July 1967, evacuated from Vietnam, and then released from the Army in October, I would have missed out on the crucial opportunity that made my career. If someone were to argue that this is all rationalization of the highest order, I wouldn't disagree. But that's how I think of it. It's how I have to think of it.

■ ■ ■

Yet another good that I find is the training I received. The Army's leadership training gave me the concepts and confidence that helped me do well in each of the civilian positions I have held. I learned and practiced the principles of leadership, including respect for the chain of command, loyalty, and a strong commitment to mission and the welfare of those under me and to setting the example. The same principles enabled me as a civilian, to forge strong teams and get things done. As a result I moved more quickly into positions of greater responsibility, gaining valuable experience on a fast-track basis. That experience gave me the confidence to start my own company.

Usertech, the company I founded in 1979 with Penny, creates user training and knowledge transfer programs needed by large corporations when they implement new information systems. Again, it was in the Army that I acquired a working knowledge of the instructional design process and its relationship to excellence in training. I learned the importance of establishing learning objectives that were essential to an organization's mission. I gained valuable experience in designing and delivering modular, audience-specific training programs with competency-based objectives. With the help of my platoon leaders and sergeants, I was able to take individual soldiers, with no knowledge about their jobs, to high levels of competency. The same process helped Usertech's team of professionals train thousands of employees at hundreds of companies, creating confidence and competency, helping those organizations enter the computer age.

Leadership training and experience gave me the confidence to start my own company. But it was the instructional design experience that gave us the tools to help take Usertech to a position of excellence in its marketplace.

■ ■ ■

In combat, situations change abruptly, dramatically. The shooting comes from the right, then the left, then behind. It may stop and then start again. There are more attackers, or defenders, than you thought. The enemy takes out your automatic weapons. All around you, the earth explodes. You lose communications. Leaders can be wounded or killed at the worst possible time. Suddenly you're cut off. You can't get choppers in. The enemy is too close in for artillery support. You're winning, then losing, then winning again. Accomplishing the mission and the survival of your force depend on quick and repetitive estimates of the situation. You have to know your soldiers, show unrelenting resourcefulness, take risks and decisive action, and generate high esprit de corps among the troops.

At Usertech, our strategies were different than in the Army. We used industry knowledge, technical skill, aggressive sales, and outstanding customer service to accomplish our mission. But the challenges and tactics were often the same. In the battle to win customers, a situation can shift unexpectedly. Your business is threatened by first one competitor, then another, each perhaps with bolder tactics, lower prices, better marketing. Customer requirements change; budgets stay fixed; deadlines are moved up, then back again. Key employees get sick or are needed elsewhere. If the sale isn't made, people may need to be laid off. I found the similarities in what it takes as a leader to help win a battle in combat and to win a customer in the high-tech marketplace to be uncanny.

Many people start a company, because they want to be their own boss and they believe passionately in their company's product or service. The same was true for Penny and me. But as I search for the good that came from starting our company, I see more. We created jobs for people. Jobs with salaries that people could count on for improving their standard of living and helping them start or raise families—and also for paying taxes. And taxes fund government programs for education, medical research, crime prevention, and national defense, among many others. I like to think there is a great amount of good that has come from starting our company, one that my experience in the Army helped us to build.

■　　■　　■

In 1976, less than a year after the official end to the "American War" in Vietnam, I went to Paris, ostensibly on business. But my personal mission was to seek out former Vietcong or North Vietnamese soldiers visiting or living in Paris. With the war finally over, I wanted to meet the enemy and talk with him, soldier to soldier, about the war. I wanted to see what good might come from the encounter. I wanted to test my belief that enemy combat soldiers were like most American combat soldiers, ordinary and decent individuals doing terrible things because of the bloody reality of ground combat. In a way, I was still searching for Charlie.

On the day before my departure from Paris, I wandered from bar to bar through the Vietnamese section of the city, hoping to find what I was searching for. I didn't know what to expect. Late in the evening, just as I was about to give up, I went into a small dimly lit cafe.

Two men were standing at the tiny bar, just inside the door. They were about five feet tall. Their snub noses, high cheekbones, coal-black hair, and height told me that they were probably Vietnamese. My gut told me they were, or had been, soldiers. I approached them and tried to introduce myself. Initially, we had difficulty understanding each other. They spoke Vietnamese, French, and a small amount of English, and I only English and a few words of Vietnamese. But with the help of the bartender, who spoke French and English, I learned that they had fought against the Americans and South Vietnamese.

Both of the men were from North Vietnam. "Comrade" Nguyen's father had been killed fighting the French at Dien Bien Phu. "Comrade" Dong came from a family of scholars in Hanoi. In 1965, soon after the Americans sent ground forces to Vietnam, they had infiltrated the south to join the Front for the Liberation of South Vietnam (the Vietcong).

The two of them spoke of many years of hardship moving from hideout to hideout in the jungle. They lived on wild vegetables and fruit, small amounts of rice and fish, bugs and insects, and an occasional, much-sought-after monkey or wild boar. They had fought in many battles, endured artillery barrages and bombings, and watched many of their comrades die. They feared daily for their lives. Each had been wounded, Dong several times.

Both were willing to die in the struggle to reunite Vietnam, to bring honor on themselves, their fallen comrades, and to "Uncle Ho." And at one time they were prepared to fight for ten, twenty, even fifty years if necessary to beat the Americans and their "puppet government" in the south. But now that the war was over and the fighting ended, they wondered how much good would come of it all.

We drank together and we talked, using the bartender as interpreter, until the early morning hours. We talked of the war, the weapons we used, and specific battles. We may have fought against each other in the Iron Triangle, but much of the time was spent talking about our families, our education, and our governments. We showed pictures of our children, wives, or girlfriends. We loosened our clothing and showed our battle scars.

Midway through the night, a Portuguese soldier, on leave from his army, joined us, and then two ex-soldiers from Senegal. The more wine and beer we all drank, the more soldierly camaraderie we shared, the more alike we seemed. It didn't matter what countries we were from, what languages we spoke, or what the color of our skin was. We had all suffered great hardship and fear and danger, longed for loved ones at home, and nurtured dreams for the future. None of us wanted to kill, but we had no choice.

We agreed that it was as easy to get drunk on patriotism as to get drunk on alcohol. At dawn, we toasted each other and cursed our respective governments for sending us off to war. We held our glasses high and shouted, *"No more wars."* Then we hugged, shook hands, and parted. I stumbled, through an early morning mist, back to the Boulevard Saint Germain and the little Left Bank hotel I was staying in.

Later in the day, with my head pounding and with little sleep, I thought about the realities of war. Politicians make the wars. It's not the men who shed blood on the battlefield who make war. It's politicians, far from the battlefield and safe, who use others for *their* noble causes. They are the ones who put Nguyen, Dong, and me into savage situations where we had no alternative but to kill each other. Were we mere pawns?

I left Paris confused, ambivalent, with good and bad feelings at war inside me. The bad feelings were aimed at politicians and governments, everywhere, that organize battles and mismanage diplomacy and brainwash patriots into believing that killing is honorable. I still felt proud to have served my country, yet increasingly angry that I had perhaps been used as cannon fodder.

My good feelings were of respect, compassion, and forgiveness towards the enemy soldiers whom I had at one time faced and fought on the ground in Vietnam.

■　■　■

As I've continued my search for the good, Penny has in her quiet way helped me more than anyone else. On Veterans Day 1978, soon after we married, I came home from work feeling down and out about my war. As I entered the house, I was met by the smells of one of Penny's gourmet meals. She and the children from my first marriage, Caroline, Suzanne, Kristin, and Stacey, were waiting for me in the dining room, sitting around the table. I could tell they were hiding something from me.

As we finished eating, Penny excused herself for a minute and returned while announcing, "Surprise!" She was carrying a carrot cake, my favorite, decorated with the words "Happy Veteran's Day, Dad." I got all teary-eyed when she and the children said, "Thanks for being a veteran." Then I opened presents.

To this day, Penny and our two children who are still at home, Topher and Annie, continue the tradition. The gift I cherish most is the Franklin Mint's miniature bronze statue of the three GIs at the Vietnam Veterans Memorial.

Penny and I have never had a significant conversation about the war. She is too honest and has too much integrity to make gratuitous comments about events that she doesn't fully understand. Instead, on those occasions when I'm tormented by memories of the war and talk about it, she quietly listens. Sometimes she touches me on my hand or shoulder, sometimes she hugs me. Then the hurt goes away.

Back in the early seventies, there were many reports in the media about Vietnam vets being ashamed of their service awards and medals. Some were reported to have thrown them away or returned them. I don't know how many men who truly *earned* combat decorations were involved in such behavior, but I suspect the numbers were blown out of proportion. Nonetheless, it's easy for me to understand their frustration and anger.

In 1986, we moved to a home in Connecticut that has a small study with a glass display case built into some bookshelves. At first, I didn't know what to use it for. I thought about displaying my combat decorations, but I was hesitant. Up until then, I had kept the medals packed in a cardboard box hidden away in our basement. I had never been ashamed of those medals. But I just didn't feel right about displaying them. The war was so divisive, and I didn't know how people would react. I also thought that seeing the medals might trigger unpleasant flashbacks in my own mind.

Penny encouraged me to put them in the display case. It was a big change. All our visitors could see them. I could see them every day. And I don't think that they have yet to cause nightmares. Do the medals destroy the ghosts of Vietnam? No. But they help keep them at bay. They remind me that years ago, I took a stand for what I believed in, something beyond self-indulgence and material gain, and that I risked my life with other men, fighting for a cause. They remind me that I was tested—that I've experienced a great deal of emotional pain. But in spite of it all, I still believe in my country and the democratic principles that we were fighting for.

■   ■   ■

As I continue my search for the good, I often think of the Vietnam veterans that have suffered severe psychological setbacks because of their combat experience. Some have dropped out of society completely. Some are said to be hopeless alcoholics. Many are homeless. Some have committed suicide. They may not have come home in a body bag, but their spirits died in the service to their country. I often pray for them. I was lucky to have a father who gave me a weapon to help fight the pain. Because of that good fortune, and the love of Penny and my children, I've survived the aftermath of Vietnam when many others have not. We cannot forget them. For even though their names do not appear on the wall at the Vietnam Veterans Memorial, they, too, have made the supreme sacrifice.

Epilogue

On the morning of Veterans Day 1999, I stood high up on the top steps of the Lincoln Memorial. In the distance, due east, stood the Washington Monument. Closer at hand, looking northeast, was the black slash of the Vietnam Veterans Memorial. A light rain was falling from a threatening sky like a gray shield overhead. Blowing from the north, a brisk wind made the fall air seem like an arctic blast. Small droplets of icy rain pricked at my face, and I could feel the cold dampness begin to penetrate my fleece vest. It's nearly eleven o'clock, I thought. Will I recognize him? Will he be able to recognize me?

Nearer to the memorial, groups of uniformed veterans meandered through Constitutional Gardens on the National Mall. Some carried unit banners and U.S. flags. Tourist groups, scouts, school groups, Gold Star Mothers, and solitary individuals from all walks of life mixed with the vets. Many of the visitors carried wreaths or bouquets of flowers. The kaleidoscopic procession of people and flowers, snaking slowly towards the memorial, was in sharp contrast to the gray and moisture-laden clouds. Somewhere beyond the massive crowd, I could hear a lonely bagpiper, shrill and beckoning.

Despite the foul weather, people had come from far and wide. Some came to mourn the loss of a family member or a buddy. Some came to remember. They all had come to honor veterans of the Vietnam War and to pay their respects to the more than 58,000 names chiseled into the black granite memorial known as the Wall. Standing alone in the shivering cold I watched the solemn spectacle unfolding. All the while I wondered, Will I be able to find him in the crowd? Will we recognize each other?

Three weeks earlier, I had opened an unexpected letter from the past. I had just recently joined the 25th Infantry Division Association, hoping that being on the association's Internet roster would connect me to men I had served with. But so soon!

The letter was from Steve Ehart. As a young lieutenant, he served with me and Alpha Company in Vietnam. He was the platoon leader for Alpha's third platoon. Courageous and cool under fire, he could always be relied on when the going got tough. We had not spoken to each other in over thirty-two years. The last time I had seen Steve was on July 9, 1967. He was waving me off as the dustoff helicopter lifted my wounded body up and away from the battlefield near LZ Zulu. I had difficulty believing that after so many years I had been thrown a lifeline, one that could connect me to someone who was there on the ground in Vietnam in that year, 1967. Someone who would understand. Someone who might even care.

"Tom—Greetings from an old subordinate," the letter began. It went on, "I saw your name and address in a recent copy of the 25th Infantry Division Association newsletter, *Flashes*, and thought you might get a kick out of these old photos. Doug Colliander (Alpha One-Six) sent me a bunch of pictures a couple of years back. These were in there. . . ." I could feel a lump forming in my throat. Reading on, I learned that Colliander, the leader of Alpha Company's first platoon in 1967, had survived Vietnam and recently died of a heart attack while mowing his lawn in Minneapolis. Colliander was also with me the day I was wounded. Like Steve he was an outstanding young officer. And I also read that First Sergeant Rutledge, Alpha's top noncommissioned officer, had recently died of complications from heart surgery. Rutledge was one of the finest noncommissioned officers I had ever served with.

The letter ended: "Hope all is well with you, and that these pictures bring back some good memories. Warm Regards, Steve Ehart." After looking at the pictures of a very young me standing next to the Second Battalion, 27th Infantry Wolfhounds sign in Cu Chi base camp, I found myself in a trance. My thoughts drifted in a dreamlike state, floating back to Vietnam, then fast-forwarded to the present.

I read the letter again and again. But strange as it may seem, I hesitated before sending Steve a response other than a polite thank-you note. I thought to myself, Do I really want to do this? I'd looked at writing *Searching for the Good* as a way to help bring some closure to my war experience. It had been a catharsis. And I think, therapeutic. Picking up with Steve where we had left off in 1967 seemed like risky business. Most of my memories of Vietnam are not good memories. I didn't know what might happen or where my emotions would take me. But I decided to forge ahead anyway, to see what would happen. After all, I said to myself, that is why I joined the 25th's association. And though my memories of the war are often painful, the memories of the men I served with are extremely positive.

I finally sent a letter to Steve with some pictures of my own. In my letter, I thanked him for writing and suggested that we get together, either when he was in my neck of the woods or I in his. I also asked that he bring me up to date on his life since Vietnam.

A few days later Steve's second letter arrived. He had stayed in the Army and retired in 1986 as a lieutenant colonel. His twenty-year career included a return in the early 1970s to Vietnam with the 173rd Airborne Brigade. And not long after his retirement he was recalled to active duty during the Persian Gulf War. Now Steve is a PGA golf professional living and working in Woodstock, Virginia. He has recently become quite active in the 25th Infantry Division Association and the Wolfhound Pack the 27th Infantry Wolfhounds' association for veterans.

The day before I received the second letter, I had receiv e-mail from Steve: "Good morning Alpha Six!" In the e-mail, b me to join him at the Wall in Washington, D.C., on Vetera a pretty neat time if you haven't been [to the Wall], and r kind of good to be a Vet. . . . No pressure intended, b' invite you along, if it works for you. Later . . . Alph

Two weeks later, there I was in Washin' shivering cold just a few steps from the · Abraham Lincoln. My heart was beating ' started slowly down the steps on my w my doubts about how I could handle the emotional impact of seeing Steve again. I told myself, I can leave now and later e-mail Steve, tell him I was there but couldn't find him. No, I thought, I can do this. Then at the bottom of the steps, I had only a short distance to go. I hesitated again, then proceeded to the memorial.

We were to meet at eleven o'clock at the bronze statue of three soldiers looking towards the Wall. As I made my way to the statue, I tried to anticipate what the day would bring. Steve had stayed in the Army and even returned to Vietnam for a second tour. I got out as fast as I could and tried to put the Vietnam experience behind me. Our lives since leaving Vietnam seemed to me to be very different. But are they? I asked myself. Perhaps not—we do have a strong common bond.

I worked my way through the dense crowd to the statue. Wearing only civvies, I felt out of place. I had discarded all of my old army threads during one of my "I want to forget" episodes back in 1970. Now I wished I hadn't done so. Most of the veterans were wearing uniforms, jungle fatigues, or some piece of distinctive garb that identified the unit they had served with in Vietnam. Many had on bush hats or ball caps with unit insignia, rank, and various other medals pinned on. Some of the vets were in wheelchairs, some on crutches. There was even a detachment of South Vietnamese and Laotian soldiers wearing camouflage fatigues. They held a large unfurled black-and-white banner that read "CIA—Do Not Forget Us." To me, they seemed very out of place.

I looked for Steve. We had made arrangements via e-mail a few days earlier. He would be wearing blue jeans, a blue Wolfhound ball cap, a black Wolfhound T-shirt over a turtleneck sweater, and a light sleeveless vest. And as agreed, I was in khaki trousers with a plaid shirt and a blue sleeveless fleece vest, and I would carry a black backpack to help him spot me. All around the statue, people were meeting and greeting each other. I looked and waited for what seemed like an eternity, but was only a few minutes. Still no Steve. Then, from behind, I heard a loud shout: "You must be Alpha Six." I turned. There he was. "Steve," I yelled. "Tom," he responded. We hugged. "I can't believe it's you," I said with tears in my eyes. The next few minutes were so emotional for me that I can't remember what we said. Then Steve suggested that we find a bench, sit down, and bring each other up to date. We had two hours until the official Veterans Day ceremonies were scheduled to begin.

We talked and we talked. The words came easily. It was fun. It was emotional. And as the years we had been apart were stitched together with our personal stories, I could see that Steve and I were more alike than unlike. We had fought together as young men, survived the crucible of ground combat, and suffered the aftermath. We each understood what the other had experienced. Our attitudes about the war were similar. But most important, we cared for each other, like brothers. After two hours of updating and reminiscing, it was as though we had never been apart. And for me there was a sense of redemption.

Steve's mother, a generous giver to the Vietnam War Memorial Fund, Inc., gave us VIP tickets for the formal ceremonies at the Wall. We had near-front-row seats. So we took temporary leave from our personal reunion and found our way to the show. John McDermott, an internationally renowned performing artist, was singing Irish folk ballads. I could feel an overwhelming sadness in the damp cold air as the tenor's haunting lyrics pulled at my heart. All eyes were fixed on the black slabs with over 58,000 names staring back at us. I tried to hold back the tears but couldn't. How could I—how could anyone—hide grief when looking at so many names of individuals cut down in the prime of their lives? And each of them had made the supreme sacrifice in a war that most Americans would rather forget.

Jan C. Scruggs, a fellow infantryman, the president of the Vietnam War Memorial Fund and the individual most responsible for getting the memorial built, was the master of ceremonies. We witnessed the presenting of the colors, the Pledge of Allegiance, the retiring of the colors, the invocation, and the welcome. There were several moving speeches, including one by Diane Carlson Evans, the founder of the Vietnam Women's Memorial Project, and a keynote by Heather French, Miss America 2000, whose own father is a disabled Vietnam War veteran. We heard two more songs by McDermott: "Danny Boy" and "The Wall," a song written by the singer himself. A bagpiper played "Amazing Grace." We watched the wreath laying and stayed to end the ceremony, a tribute to the fallen: a lone bugler atop the vertex of the Wall playing Taps in the drizzling rain. More tears.

The last American soldiers left Vietnam almost twenty-five years before the ceremony on that day in November 1999. Yet one might have thought, from the outpouring of emotion, that the war had just ended. Several years before I had received, as a gift, the Collins Publishers 1987 edition of *The Wall, Images and Offerings from the Vietnam Veterans Memorial*. On the inside cover of the book, it's written that "the Vietnam War Memorial has become America's wailing wall." And so it seemed to me on Veterans Day 1999. I can think of no better way to describe it.

When the formal ceremonies ended, we stood silent for a few minutes, alone with our thoughts. Then as the crowd dispersed, we linked up with Bob Babcock, an old ROTC buddy of Steve's, who had served as a platoon leader in the Fourth Infantry Division in Vietnam. Our small group hung out at the memorial for another half hour or so, talking with Gold Star Mothers, taking pictures, and meeting other comrades in arms from 25th Division and Wolfhound units. Then we visited the Vietnam Women's Memorial, where I met and spoke with Diane Carlson Evans.

I told Diane the story of the two nurses who had helped protect me and the other wounded during the mortar attack on the 12th Evac. While speaking with her, I had the strange feeling that I was in some way connecting with the nurses who had been with me during the attack. Perhaps it was a genuine warmth and sincerity that I sensed in Diane, born of her own experiences as a nurse in Vietnam. I choked up several times during our brief visit.

After my visit with Diane, we decided to get some antifreeze into our blood before we all became stacks of ice. I'm not sure if it was the weather or if it was all the emotions that I had experienced over the previous four hours, but I was ready for a drink. Steve led us to a favorite watering hole, a T.G.I. Friday's restaurant, near the campus of George Washington University and just a few blocks from the memorial.

The hostess seated us without delay. It was three o'clock. And after we ordered burgers and the first of many rounds of drinks, the war stories—most of them true—started flying fast and furious. The strangest of all the stories we heard that day is very true and stranger than fiction.

While Steve and I served with Alpha Company, a young man named Frank Clouse was a member of Steve's platoon. But Clouse was not Clouse, he was Paul Mahar, a boyhood best friend of Frank Clouse. When Clouse, who was serving in the Army at the time, received orders for Vietnam, he went AWOL rather than leave his wife and go to war, where he could die. If he'd been caught, he would have gone to jail and ruined his life and career. Instead, he and his friend Paul Mahar concocted a scheme that would keep Clouse's record clean.

They switched identities. Mahar donned Clouse's uniform, destroyed his ID card, and reported to Fort Dix, New Jersey. The plan was to tell the Army that he was Clouse and that he had lost his ID card. Then the Army would declare him ineligible for combat because he had a metal pin in his left arm that the Army missed during his induction physical exam. In fact, Mahar had tried to join the Army with Clouse but was declared 4-F because of the pin in his arm.

As they say, the best laid plans. The Army bought the story that Mahar was Clouse. But he was told he had to go to Vietnam in spite of the pin in his arm. So Mahar, who had not received a single day of Army training, shipped out for Vietnam, where he was assigned to Alpha Company 2/27 Infantry Wolfhounds. He served his time in our front-line unit with honor, was decorated for courage, and came home unharmed—as Sergeant Frank Clouse.

Back in 1967 none of us knew Clouse was not Clouse but instead was Paul Mahar. By 1994, after Mahar had decided to come clean with his story, it was featured in the press and on network television. The television show included several snapshots of Mahar as Clouse, provided by Sergeant Gary Pearse, Steve Ehart's platoon sergeant in Vietnam.

Steve had just recently learned of the big switch after talking with Alfred "Luke" Serna, a squad leader with Steve's platoon. One of the snapshots shown on television was a picture of Mahar sitting on an Army cot with then Sergeant Luke Serna. A plea went out for anyone who recognized Serna or Clouse (Mahar) to contact NBC. And as luck would have it, Serna's sister saw the program. She called Luke, who then contacted the network to provide information for a follow-up to the original story.

But there was another story I heard over those drinks at T.G.I. Friday's that would prove even more extraordinary for me. Bob Babcock and Steve were talking about another ROTC buddy of theirs named Calvin Neptune. As a second lieutenant in the Medical Services Corps (MSC), he had served in 1967 with the 25th Division. Steve commented that he had heard that Neptune had been hit by a mortar outside his hootch in base camp and sent back to the United States.

I interrupted the conversation to tell Steve and Bob about the mortar attack on Cu Chi base camp that I describe in the chapter titled "Why?" I couldn't believe my ears. Was it possible that Cal Neptune was the same MSC lieutenant whose name I had forgotten? Is he the person with the fictitious name, Lieutenant Donald Young, whom I refer to in several chapters. Could he be the one who was with me on that horrible night, March 15, 1967, when Cu Chi base camp was mortared? Is he still alive? He couldn't be. The medics told me that the lieutenant I helped to the aid station was dying. For thirty-two years I assumed that he was dead. And for thirty-two years I have felt guilty for it being him and not me that took most of the shrapnel from the shell burst.

It was too coincidental. There just couldn't be two MSC lieutenants hit by a mortar round during the same month and in the same manner. Particularly since Army regulations authorized that only one be assigned to an infantry battalion like the Second Battalion, 27th Infantry Wolfhounds. I had to learn the answers to my questions: Was Cal Neptune the MSC lieutenant who was with me on March 15, and is he still alive?

But at T.G.I. Friday's that night, talk wound down. We decided to head home. Steve and I were the last to leave. It was past nine in the evening. We had been talking for over six hours. After finding our way with some difficulty to Washington's Foggy Bottom Station, we took trains in opposite directions, both heading for home, Steve's in Virginia, mine in Connecticut. What had started as a melancholy day, filled with the sadness over the thought of the Vietnam War and the lives it took and wrecked, ended on a very high note. I had experienced my first reunion with an old Army buddy and it felt good. Very good. I could tell that we would pick up where we left off many years ago. In fact, we already had. And we both now know that we will be there for each other in time of need—twenty-four hours a day, seven days a week—just as we had been there for each other thirty-two years earlier, fighting to survive in the green jungles and rice paddies of Vietnam.

After returning home from Washington, I was eager to contact Cal Neptune. Steve and I exchanged e-mails. He suggested that I access the Wolfhound Pack's website and search through the Headquarters Company partial roster of veterans who had served in Vietnam. He thought Cal's name would appear with a link to his personal e-mail address. I accessed the Web site and searched through the roster. Sure enough, they were there, I found his name and e-mail address.

Then I sent an e-mail to Neptune:

> "Calvin, for a very brief time in Nam I was the hootch mate with an MSC Lt. who was hit badly during a mortar attack that took place on March 15, 1967. The first rounds landed very near our hootch. As I recall, I helped him to the aid station where I got sick seeing how bad the Lt. was hit. . . . I never saw him again and was told he died. Are you that person? I hope so."

The next day I received an e-mail response from Cal:

> "Wow! What a surprise message. Yes, I am that MSC 2Lt. who was with you that night, Mar. 15, 1967. And yes I was/am one fortunate person. I thank you and everyone else that got me the care I needed. . . . Initially, the blood loss I experienced was the first threat to life, so the doc said. So your and everyone's timely action surely saved my life. . . ."

I still had trouble believing that Cal was alive. But there it was in black and white. He had spent almost a year in Fitsimmons Army General Hospital before being released with a medical profile that prevented certain assignments. Like Steve, Cal stayed in the Army as a career. Now retired, he is in private practice in the Denver area doing psychological counseling. We correspond on a regular basis over the Internet.

For many years, I have felt a strong sense of guilt thinking that Cal was dead. I still feel very bad about the pain, suffering, and long convalescence that he must have endured. But the guilt over his death is now gone. One of the demons of the war has been slain— with the help of an old Army buddy, the Internet, and America Online.

I don't know how many more chapters there will be in the story of my reunion with Steve—and the good that will come from it. But I'm confident that there will be many more and a great deal of good. Through him, I have already made contact with my battalion commander in Vietnam, now a retired three-star general; two of the sergeants, Alfred "Luke" Serna and Gary Pearse, who served with Steve and me; and, of course, Cal Neptune. Our network is expanding. And, as we enter the new millennium, each of us is attempting to contact as many Wolfhounds as possible. The Wolfhound Pack is planning a large reunion in mid-September 2000 in St. Louis. Many of us plan to be there, together again.

Each time that I encounter someone with whom I served in combat, I sense a profound healing process. Yes, it was a lousy war. But that reality loses its painful grip on me when I reunite with fellow comrades in arms—and I see anew the quality of the men who fought alongside me. I remember our dedication to cause and to our country. But above all else, I remember the dedication and love we had for each other during that sad war in a far-off place called Vietnam.

Glossary

4-F: A military classification designating that an individual is exempt from military service for physical or medical reasons

Airborne: A military term used to describe troops or units that enter a field of battle by parachuting from an airplane

Air Strike: An attack by military aircraft, fighters and bombers; often done in support of ground troops

AK-47: The assault rifle designed by the Russians and used against the Americans by the North Vietnamese and Vietcong

Alpha: The Army's designation for the letter "A," as used in Alpha Company for Company A; also used as the abbreviation for Alpha Company

Alpha Company: Company A in an infantry battalion

Alpha Six: The radio call sign for the company commander of Alpha Company

Ambush: A surprise attack launched from heavily concealed positions; generally on a column of troops moving on a trail, on a road, or through a valley

Ann-Margret: A popular and shapely American singer and actress who accompanied Bob Hope on tour in Cu Chi, South Vietnam, to entertain members of the 25th Division; also a portion of the 25th Division's base camp defensive perimeter named in honor of the actress

AO: The abbreviated form of *Area of Operations*

Ao Dai: The traditional long and snug-fitting silk garment worn by Vietnamese women

APC: An armored personnel carrier; a box-shaped, heavily armored tracked vehicle with a top-mounted .50-caliber machine gun; used to transport troops in a mechanized infantry unit

AR-15: A small full-automatic rifle, similar to a submachine gun, used by some American infantrymen in lieu of the M-16

Arc Light: The code name used in Vietnam for a B-52 bomber attack

Area of Operations: A geographical area assigned, by higher headquarters, to an Army unit in which it conducts military operations; abbreviated as *AO*

ARVN: The South Vietnamese Army; officially named the Army of the Republic of Vietnam

AWOL: Absent without Leave; an unauthorized absence from an assigned place of duty; results in a disciplinary action, sometimes severe

B-24 Liberator: A long-range bomber plane used by the Americans in Europe and the Pacific during World War II

B-52: The high-altitude bomber plane used extensively by the Americans during the Vietnam War for bombing Vietcong and North Vietnamese sanctuaries and invasion routes

Bamh Bamh: Slang for Vietnamese beer

Battalion: A military unit, normally commanded by a lieutenant colonel, consisting of a headquarters and four or more companies of approximately 160 soldiers each

Battery: A unit in an artillery battalion; similar to an infantry company, but with fewer soldiers

Beachhead: A secure area of beach established after an attack by an amphibious landing force

Beaucoup: Many or a lot, as in beaucoup Vietcong; also spelled boo coo

Bennett, Tony: A very popular American male vocalist during last half of the twentieth century

Bird Dog: Military slang for an L-19 (also O-1E) light, single-engine airplane used in Vietnam to locate targets for tactical air strikes; propeller driven

Body Bag: A plastic bag used to carry troops killed in action from the field

Booby Trap: A cleverly designed hidden device, usually an explosive, such as a hand grenade or land mine that is activated by a trip wire or pressure-sensitive blasting cap; used extensively by the Vietcong to kill or maim American troops

Boom-Boom: Slang for quick sex

Brigade: An American military unit, normally commanded by a full colonel, with a headquarters and three or more battalions

Buck Sergeant: A sergeant with three stripes; lowest in rank of sergeants

Bunker: A reinforced camouflaged shelter, partially or all underground, from which troops fire on advancing enemy troops; other bunkers are used solely for protection against bombing or artillery attacks

C-4: A very powerful plastic explosive detonated with a fuse and blasting cap

Cape Canaveral: The site on the east coast of Florida from which the National Aeronautics and Space Administration (NASA) launches rockets for space exploration

Castro, Fidel: The anti-American Communist dictator who came to power in Cuba in 1959

Chagres River: A large river in Panama that is part of the Panama Canal route

Charlie: Slang for the VC (Vietcong); taken from "Victor Charlie," the Army's phonetic designation for VC used in radio communications

Chevy: Slang used extensively in the fifties for a Chevrolet automobile produced by General Motors Corporation

Chicom: Chinese Communist, as in Chicom grenade; usually refers to weapons produced by China and supplied to the Vietcong or North Vietnamese Army

Chopper: GI slang for a helicopter

CIA: The American Central Intelligence Agency; allegedly played a significant role during the Vietnam War by sponsoring covert operations against the North Vietnamese

Civvies: Army slang for civilian clothes

Claymore Mine: A powerful aboveground antipersonnel mine, detonated with an electric charge by a soldier; usually used in front of a defensive position or during an ambush

Cluster Bombs: Small baseball-size bombs, released in large clusters, that filter down through heavy vegetation over a wide area before detonating; used extensively in Vietnam by the Americans

CO: Commanding Officer

Cold War: The period of time between the end of World War II and the early 1990s, during which there was intense hostility between the Communist allies led by the USSR, known as the Eastern Bloc, and the democratic nations led by the United States, known as the Western Bloc; the period has been characterized as one of the most dangerous in world history because of the nuclear arms race and the potential for the destruction of humankind in an all-out nuclear war

Combat Air Assault: An insertion, using helicopters, of combat infantry troops into an AO; often led by a company officer, usually a captain or a lieutenant

Command Post: The location in a defensive perimeter or during offensive operations from which the senior commander directs the action; abbreviated as *CP*

Communist: One who believes in Communism or the teachings of Karl Marx; used generally to describe the people, soldiers, and armies of Communist nations who were the enemies of freedom during the Cold War

Company: An American military unit commanded by a captain consisting, at full strength, of four platoons of forty soldiers each; usually identified by a letter of the alphabet, such as Company A, B, C, or D, and also by Alpha, Bravo, Charlie, or Delta Company; in Vietnam, a company was often understrength and operated with only two or three platoons

Company Commander: The officer who commands a company; usually a captain; sometimes called "the old man"

Company-Grade: As in company-grade officers; the captain, first lieutenants, and second lieutenants who serve at the company level

Comrade: A fellow soldier or fellow Communist

Cordite: The explosive powder often in bombs, artillery, and mortar shells

CP: The abbreviated form of *Command Post*

C Rations: Canned and packaged food provided by the Army to troops in the field; favorites of most GIs in Vietnam were beans and franks, pound cake, canned peaches, and chocolate

Cu Chi: The location of the 25th Infantry Division's large base camp in South Vietnam; huge Vietcong tunnel complexes surrounded the camp

Custer, General George Armstrong: Civil War hero and Indian fighter who, in 1876, led the Seventh Cavalry Regiment into an Indian ambush at the Little Bighorn River in Montana; none of Custer's troops survived what was to become known as "Custer's Last Stand"

Defcon: Defensive concentration of artillery fire; preselected and preregistered artillery targets that are established outside a military unit's defensive perimeter to facilitate timely and accurate fire support when the unit is under attack

Defensive Perimeter: The line of manned foxholes, bunkers, weapons, mines, barbed wire, and other obstacles that surrounds a military unit when in a defensive posture

Didi Mau: Vietnamese slang for "get out of here quickly" or "hurry up"

Dien Bien Phu: The place in North Vietnam where, in 1954, Communist-led Vietminh (predecessors of the Vietcong) defeated the French in one of the most historic battles in military history; it put an end to French colonial rule in Indochina

Division: A very large military unit consisting of several brigades and other supporting units; usually commanded by a brigadier general; can be 15,000 to 20,000 soldiers

DMG: Distinguished Military Graduate; an individual who graduates from the Army's ROTC program with top honors

Door Gunner: The helicopter crewmen firing an M-60 machine gun from the open door of a Huey helicopter; there are two door gunners, one on each side of the helicopter

Doves: Term used extensively during the sixties to describe individuals who were against the use of U.S. military forces in Southeast Asia

Dustoff: A medical evacuation from the field by helicopter; usually for soldiers wounded by enemy fire

E&E: Escape and evasion, as in escaping from captivity and evading the enemy attempting to find and recapture you

Eagle Flight: A single helicopter attempting to locate an enemy force by flying at a low altitude to get the enemy to fire on it and thus reveal its position; always supported with gunships and troop-carrying helicopters

Evac: Evacuation from the field, usually when wounded; also the abbreviation for a type of military hospital near the field of operations, as in 12th Evac

Extraction: Withdrawal from the field or AO by helicopter

F-100: The North American "Super Sabre," used extensively in South Vietnam in ground-support missions such as enemy troop concentrations, trails, roads, and bridges.

FAC: Abbreviation for *forward air controller*

Fatigues: A dark green or camouflaged combat uniform, as in jungle fatigues

Field of Fire: The area covered by direct fire weapons such as machine guns and rifles; also interlocking or overlapping fields of fire

Firebase: An artillery fire support base from which infantry troops can be supported by artillery; in Vietnam, very often temporary

Firefight: An engagement with the enemy; sometimes only a brief exchange of fire, at other times a fierce battle

Fire Mission: A request for artillery or air support, including map coordinates of the target, sent by a forward observer to the artillery or supporting aircraft

Flak Jacket: A bullet-proof, sleeveless jacket or vest that protects the body from gunfire and shrapnel

FNG: Fucking new guy; a pejorative term to describe soldiers who had just arrived in Vietnam and were new to their units; seasoned troops were fearful that an FNG might do something stupid and get them killed

FO: Abbreviation for *forward observer*

Forward Air Controller: The person who directs and controls air strikes, usually in support of ground troops

Forward Observer: The soldier, usually an artilleryman in the field with the infantry, who calls in map coordinates by radio for an artillery firebase to use during a fire mission; the forward observer, typically a second lieutenant, stays close to the senior commander of the ground troops

Fragging: The intentional killing of a fellow soldier or superior officer with a fragmentation grenade; there were reported cases of fragging late in the Vietnam War

Free-Fire Zone: An area in Vietnam that was presumed to be an enemy sanctuary and free of civilians, where troops could fire at will or planes could bomb at will without fear of harming noncombatants

Free World: The free nations aligned against the Communists during the Cold War; also called the Western Bloc

Friendly Fire: Used to describe American air, artillery, or ground fire that mistakenly hits American troops, as in killed by friendly fire

Fulda Gap: A gap in the mountains separating western Germany from the Soviet armies of Eastern Europe; during the Cold War believed to be a prime potential invasion route for the Communists

G-1: The military headquarters organization at division level charged with the responsibility for all personnel activities; includes recruiting, assignment, and promotion of individuals in the division

Gatling: As in Gatling gun; a machine gun with a cluster of barrels that fire in rapid sequence as the barrels are rotated

Garrote: A length of wire used to kill silently from behind, by strangulation

GI: An abbreviation for "government issue"; used extensively as slang for U.S. soldiers, particularly enlisted men

Gook: A pejorative term for the Vietcong and sometimes all Vietnamese

Green Berets: The name, taken from their headgear, of the Army's elite Special Forces units trained in counterinsurgency, antiterrorism, and other clandestine operations

Grunt: Slang for an infantryman or foot soldier

Gulf War: A brief war in the Persian Gulf, in 1991, stemming from the 1990 Iraqi invasion of Kuwait; a coalition of United Nations forces led by the United States bombed Iraq and forced its troops out of Kuwait with the use of highly mobile ground troops

Gunship: An attack helicopter that is mounted with machine guns and rockets; used extensively in support of ground troops during combat air assaults, eagle flights, and extractions

Hand Grenade: A deadly explosive device thrown by hand; often used in Vietcong booby traps

Hanoi Hannah: The fictitious name used by Vietcong and North Vietnamese females during taped propaganda broadcasts, often played over loudspeakers in the jungle, aimed at destroying American soldiers' will to fight

Hawks: Term used extensively during the sixties to describe individuals that favored the use of U.S. military forces in Vietnam

Helipad: A landing area for helicopters; often cement or steel with a large letter "H" in the center

Helping-Hands: A program aimed at winning the hearts and minds of South Vietnamese villagers and peasants by distributing food, clothing, and medical supplies to the needy

Heston, Charlton: A Hollywood movie star

Ho Bo Woods: A Vietcong sanctuary in the Iron Triangle northwest of Saigon (now Ho Chi Minh City)

Ho Chi Minh: The Communist revolutionary leader and president of North

Vietnam during most of the Vietnam War; affectionately called "Uncle Ho" by many of his followers

Ho Chi Minh City: The name given to Saigon, the former capital of South Vietnam, after the fall of South Vietnam to the Communists in 1975

Ho Chi Minh Trail: A vast network of roads and hidden jungle trails running south from North Vietnam through Cambodia and into South Vietnam; used by North Vietnam to move troops and war materials south during the Vietnam War

Hootch: A small, simple dwelling often constructed of sticks, mud, and dry grasses or straw; a peasant hut

Hope, Bob: A very popular American entertainer who took the time to visit and entertain U.S. armed forces installations all over the world; a comedian and actor

Huey: The name used by soldiers for the UH-1 helicopters; also called a "slick" if used for transporting troops and a "gunship" if mounted with rockets and extra machine guns

Humpin' the Boonies: Moving slowly, day after day, through endless swamps, rice paddies, jungles, hamlets, and small villages searching for Vietcong or NVA troops

Incoming: Term used when a unit is receiving enemy fire, particularly mortar or artillery shells

In-Country: Army slang meaning in the country of Vietnam

Indochina: The area in Southeast Asia that includes, among others, the countries of Vietnam, Cambodia, and Laos

IOBC: Infantry Officer Basic Course

Iron Curtain: The extensive manned line of fortifications, land mines, tank obstacles, barbed wire, and other barriers that separated Communist Eastern Europe from Western Europe during the Cold War

Iron Triangle: A Vietcong-infested area north of Saigon (now Ho Chi Minh City) that was in the Second Battalion, 27th Infantry Wolfhounds' area of operations

Insertion: Moving troops into an enemy-controlled area; usually by helicopter

IV: Intravenous, as in intravenous bottle used to inject plasma, saline solutions, and medications directly into blood veins

JFK: President John F. Kennedy

Joint: A self-rolled marijuana cigarette

***Kaserne*:** The German word for an army post

Khmer: Khmer Rouge; the Cambodian Communists

KIA: Killed in action; sometimes "kangaroo" in radio transmissions

L-19: A light, single-engine propeller-driven airplane, also called an O-1E, used to locate targets for tactical air strikes; also known as a *Bird Dog*

Land Mine: A small but very powerful explosive placed just under the surface of the ground; used against foot soldiers and vehicles such as trucks and tanks; most often pressure detonated but sometimes detonated by radio signal or electrical current

Landing Zone: A clearing in the jungle, woods, or rice paddies where helicopters can land; usually prepared for air assaults, insertions, extractions, and dustoffs; also known as the *LZ*

LAW: Light antitank weapon; portable olive-drab tube, with a plastic sight, rubber trigger, and one round of ammunition; used by extending the tube, aiming, shooting, and then throwing it away

Lederhosen: German for leather shorts with a bib and shoulder straps; often decorated with elaborate needlework; popular in Bavaria

Lift: A flight of troop-carrying helicopters flying into or out of a landing zone, as in it took three lifts of six helicopters

Listening Post: A guard position placed forward of a defensive perimeter to provide early warning of enemy troops; ideally manned by three to four soldiers but sometimes by only two

LZ: Landing zone

M-16: The standard-issue American full and semiautomatic 5.56 mm combat assault rifle used by the Americans and South Vietnamese armies; twenty-round magazine

M-60: The standard-issue American 7.62 mm light machine gun; carried by the infantry

M-79: An American single-shot portable grenade launcher that propels a 40 mm shell with a kill radius of five meters; looks like a toy rifle or sawed-off shotgun

M-113 APC: The armored personnel carrier used in mechanized infantry units

Magazine: A spring-loaded container for holding bullets or cartridges that are fed automatically into the chamber of a weapon, such as an M-16 or AK-47

Mamasan: Slang for an elderly Vietnamese woman

McNamara, Robert S: Secretary of Defense under Presidents Kennedy and Johnson; one of the chief architects of America's strategy for fighting the Vietnam War

MEDCAP: Medical Civic Action Program; program that provided medical aid for remote Vietnamese villages and hamlets

Medevac: Evacuation from the field for medical reasons, such as wounds received in action; also called a *dustoff*

Medic: A soldier with medical training who administers first aid in the field

MO: Method of operating

Mortar: A small, portable artillery piece consisting of a tube, a tripod, and a base plate; used by ground troops for close-in fire support

MP: Abbreviation for Military Police and for Military Policeman

Mr. Mom: A 1980s American film in which the father of a family takes on the traditional role of the mother

Nam: Soldiers' slang for Vietnam

Napalm: A flammable, sticky substance like jelled gasoline that is dropped from attack airplanes in canister-like bombs or is used by infantrymen on the ground with flamethrowers

NATO: North Atlantic Treaty Organization

NBC: National Broadcasting Company

NCO: Abbreviation for *noncommissioned officers*

Noncommissioned Officers: Individuals in the army holding rank, but not that of a commissioned officer; includes sergeant, staff sergeant, sergeant first class, master sergeant, and sergeant major

No Time for Sergeants: Broadway play and film comedy about a country boy drafted into the Air Force who through a basic ignorance turns his unit upside-down

Nouc Mam: A condiment made from fish oils used by the Vietnamese on much of what they eat; has a strong pungent odor

Numma One: Vietnamese slang for the best, as in GI numma one, VC numma ten

Numma Ten: Vietnamese slang for the worst, as in GI numma one, VC numma ten

NVA: The North Vietnamese Army

OPA: The Army's Office of Personnel Administration in Washington, D.C.

Pacification: A general term for a number of programs, like MEDCAP and Helping-Hands, aimed at winning the hearts and minds of the South Vietnamese villagers

Papasan: Slang for an elderly Vietnamese man

Perimeter: See *Defensive Perimeter*

PGA: Professional Golfers Association

Piaster: A unit of the dong, Vietnam's currency

Pineapple: Slang in the 25th Division for native Hawaiians serving in the division, as in "He is a pineapple"

Plain of Reeds: An area in the former South Vietnam northwest of Saigon (now Ho Chi Minh City), near the Cambodian border

Platoon: An American military unit commanded by a platoon leader who is typically a lieutenant; at full strength consists of four ten-person squads; normally part of a company

Point: The front position in a column of soldiers, as in walking point

Point Man: The lead individual who is walking point in a column of soldiers; a very risky position particularly in jungle terrain offering excellent cover for enemy snipers, mines, and booby traps; usually the first person shot at by the enemy

Pop Smoke: To ignite a smoke grenade used to mark a ground unit's position or a landing zone; smoke grenades come in many colors: orange, yellow, red, purple, green

POW: Prisoner of war

PRC-25: A field radio carried at the platoon and company levels, used for communications between the company commander and his platoon leaders; also used to communicate with battalion headquarters and to call in artillery support

Puff the Magic Dragon: A converted AC-47 cargo plane with Gatling-type rotating machine guns called miniguns and capable of firing 6,000 rounds of tracer ammunition per minute; the stream of red tracers looked like fire from a dragon's mouth

Punji Pit: A well-camouflaged hole or trench in the ground with poisoned bamboo spikes sticking up; used by the Vietcong to injure unwary American and South Vietnamese troops who might fall in

Quonset Hut: A corrugated metal building shaped like a half- or semi-cylinder; used to house troops in camp, for medical facilities in field hospitals, and for numerous other military purposes

RA: Regular Army; as opposed to the Reserve Army

Ranger: A soldier with advanced specialized training in certain kinds of operations, such as counterinsurgency and reconnaissance, and survival skills

Recon: An abbreviated form of reconnaissance or reconnoiter, as in recon platoon or recon the enemy

Reveille: The wake-up signal typically played on a bugle early in the morning at military installations

Rifleman: A soldier armed with a rifle, as in the infantry; also an infantryman or a grunt

Rocket-Propelled Grenade: A small but powerful rocketlike grenade launched from a tube; used extensively by the Vietcong and NVA troops against the Americans and South Vietnamese; also called *RPG*

Rome Plow: A massive excavating vehicle used to remove trees and other vegetation that might conceal the enemy

ROTC: Reserve Officers Training Corps

Round: A bullet, as in a round from an M-16 or an AK-47

RPG: Abbreviation for *rocket-propelled grenade*

RTO: Radio telephone operator; a soldier that carries the radios needed for effective field communications

Ruff-Puffs: Pejorative for the South Vietnamese village militias at the region and province level; they often had their families with them at their outposts; in some battles members of the militia were reported to have changed sides and fought for the Vietcong

S-3: The letter-number designation for the battalion-level staff operations officer; responsible for coordinating the activities of battalion units during combat operations

Saigon: The capital city of South Vietnam until the fall of the country, in 1975, to the Communists; renamed Ho Chi Minh City by the Communists

Sapper: A Vietcong soldier willing to risk his life on suicide-like missions by storming an American position, such as a command post or bunker, with high explosives to destroy it

Satchel Charge: An explosive charge, often dynamite, more powerful than a hand grenade, packed in a canvas bag with handles used to throw it; used by sappers

Search and Destroy: A military operation designed to sweep an area to find and destroy the Vietcong or NVA but not to hold territory

Self-Propelled Howitzer: A tracked vehicle used in Vietnam with a built-in artillery gun; delivers either a 105 mm or a 155 mm shell in support of ground troops

Sergeant: See *Noncommissioned Officers*

Sergeant Bilko: The archetypal conniving Army sergeant made famous in the 1950s television comedy of the same name and revived in a 1990s feature movie; Phil Silver, who played Bilko in the 1950s, described Bilko as "the king of the motor pool, lord of the mess hall, scourge of the orderly room. Even the colonel quails before Bilko."

Sergeant York: World War I hero and winner of the Congressional Medal of Honor

Sgt.: Abbreviation for sergeant

Shell: A high-explosive projectile used in artillery howitzers, mortars, cannons, or other large guns

Short-Timer: A soldier with very little time remaining in Vietnam, usually less than a month

Shrapnel: Sharp, jagged pieces of metal sent flying through the air from explosions made by artillery shells, bombs, mortar shells, hand grenades, mines, and rockets

Slick: A troop-carrying Huey helicopter

Sock Hop: The name for a dance in the 1950s that was typically held in a high school gymnasium; dancers wore socks only, no shoes, to protect the floor of the gymnasium

Sortie: A flight by one military aircraft

Soviet: Concerning the former USSR, as in Soviet armies or Soviet ideology

Special Forces: See *Green Berets*

Sputnik: The first earth-orbiting satellite; launched by the Russians in 1958

Stealth: To move quietly or secretly, as in using stealth to move through the jungle

Steve McQueen: The American movie star who played Seaman Jake Holman in *The Sand Pebbles*

Strategic Air Command: The military organization with the mission of deterring nuclear war by maintaining a superior force of aircraft ready to strike anywhere in the world within minutes; also known as the SAC

Taps: A bugle call performed at burial ceremonies for soldiers and sailors; also sounded at the end of the day or evening to signal the time for returning to barracks or quarters

Tet Offensive: The wide-scale offensive launched in January 1968 by the Vietcong and NVA during which military installations, cities including Saigon, and government facilities all over South Vietnam were attacked; the offensive was militarily unsuccessful but a major political victory that forced the United States to rethink its objectives in Vietnam; Tet is the Vietnamese New Year

T.G.I. Friday's: Thank God It's Friday's; a restaurant chain

The Old Man: The company commander in a combat outfit

The World: Slang used extensively by American soldiers in Vietnam for the United States or any other civilized country outside of Vietnam

TOC: Tactical Operations Center

Top Brass: Army slang for senior officers; also higher-ups in any organization

Tour of Duty: The period of time a soldier spends in the service or at a particular duty station; the typical tour of duty in Vietnam was twelve to thirteen months

Tracer: A round of ammunition that is coated with a flammable substance that makes it glow brightly, thus revealing the direction of the firing; American tracers were red, NVA tracers sometimes green

Trip Flare: A flare that is triggered by an individual stepping on a trip wire hidden on the ground; provides early warning of attacking troops and illuminates their approach

Tunnel Rat: Small American soldiers who searched Vietcong tunnels; a very risky job requiring substantial courage

Uncle Ho: Nickname for *Ho Chi Minh*

VC: Abbreviation for *Vietcong*

Vietcong: The Vietnamese Communist guerrillas fighting with the North Vietnamese to overthrow the established pro-American government in South Vietnam; also referred to as VC, Victor Charlie, Charlie, and gook

Vietminh: The predecessors to the Vietcong who fought against the French in Indochina and defeated the French at Dien Bien Phu

War Zone C: A large area in the Wolfhound area of operations northwest of Cu Chi and adjacent to the Cambodian border and NVA infiltration routes

Wayne, John: A tall, handsome, and rugged movie actor starring in larger-than-life, he-man roles in many westerns and war movies; starred in the movies *The Green Berets* about the Special Forces in Vietnam and *The Sands of Iwo Jima* about World War II in the Pacific

White Phosphorus: A highly incendiary chemical used in artillery shells, rockets, and grenades; sticks to the skin and burns through it; also called *Willy Peter* or *WP*

Willy Peter: Abbreviation for *White Phosphorus*

Wimp: Not manly

Wolfhounds: Name given to the 27th Infantry Regiment after it fought the Bolsheviks in Russia; like Russian Wolfhounds the regiment is ferocious towards its enemies and kind to its friends

WP: Abbreviation for *white phosphorus*

Author's Notes

T his is a book written from memory about events that took place many years ago—events that still live for me in the pages and chapters of my life. In writing it, I have been as faithful to the truth as memory and rigorous soul-searching permit. I have labored hard to present my journey to war in story form as experienced by me, and others who fought alongside me, in those early years of the Vietnam war. In the chapters of the book that describe firefights and battle actions in Vietnam or the years of my first marriage, I present the facts as I best recall them. However, given the tricks that memory and human emotion sometimes play on us, it's possible that specific events, as described, may well include a blending of details from several events. And dialogue, where present, does include constructs that reflect my best recollection of actual discussions.

In chapters that follow the chapter titled *Willow Run,* I occasionally refer back to Willow Run. On some occasions the reference is to the community values, or the spirit, of Willow Run. In others, the reference is to a *place-in-time* that often includes my formative years in the neighboring communities of Belleville and Ypsilanti, Michigan.

For family members, well-known public figures, Bob Babcock, Bob Bott, Frank Clouse, Lieutenant Doug Colliander, Lieutenant Steve Ehart, Diane Carlson Evans, Specialist Bert Hale, Harry Hidenfelter, Major General T. H. Lipscomb, Paul Mahar, Sergeant Frank Maki, Colonel George Murray, Lieutenant Calvin Neptune, Colonel John Norvell, Sergeant Gary Pearse, Beverly

Pink, First Sergeant Charles Rutledge, Sergeant Alfred "Luke" Serna, Lieutenant Mike Tarantola, and Army Chaplain Tucker, real names are used. For all the other individuals I've written about, I have used pseudonyms and made minor alterations to their personal attributes to protect their privacy.

To help me remember dates and confirm my recollection of key historical events, I referred to *The World Book Encyclopedia* published by World Book, Inc. and to *The Sixties—The decade remembered now, by the people who lived it then,* published in 1977 by Random House/Rolling Stone Press.